THE MUSICAL SALVATIONIST

The World of Richard Slater (1854–1939)
'Father of Salvation Army Music'

Music in Britain, 1600–1900

ISSN 1752–1904

Series Editors:
RACHEL COWGILL & PETER HOLMAN

This series provides a forum for the best new work in this area; it takes a deliberately inclusive approach, covering immigrants and emigrants as well as native musicians. Contributions on all aspects of seventeenth-, eighteenth- and nineteenth-century British music studies are welcomed, particularly those placing music in its social and historical contexts, and addressing Britain's musical links with Europe and the rest of the globe.

Proposals or queries should be sent in the first instance to Professor Rachel Cowgill, Professor Peter Holman or Boydell & Brewer at the addresses shown below. All submissions will receive prompt and informed consideration.

Professor Rachel Cowgill,
School of Music, Cardiff University, 31 Corbett Road, Cardiff CF10 3EB
email: cowgillre@cardiff.ac.uk

Professor Peter Holman, School of Music, University of Leeds, Leeds, LS2 9JT
email: p.k.holman@leeds.ac.uk

Boydell & Brewer, PO Box 9, Woodbridge, Suffolk, IP12 3DF
email: editorial@boydell.co.uk

ALREADY PUBLISHED

Lectures on Musical Life
William Sterndale Bennett
edited by Nicholas Temperley, with Yunchung Yang

John Stainer: A Life in Music
Jeremy Dibble

*The Pursuit of High Culture: John Ella and
Chamber Music in Victorian London*
Christina Bashford

Thomas Tallis and his Music in Victorian England
Suzanne Cole

The Consort Music of William Lawes, 1602–1645
John Cunningham

Life After Death: The Viola da Gamba in Britain from Purcell to Dolmetsch
Peter Holman

THE MUSICAL SALVATIONIST

The World of Richard Slater (1854–1939)
'Father of Salvation Army Music'

Gordon Cox

THE BOYDELL PRESS

© Gordon Cox 2011

First published 2011
The Boydell Press, Woodbridge

ISBN 978 1 84383 696 4

The Boydell Press is an imprint of Boydell & Brewer Ltd
PO Box 9, Woodbridge, Suffolk IP12 3DF, UK
and of Boydell & Brewer Inc.
668 Mt Hope Avenue, Rochester, NY 14620, USA
website: www.boydellandbrewer.com

A catalogue record for this book is available
from the British Library

Designed and typeset in Adobe Minion Pro by
David Roberts, Pershore, Worcestershire

Printed and Bound in the United States of America

Dedicated to the memory of my parents,
Gordon and Margaret Cox,
Salvation Army Officers

🎵 Contents

Illustrations

Foreword

RICHARD Slater, justly termed some decades ago as the 'Father of Salvation Army Music', has been, for much my life, both a fascinating character and an icon. Born in mid-Victorian London, composer and orchestral musician, radical thinker, educator, diarist – his role in shaping the basis of the movement's musical evolution is historically vitally significant. Yet beyond his vast output of articles and music, what we know of him has hitherto been almost all contained in a small, though substantial, biography by Arch. R. Wiggins, published in 1945. Beyond copious writings about William and Catherine Booth, the Salvation Army's founders, and at least two Heritage Centres, there is a general respect for, but little real interest in, the movement's history, heritage and traditions, which may be due to the largely activist nature of the membership's involvement and a tendency to highlight the pioneers. It is a heartening sign that there is now a thriving Salvationist Historical and Philatelic Society.

In introducing Gordon Cox's excellently researched and presented book about Slater I trust that I may be pardoned for a subjective input, bearing in mind my foregoing comments and the need to fill in extra areas of his life and philosophy. I regret that I am one of the many who, in youth, failed to question those who have 'been there', or had personal knowledge of events and people. In the familiar area of ancestry, for instance, we now have to trawl through documents to secure information which was once easily available from family members. I knew Slater's biographer and have worked with men who had connections with him. Now an octogenarian, I succeeded to his editorial chair (much later!); in times past I have visited (and cleaned) his grave, photographed his little rented house in Westgate-on-Sea (now demolished) and once talked with his then surviving next door neighbours. I have paced the road in King's Cross where he once lived, visited one daughter and corresponded with the other, played over his unpublished songs yet picked up practically nothing which could supplement his official biography. So for me this book is excitingly informative, not least on account of Gordon Cox accessing the Slater diaries and unearthing further material about his earlier years. As is made clear in the book, my mention of those diaries has led to a much richer result than perhaps our first encounter promised.

Although by the early 1880s Salvationist brass bands were evolving strongly, one cannot think that, in those formative years, Slater could possibly have envisaged the thousands of instrumentalists and choir members which were an international feature by the time of his death in 1939. By then, Salvationist musicians had long been making records and broadcasts, had performed in the presence of royalty, and a hugely commercially successful publishing programme was in place. Yet back in 1882 William Pearson had written a song which contained the visionary line *With a thousand bands and a thousand drums* ... The strength of the foundations laid by Slater and his colleagues is confirmed by the fact that so many of these groups have survived world wars and the changes of political regimes and economies.

Gordon Cox has a pedigree embedded in The Salvation Army. Although he is not a member of that movement, his parents were full-time officers and his grandfather was a highly respected bandmaster for many years. So with that heritage it is not surprising that he has an understanding of what Salvation Army music is about. He explores a wide historical field: from the beginnings to the cultural expansions which put his central character in context. The later chapter on Eric Ball gives insight into an outstandingly innovative composer who, from the late twenties until just after World War II exerted a strong influence on the progress of the Salvation Army's music and continued to contribute to it for many years after that. There can be no doubt, even to the present day, that Richard Slater and the musical pioneers got it right and instituted a unique example of the art of music in the service of the spiritual power to which they were committed. A commitment which, in motivation and practice, continues to be evidenced by their successors, among which I am honoured to be included.

Lieutenant-Colonel (Dr) Ray Steadman-Allen
Editor-in-Chief, The Salvation Army Music Editorial Department, 1967–1980

Acknowledgements

M ANY people have contributed to the completion of this book. First and foremost I would like to thank Stella Taylor. She generously granted me access to the diaries of her great-grandfather, Richard Slater. Both she and her husband Doug have been most hospitable to me, and have put themselves out in many ways in order that I might pursue my interest in Slater's life and work. I am most grateful to them.

Special thanks are due to a number of eminent Salvationists with whom I was privileged to talk and correspond about the Army and its musical culture, including Ray Steadman-Allen (a distinguished successor of Slater as Head of The Salvation Army's Music Editorial Department, 1967–80), Michael Clack, Stephen Cobb, Ronald Holz, David Lambert-Gorwyn and Roy Terry. Their enthusiasm and conviction regarding the Salvation Army and its mission helped illuminate much of my archival research. Particular thanks also to Ray Steadman-Allen for so readily agreeing to contribute a foreword to the book.

I am indebted to a number of family members, friends and colleagues who read and critically commented on portions of the book. They are Stacia Beeney, Alistair Cox, Brendan Cox, James Garnett, Stephanie Pitts, Jane Southcott, and Robin Stevens. I would also like to thank the following for their help in dealing with some of my specific queries: Ian Barton, Donald Bibey, Laurie Bovey, Vic Gammon, Trevor Herbert, Eric Rapp, Dave Russell and Colin Waller. Also to Stephen Allen, Alan Cross, and Michael Thomas for technical assistance. Any errors of fact or interpretation remain my responsibility.

Much of the research was carried out in The Salvation Army International Heritage Centre in London. I owe a special debt to Gordon Taylor, the Centre's archivist, for his guidance arising from his profound understanding of the Army's history. Also to Alex von der Becke, Photo-Archivist of the Centre, for helpful advice on illustrations. I would like to extend special thanks for the help received from the following archives and libraries: Bishopsgate Library; Bodleian Library, Oxford; The British Library, including the Newspaper Library and the Sound Archive; Camden Local Studies and Archive Centre; Guildhall Library; South Place Ethical Society Library at Conway Hall; The National Archives; University of Reading Library. Thanks too, to conference audiences at the universities of Exeter and Sheffield where I first presented my ideas.

I am particularly indebted to the International Heritage Centre (Gordon Taylor) for permission to reproduce the images relating to Slater and then through to Eric Ball (Plates 1–8), to Gavin Holman of *The Internet Bandsman's Everything Within* for permission to use the photograph of the Chalk Farm Band (Plate 9), and to Salvationist Publishing and Supplies (Trevor Caffull) for permission to include the music examples.

I also thank the Finzi Trust for awarding me a Travel Scholarship in 2007/8, which enabled me to extend my research to encompass the life and work of Richard Slater.

I am indebted to Rachel Cowgill, the Series Editor, for her penetrating critiques of the manuscript in its various drafts, and to Michael Middeke of the Boydell Press for his faith in the project, and to Catherine Larner and David Roberts for seeing the book through to publication.

Finally, for her constant encouragement and belief in the value of my work over the years, I am deeply grateful to my wife Sheila.

Abbreviations

BJ	Band Journal (of the Salvation Army)
FO	*Field Officer*
FS	Festival Series (of the Salvation Army Band Journal)
ISB	International Staff Band
OF	Order of the Founder
RSd	Richard Slater Diaries
SA	Salvation Army
SP&S	Salvationist Publishing and Supplies
SS	Second Series (of the Salvation Army Band Journal)

Introduction

In this book I present a social history of music-making in the Salvation Army from its beginnings in 1878 until the outbreak of the Second World War in 1939. What makes the study distinctive is that I relate this history to the musical world of Richard Slater (1854–1939), popularly known as the 'Father of Salvation Army Music'.[1] Fundamentally I view Slater's achievement as fashioning the musical life of the Salvation Army into a musical world characterised by self-sufficiency and a sense of boundedness.[2] It was to be based upon an active and effective policy of encouraging musical participation and musical education.

The Introduction will outline some of the pertinent literature relating to the history of the Salvation Army. It will then describe my search for and discovery of sources, and will focus upon methodological and editorial procedures. Such an account should emphasise Stephen Yeo's observation that 'history is always made to look tidier for the reader than it appears to the writer before he boils it down into paragraphs'.[3] Finally the chapters will be outlined, and I shall discuss some of my own reasons for embarking on this quest

The Salvation Army was founded in East London by William Booth in 1878. Its mission was to evangelise the 'undeserving poor'. It was E. P. Thompson's contention in 1965 that the Salvation Army deserved serious attention from historians, not least because it is rich in materials for the understanding of revivalism and the phenomena of conversion and self-dedication.[4] A number of landmark studies have been published both following up and extending the spirit of Thompson's suggestions.[5] These have focused on the following aspects: the

---

[1] See A. R. Wiggins, *Father of Salvation Army Music: Richard Slater* (London, 1945). Wiggins quotes from a reminiscence of Archie Burgess, a Salvation Army officer and concertina player, who remembered Bramwell Booth introducing Slater to a Bandmasters' Council at the Clapton Congress Hall in the early years of the twentieth century as follows, 'Now I am going to ask the Father of Salvation Army Music, Major Slater to speak to you' (p. x.).

[2] For illuminating discussion regarding musical worlds, see R. Finnegan, *The Hidden Musicians: Music-Making in an English Town* (Middletown, CT, 2007).

[3] S. Yeo, *Religion and Voluntary Organisations in Crisis* (London, 1976), p. ix.

[4] E. P. Thompson, 'Blood, Fire and Unction', *New Society*, 13 Mar. 1965, pp. 25–6.

[5] See R. Robertson, 'The Salvation Army: The Persistence of Sectarianism', in *Patterns of Sectarianism: Organisation and Ideology in Social and Religious Movements*, ed. B. Wilson (London, 1967), pp. 49–105; A. Briggs, 'The Salvation Army in Sussex, 1883–1892', in *Studies in Sussex Church History*, ed. M. J. Kitch (London, 1981), pp. 189–208; V. Bailey, '"In Darkest England and the Way Out": The Salvation Army and Social Reform and the Labour Movement', *International Review of Social History* 29:2 (1984), pp. 133–71; G. Horridge, *The Salvation Army in its*

influence of William and Catherine Booth; the growth of the movement in its early years, often in the face of sustained opposition; its roots in Methodism and the influence upon it of American revivalism; the Army's constitutional crisis in 1929; the social class basis of its membership; connections with popular culture; the influences of militarism and temperance; the role of women; the relationship between its evangelism and social work and the possible alliance with socially radical movements. In addition to these studies are the in-house histories of the Salvation Army by Robert Sandall and Arch Wiggins covering the years 1865–1914, particularly important as the official chronicles of the historical record.[6]

Somewhat surprisingly, the Salvation Army's musical tradition has been relatively little explored. A pioneering musical study was undertaken by Ray Steadman-Allen between 1965 and 1966, when he was Head of the Army's Music Editorial Department. Entitled 'The Evolution of Salvation Army Music', it comprised 15 articles published in weekly instalments in *The Musician*.[7] In its comprehensiveness of treatment covering congregational singing, vocal music production and the expansion of the scope of instrumental musical genres, it remains the first port-of-call for any serious researcher.

Very different in style are the historical snapshots of Salvation Army bands and songsters across the world by the Salvationist musician and journalist, the late Brindley Boon. Published in 1966 and 1978 respectively, they contain valuable nuggets of information alongside entertaining anecdotes. His history of the Salvation Army's International Staff Band, is in similar vein.[8]

A particularly significant social and musical history of Salvation Army Bands

Early Days, 1865–1900 (Godalming, 1993); N. Murdoch, *Origins of the Salvation Army* (Knoxville, TN, 1994); D. Rapp, 'The British Salvation Army, the Early Film Industry and Urban Working-Class Adolescents, *Twentieth Century British History* 7:2 (1996), pp. 157–88; R. Hattersley, *Blood & Fire: William and Catherine Booth and Their Salvation Army* (London, 1999); P. Walker, *Pulling the Devil's Kingdom Down: The Salvation Army in Victorian Britain* (Berkeley, CA, 2001); R. J. Green, *The Life and Ministry of William Booth, Founder of the Salvation Army* (Nashville, TN, 2005); A. Woodall, *What Price the Poor? William Booth, Karl Marx and the London Residuum* (Aldershot, 2005); J. Larsson, *1929: A Crisis that shaped the Salvation Army's Future* (London, 2009).

[6] R. Sandall, *The History of the Salvation Army*, vol. 1: *1865–1878* (London, 1947); vol. 2: *1878–1886* (London, 1950); vol. 3: *1883–1953: Social Reform and Welfare Work* (London, 1955); A. Wiggins, *The History of the Salvation Army* vol. 4: *1886–1904* (London, 1964); vol. 5: *1904–1914* (London, 1968).

[7] R. Steadman-Allen, 'The Evolution of Salvation Army Music', *The Musician*, July 1965 – Feb. 1966.

[8] B. Boon, *Play the Music Play! The Story of Salvation Army Bands* (London, 1966); *Sing the Happy Song!: A History of Salvation Army Vocal Music* (London, 1978); *ISB: The Story of the International Staff Band of the Salvation Army* (Bristol, 1985).

is contained in the chapter 'God's Perfect Minstrels: The Bands of the Salvation Army', written by Trevor Herbert, in his authoritative edited collection, *The British Brass Band*, published in 2000.[9] Herbert, a non-Salvationist, is an authority on brass instruments, their history and repertoire. His chapter has an ambitious range, covering the function of Salvation Army bands, the tensions between aesthetic and doctrinal principles, the centralised control of the repertoire, and the international spread of the Army and its banding culture. In a sense it brought the Salvation Army's musical traditions to the attention of the wider world. Also in the same year was published the very first specific entry on the Salvation Army in the second edition of Grove's *New Dictionary of Music and Musicians*. Written by Steadman-Allen, it also reinforced the sense of the opening up of this particular musical world.[10]

The most recent contribution to the field has been the two-volume *Brass Bands of the Salvation Army* (2006, 2007) by the American academic and Salvationist, Ronald Holz.[11] In addition to an in-depth history of Salvation Army bands in the UK up to the present, he also includes regional and national essays by informed contributors, on the tradition in Australia, Canada, New Zealand, Sweden and the USA. A further notable feature of the first volume is the rich assemblage of archival photographic illustrations, which provide a real sense of historical perspective. The second volume breaks new ground in its close musical analysis of key works from the Salvation Army band repertoire in the post World War II era. *Brass Bands of the Salvation Army* is an indispensible resource.

My initial interest in the Salvation Army as a possible area for research arose from my reading of Lucy Green's study *How Popular Musicians Learn* (2002), which particularly intrigued me through its exploration of 'informal' methods of musical instruction and training.[12] Certainly similar informal methods of musical training in some brass bands were still evident in the late 1980s.[13]

[9] T. Herbert, 'God's Perfect Minstrels: The Bands of the Salvation Army', in *The British Brass Band: A Musical and Social History*, ed. T. Herbert (Oxford, 2000), pp. 187–216.

[10] R. Steadman-Allen, 'Music of the Salvation Army', in *New Grove Dictionary of Music and Musicians*, 2nd edn, ed. S. Sadie (London, 2000), vol. 22, pp. 183–4 (hereafter *New Grove 2*).

[11] R. Holz, *Brass Bands of the Salvation Army: Their Mission and Music*. 2 vols (Hitchin, 2006–7). Other important historical studies of Salvationist music by Holz include: 'The History of the Hymn-Tune Meditation and Related Forms in Salvation Army Instrumental Music in Great Britain and North America' (Unpublished PhD dissertation, University of Connecticut, 1981); *Erik Leidzén: Band Arranger and Composer* (Lewiston, NY, 1990); *The Proclaimers: A History of the New York Staff Band, 1887–2007* (New York, 2007).

[12] L. Green, *How Popular Musicians Learn* (Aldershot, 2002).

[13] See Finnegan, *The Hidden Musicians*, p. 49.

Through my own personal experience of growing up in the Salvation Army I knew how effective and powerful such informal methods could be. I decided to visit The Salvation Army International Heritage Centre, at the William Booth College in South London, to see what kind of sources were available to undertake a focused historical study of the musical instruction and education of Salvationists. What I encountered was a wealth of published materials contained within the organisation's periodicals, aimed specifically at Salvationist musicians, including the *Local Officer*, the *Musical Salvationist*, the *Bandsman and Songster*, *The Musician*, and more generally the *War Cry*. In addition I found numerous instrumental tutors, pedagogical texts, as well as a fictional account of musical learning within an Army band. The most intriguing work that I came across at this time was the *Salvation Army Dictionary of Music* [1908] 'compiled by Brigadier Slater'.[14] I was aware of Richard Slater's reputation as 'Father of Salvation Army Music', and the more I read of his educational thinking the more I became intrigued by his sense of vision, and his energy.

Through my immersion in the periodical literature a theme related to 'education' emerged, notably 'participation'. This was stimulated by Stephanie Pitts' book *Valuing Musical Participation* (2005), in which she investigated the experiences of musical participants in a variety of contexts, including a Gilbert and Sullivan festival, a contemporary music summer school and a chamber music festival.[15] It struck me that the notion of musical participation could be a valuable focus for my Salvationist history as I had become aware of the multi-faceted opportunities for musical participation which the Salvation Army offered its recruits, not only in brass bands but in a plethora of instrumental and vocal ensembles. Moreover, alongside accounts of musical activities there were countless details included of these Salvationist musicians, most notably a long-running series in the *Bandsman and Songster* listing the occupations of over 1,000 band members. It struck me forcibly that the notion of musical participation could be a rich seam in my investigation.

The problem at the time was that all my sources were 'official' ones, and both the Army's periodicals and in-house biographies and histories were somewhat propagandist and hagiographic, understandably so considering their function. But I needed to search out some primary sources that would provide scope for encountering personal reflections, disagreement and honest debate. I became increasingly determined to investigate the life of Richard Slater, and was fortunate enough to gain a Finzi Scholarship Award in 2007, which provided me with

---

[14] R. Slater, *Salvation Army Dictionary of Music: To meet the Needs of Bandsmen and Songsters* (London, [1908]). Richard Slater also assembled a 'History of Salvation Army Music: Vocal and Instrumental'. The two unpublished volumes contain a mixture of typed and handwritten entries. Compiled in 1925, much of the detail is also contained in Slater's other writings. The two volumes are held in The Salvation Army International Heritage Centre.

[15] S. Pitts, *Valuing Musical Participation* (Aldershot, 2005).

resources to extend the scope of my research.[16] My initial search for information about Slater was frustrating. I managed to track down details of his family line by trawling through census data, but apart from that I found little information. I had already read Wiggins' 80-page biography of Slater entitled *Father of Salvation Army Music*. Published in 1945, it intrigued me with its references to Slater's early fascination with secularism and free-thought before his conversion. There were also a few tantalising quotations from his diaries. It appeared that Slater had been an inveterate diary-keeper. According to Wiggins 'no man kept a diary more meticulously and faithfully than he'.[17] However, although I made numerous enquiries, the whereabouts of the diaries appeared to be unknown.

I had become reconciled to writing a study of his life, as Carolyn Steedman puts it, 'out of absence and silence, out of records missing and lost',[18] when through following up a chance suggestion made to me by Ray Steadman-Allen, I managed to locate the 24 volumes of the diaries covering Slater's whole life, held in safe keeping by Slater's great-granddaughter Stella Taylor (née Rolfe). When I contacted Stella, she kindly agreed that I could have access to the diaries for the purposes of my research.

The Slater diaries include a description of his early years, and from 1871 until his death a highly detailed account of his daily life, including discussion of his work, family, friends and acquaintances, ideas, music criticism, lists of books read, his walking tours, his health etc. For Slater, the reasons for writing his diaries were clear:

> This account of my life was written in the <u>first instance</u> to satisfy my own mind's desire to have as complete a record as possible, in the <u>second place</u>, I thought my children, relatives and friends would find it of interest and service in the future; and thirdly, I have some hope that it might prove of public interest for publication, at least in some modified form in years to come. That hope has support in the fact that out of such disadvantages as bad sight, great poverty, narrow circumstances, and, being fatherless, I have risen at least to some distinction and reputation for various kinds of musical and literary work, and by my long connection with the musical side of the Salvation Army I think the record is such as to become of lasting value in connection with the history of the Army. (Richard Slater Diaries, vol. 1, Introduction, p. x)

The 24 volumes plus index which comprise the diaries are indeed a rich

---

[16] See G. Cox, '"A Natural Pedagogue": The Life-Long Educational Quest of Richard Slater (1854–1939), "Father of Salvation Army Music", as described in his Manuscript Diaries', unpublished report of the Finzi Scholarship Award. Submitted to the Finzi Trust, 30 Apr. 2008.

[17] Wiggins, *Father of Salvation Army Music*, p. 7.

[18] C. Steedman, *Master and Servant: Love and Labour in the English Industrial Age* (Cambridge, 2007), p. 9.

resource. Slater numbered each volume consecutively 1–24. In addition to the 24 volumes, there are three small supplementary volumes (volumes 1a, b, c). The diaries up until 1905 were transcribed by Slater into longhand from earlier volumes, no longer extant, written in shorthand. He completed this transcription in 1908. Also included is a retrospective account of his early years. Although he had intended to compile a straight chronological account, in fact he was considerably less systematic, and frequently entries appear out of sequence. The diaries after 1908 are more chronologically ordered (although not completely). For the researcher, reading the diaries is rather like riding on a dizzying switchback, going constantly forward and then back. At least half of the 24 volumes are over 500 pages long, and at times I had to agree with Carolyn Steedman in her astute observation that 'too much documentation poses its own problems'.[19]

As a result of working with the diaries and realising their richness of detail, I became convinced that my study should expand from my original intention which had been to focus upon the years of Slater's active service in the Salvation Army (between 1884 and 1913), to encompass the years from his birth (1854) to his death (1939), as this would provide an effective frame for a wider history of Salvationist music-making. I believe that knowing something of his remarkable life before he became a Salvationist provides an intellectual and social context within which to place the Salvation Army and its music-making, and, of course, to understand something of the motivations and character of the 'Father of Salvation Army Music'.

It was at a fairly late stage that through the good offices of the Salvation Army's International Heritage Centre I was able to work with a further crucial unpublished primary source, the six volumes of the proceedings and the final report of the influential Commission of Enquiry into Salvation Army Music which met between 1915 and 1916.[20] These proceedings and report had been rescued from the bombed International Headquarters building in London in May 1941, when most of the Army's other historical records were lost. They provide a verbatim account of the evidence presented by a variety of leading Salvationists concerning the state of Salvation Army music-making at that time. As a primary source these volumes were invaluable, providing rare glimpses into the ongoing debates within the Army about its musical life.

To account for the progress of Salvation Army music-making in the inter-war years I went back to the Salvationist periodicals as an invaluable record, and for a commentary decided to use Richard Slater's entries in his diaries on those occasions when he felt impelled to state his views on the musical life of the organisation to which he had devoted most of his working life. These years were

---

[19] Ibid., p. 8.

[20] The Salvation Army, 'Report of the Commission of Enquiry into Matters Relating to Salvation Army Music' (unpublished, 1916); 6 vols of the Proceedings, and the Report: The Salvation Army International Heritage Centre.

dominated by Eric Ball (1903–1989) who was to become the leading composer, conductor and adjudicator in the brass band world, and I supplemented my sources to include evidence from his writings and from recorded interviews that he gave.

As far as editorial and presentational procedures are concerned, some explanation is required of my referencing to the Richard Slater Diaries which I abbreviate as 'RSd'. My extracts from the diaries are exact, including any underlinings, and occasional misspellings. I have taken the decision to reference the diary entries in the text, rather than as footnotes, so as not interrupt the flow for the reader, and also to avoid an unmanageable number of footnotes. Every quotation from the diaries will include the volume number and the date of entry e.g. RSd, v. 24, 1 Nov. 1939. On occasion Slater does provide an end-of-year review in his diaries, in which case I designate this as 'annual review' preceded by volume number and the year e.g. RSd, v. 9, 1904, annual review. When Slater came to compile his diary he also included a retrospective account of his early life entitled 'Early Memories'. References to this account omit the date of the entry, as the material is drawn from memory, and the volume and page numbers are included, e.g. RSd, 'Early Memories', v. 1, p. 158.

In my referencing of musical scores for band, I refer to four series of Salvationist publications for bands in the text: the Band Journal (BJ 1884–present, now termed the Ordinary Series); Second Series for smaller bands (SS 1921–present, now termed the Triumph Series); Festival Series for more advanced bands and music (FS 1923–2006); Judd Street Collection superseding the Festival Series (2006–present). I simply provide the specific numbering of the item: e.g. Slater's *The Italian March* (BJ 490), Marshall's *Army of the Brave* (FS 6). This will aid in locating the scores referred to. For works warranting closer discussion I shall also include the date of publication. Readers will notice that occasionally Salvation Army bands are referred to by number e.g. Reading 1, Reading 2. This applied when there was more than one corps (worship centre) in a town: the numbering was according to whether the corps was the first to be established, or the second etc.

I have adopted the following editorial conventions. Although the legal name of the movement is The Salvation Army, as is common practice I forego the capitalisation of the definite article, and occasionally to prevent too much repetition I use the term, 'the Army'. I do not, however, use the popular abbreviation 'S.A.' unless directly quoting from another source which does employ it. I have generally omitted the ranks of Salvation Army officers, as these changed rapidly due to promotions. I have, however, retained them when quoting from transcripts, and occasionally when it was needed to emphasise the seniority of an individual. Any interpolations of my own in quotations are enclosed within square brackets, e.g. [*sic*], or when I omit words or phrases within a quotation, e.g. […]. In the opening chapter I have provided a glossary of Salvationist terms, to aid non-Salvationists in their reading of the book.

Now for some description of the book's structure and content. Chapters 1–5 relate to the years between 1854–1913, from Richard Slater's birth to his retirement from active service in the Salvation Army. Chapters 6–8 deal with the First World War years, followed by the inter-war years 1919–39, concluding with Slater's death. Finally there is an Afterword which brings the story up to date.

Chapter 1 introduces the reader to the Salvation Army, with an account of its early history, its beliefs and practices, some account of the musical context at the time, William Booth's views on music in the service of religion, and the Army's first band. The chapter serves as a backdrop for the rest of the book. Chapter 2 is based upon Richard Slater's own extensive account of his early life contained within his diaries. This casts light on his childhood and his self-education in music, literature and the science of human character. All this led him to work as a music teacher, and then as lecturer on phrenology and music in working men's clubs, leading to his first tentative contacts with the Salvation Army.

Chapter 3 focuses upon Slater's decision to enter the Salvation Army as a full-time officer and his leadership of the Musical Department of the Salvation Army from 1883 until his retirement in 1913. He was responsible for overseeing an extensive publishing programme of original vocal and instrumental music, and for composing much of it. The chapter details the numerous battles Slater was involved in with the Army authorities who were worried that the musical development of its troops might deflect them from their primary mission of evangelisation. As a contrast to the internal workings of the Salvation Army's Musical Department, a full account is provided of George Bernard Shaw's encounter with the Salvation Army in 1905, which received considerable newspaper coverage, and resulted in a confidential critique of the Army's music by Shaw. The chapter concludes with an account of Slater's relationship with William Booth, and his fight to receive the copyright fees he believed were owed to him by the Army.

Chapter 4 examines musical participation amongst Salvationists, itemising the extent and diversity of instrumental and vocal groupings, as well as linking all this with the essentials of religious conversion and commitment. The chapter also investigates the occupational backgrounds of over 1,000 Salvationist band members, which contributes to the debate about the extent to which the Salvation Army was a grass-roots working-class musical religious movement.

Chapter 5 addresses ways in which Salvationist musicians acquired their musical skills and knowledge. Central to Richard Slater's cause was the effective musical education of his troops. Through competitions, examinations, published tutors and musical instruction books, Slater created a powerful means of education, which ensured a musical self-sufficiency amongst the Army's musicians, whether as performers, composers or arrangers. The chapter concludes with a number of educational life histories of some leading Salvationist musicians.

World War I forms the backdrop for Chapter 6, which commences with a description of the International Congress of 1914, which demonstrated the musical growth of the Salvation Army across the world. The following year a

Commission of Enquiry into the Army's musical life was set up, and surviving records present a valuable series of commentaries on the state of Salvation Army music at that time from musical experts, local music leaders, and officers. The report looks both forwards and back. The chapter then proceeds to assess the impact of the First World War on Salvationist musicians both at home and abroad. There was an enhancement of the public role of Salvation Army Bands, but at the same time membership of musical sections were severely depleted through enlistment.

Chapter 7 surveys developments between 1919 and 1939, years which were dominated by the work of Eric Ball as a composer and conductor. Other significant composers included Philip Catelinet, Bramwell Coles, and George Marshall, all of whom together with Ball were members of the Music Editorial Department. On the one hand, honours and recognition poured in for Salvation Army bands, with their admired technical skills and increasing musical sophistication; but on the other hand external and internal tensions surfaced. A key development during these years was the growing involvement of Salvation Army bands in broadcasting and recording, in both of which Eric Ball was a considerable force as conductor and composer.

Chapter 8 depicts the final years of Richard Slater's life including his efforts to publish his research on Wagner, and his general political sympathies. This is followed by an assessment of his life and work, paying particular attention to his creation of a musical world, his contribution to the development of Salvation Army bands, the provision of an appropriate Salvationist musical repertoire, and meeting the educational needs of Salvationist musicians.

In the Afterword, a view of Salvation Army music today is presented. There are clear indications that in the 21st century there has to be adaptation and sometimes profound change, but I argue that what remains is a steadfast conviction amongst musical Salvationists that music remains one of the Army's defining symbols.

M Y personal motivation in undertaking this study lies in my own biography. My childhood in the 1950s was dominated by the sound world of the Salvation Army. I had been born into a Salvationist family. My parents were full-time Salvation Army officers, and my paternal grandfather had been Bandmaster of the Exeter Temple Band for 54 years, a Salvation Army record at the time. Growing up in the Army meant that I received a rich musical education. I became a self-taught bandsman and took my place in a community which was both socially and musically a separate world. I was able to develop my skills as a pianist at Salvationist meetings, and learnt through necessity the arts of instant keyboard harmonisation and improvisation. I became acutely aware that this musical world, with its spontaneity and informality seemed separate from the musical culture into which I was being inducted through piano lessons and music theory instruction. It was a bicultural musical existence. On leaving school I won a place at the Royal Academy of Music, and this sense of bifurcation increased in my mind. By the time I completed my studies I was no longer a Salvationist, but my experience within the movement triggered a lifelong fascination with such matters as the relationships between music and religion, music and social change, and formal and informal styles of music-making and musical education. I went on to explore these in my studies in folklore at the Memorial University of Newfoundland, and in my doctoral studies in music education history at the University of Reading.[21] A consideration of these relationships now provides the underpinning of this historical study of Salvationist musical culture.

As far as my own role in writing this book is concerned I feel some creative tension. In my formative years I was an 'insider' in the Salvation Army, but now I am a cultural 'outsider', looking on and reflecting. Bruno Nettl in his classic text *The Study of Ethnomusicology* (2005) mentions the idea of joint research by an insider and an outsider as a way of bridging chasms.[22] I trust that my perspectives as both insider and outsider will sharpen and enliven the narrative and thus enable me to do justice to the unique musical worlds both of Richard Slater, and the Salvation Army.

---

[21] I have pursued some of these themes in my previous books. See G. Cox, *Folk Music in a Newfoundland Outport* (Ottawa, 1980); *A History of Music Education in England, 1872–1928* (Aldershot, 1993); *Living Music in Schools, 1923–1999* (Aldershot, 2002).

[22] B. Nettl, *The Study of Ethnomusicology: Thirty-one Issues and Concepts*, 2nd edn (Champaign, IL, 2005), p. 158.

CHAPTER 1

The Origins of the Salvation Army and its Musical World

THERE was no mistaking the palpable sense of excitement and anticipation amongst the Salvationists of the cathedral city of Exeter as they celebrated their 12th anniversary in 1893. Their Commanding Officer, Captain George Kendall, put it like this in a pamphlet specially prepared for the occasion:

> The strength of Exeter Corps this Anniversary speaks volumes for its success; in fact ever since the Colours were unfurled, there has been a ceaseless flow of success; its converts must be counted by thousands, members of all denominations have been recipients of much spiritual good through its instrumentality.[1]

Kendall reeled off the statistics: 418 soldiers on the roll; 252 conversions within a year; open-air services attended by 500 individuals weekly; Sunday congregations numbering 3,500; week night attendance totalling 1,100. A section was devoted in the pamphlet to 'Our Band'. Kendall made a special point about the 24 bandsmen:

> Their services [...] are devoted to the cause, without the slightest return whatever in the shape of pay. Not even their bandmaster who is responsible for the musical efficiency of the band, receives one penny for his services; but does his duty to the men and the cause out of love for the same.[2]

However, there was a warning against complacency, there was still much to do:

> Crowds are yet unsaved [...] in a multitude they crowd our thoroughfares, listen at our open-air services, follow our band, and flock to our temple [...] Thus with the fire of holy zeal, prompting our service of love, we will 'Go Forward'.[3]

Such reports of progress were not unique to Exeter, nor indeed to Britain, for by 1890 the Salvation Army had invaded 34 countries, and this overseas expansion made it the fastest-growing Christian sect in an age of missions.[4] By 1900 it was reckoned the Salvation Army had a membership in Great Britain of an estimated 100,000.[5]

---

[1] G. Kendall, *The Salvation Army, Exeter Corps: 12th Anniversary Review* (Exeter, 1893), p. 7.

[2] Ibid., p. 2.

[3] Ibid., pp. 3, 4.

[4] Murdoch, *Origins of the Salvation Army*, p. 136.

[5] A. D. Gilbert, *Religion and Society in Industrial England* (London, 1976), p. 42.

In this chapter, in order to provide an overall context for the book, I shall investigate some of the historical circumstances that underpinned the Salvation Army's advance in William Booth's lifetime, one of the outcomes of which was the creation of a distinctive musical world in which Salvationist musicians were empowered to express both exhilaration and reflection in their evangelical mission. I shall focus on the following aspects: William Booth and the founding of the Salvation Army, together with a brief outline of its organisation, beliefs and practices; the plebeian musical tradition from which the Salvation Army drew much of its sustenance; the growth of Salvation Army music with reference to Booth's views on singing and the development of a vocal repertoire based partly on secular tunes; the beginnings of what was to become the iconic musical symbol of the movement, the Salvation Army band.

✌ William Booth (1829–1912) and the Salvation Army

The 19th century in Britain was in many ways 'the Evangelical century'.[6] Christian Evangelicalism had one aim: to bring everyone to conversion. Such conversions focused the individual upon personal salvation, ideals of moral behaviour, and manifestations of outward piety. Underpinning this evangelical rebirth was the notion of the individual as a 'free moral agent'. As Callum Brown argues, personal conversion was democratic, and had the effect of moving religion out of the control of civil-ecclesiastical powers. It deregulated religion, thereby creating a demand for a plurality of churches competing one with another for the religious affiliation of the people.[7]

The so-called 'salvation revolution' coincided in the 1790s and 1800s with the industrial revolution and its accompanying rapid urbanisation. New social problems had been created, particularly within the new urban working class, including the breakdown of social relationships, children having to work long hours six days a week, and increasing prostitution and drunkenness. It is within this context that evangelicalism has to be seen. It became immediately popular amongst the new working classes, and it imbued women as well as men with a sense of spiritual equality. But evangelicalism also provided a moral package suited to the regulation of the 'lower orders' who were now out of reach of institutional control.[8] Christian evangelicals led the way as far as philanthropy was concerned, believing that the gospel and humanitarianism were complementary to each other. This philanthropic tradition was most notably represented by the prison reform work of Elisabeth Fry, and the care of orphans by

---

[6] C. Brown, *The Death of Christian Britain: Understanding Secularization* (London, 2001), p. 43.

[7] Ibid., pp. 36–9.

[8] Ibid., pp. 41–2.

Dr Barnardo.[9] Indeed, the churches were the most obvious source of help in a society which, until shortly before the First World War, lacked a state welfare system. In the churches of Reading for example, individual congregations provided a variety of agencies dealing with visiting the sick, encouraging sewing for the poor, setting up soup kitchens, Provident Clubs, Coal and Clothing Clubs, Loan Blanket Societies, Infants' Friends Societies, Penny Banks and maternity groups.[10]

One of the outcomes of the 'salvation revolution' was the Salvation Army. Any consideration of this remarkable movement must start with acknowledging the role of its charismatic founder, William Booth. Born in Nottingham on 10 April 1829, Booth at the age of 13 was apprenticed to a Unitarian pawnbroker, across whose counter he daily faced profound and chronic poverty. He imbibed both Chartism and Methodism in his youth, and they played a crucial role in his later decision to take the gospel to the poor and socially unacceptable.[11] In 1849 William Booth arrived in London to search for work. He eventually became a minister in the Methodist New Connexion, and on 17 June 1855 married Catherine Mumford, who was to exert a profound influence upon him. Eventually he became disillusioned with the New Connexion and worked as an itinerant preacher.

In 1865 he began preaching in the East End of London and founded the Christian Mission, which was intent on reaching the urban working class. The Mission was distinctive because of the authority it gave to women, its emphasis upon holiness theology, and its strict hierarchical structure.[12] Much of the Booths' theology was influenced by American revivalists, most notably James Caughey, Charles G. Finney and Phoebe Palmer, all of who preached at some point in England.[13] Their methods converted sinners through advertising meetings in rented halls, preaching and praying for specific results, bringing sinners to open confession of sin at a penitent form, and training converts to win others. Coupled with this was the close link with British Methodism and the thinking of John Wesley. William Booth, according to Roger Green, was 'rooted and grounded in Wesley's theology and tradition'.[14] The Booths' Wesleyanism stood mid-way between extreme Calvinism and such mid-19th-century

---

[9] D. W. Bebbington, *Evangelicalism in Modern Britain: A History from the 1730s to the 1980s* (London, 1989), p. 120.

[10] Yeo, *Religion and Voluntary Organisations in Crisis*, p. 58.

[11] See Woodall, *What Price the Poor?*, pp. 6–42.

[12] Walker, *Pulling the Devil's Kingdom Down*, p. 20.

[13] Murdoch, *Origins of the Salvation Army*, p. 1.

[14] Green, *The Life and Ministry of William Booth*, p. 36. With regard to its Methodist roots, Hugh McLeod makes the point that the Salvation Army was 'heir to the Primitive Methodist tradition of plebeian evangelicanism'. See H. McLeod, *Religion and Society in England, 1850–1914* (Basingstoke, 1996), p. 164.

expressions as transcendentalism and free thought. Faith, repentance and restitution for past wrongs brought conversion and this led to holy living. Thus salvation included both new birth (conversion) and an experience of holiness (entire sanctification).[15] Along with biblical trustworthiness and Trinitarianism[16] these doctrines became the creed of the Christian Mission. It was somewhat later, that Booth dispensed with the sacraments of baptism and communion, in a similar way to the Quakers. A fundamental policy of the Mission was to establish an equal place for women within its ranks. Such thinking was influenced by Catherine Booth, whom Hattersley has described as 'the most formidable woman of the nineteenth century'.[17]

With reference to hierarchical structure, a Deed Poll was approved by the Mission's Annual Conference and registered as the Foundation Deed in 1875.[18] This gave William Booth unique and exceptional powers. The Mission was to be overseen and directed by one person, Booth himself. A fear developed later that his successors as President or Chairman of Conference would automatically be members of his family, in effect it would be a family-run concern.[19]

Gradually the use of military titles grew within the Mission, so that Booth was sometimes known as 'General of the Hallelujah Army'. The story is recounted that one of Booth's great allies and colleagues, George Scott Railton, was discussing with William and his oldest son Bramwell the preparation of the yearly appeal:

> Railton read 'We are a volunteer army'. Bramwell interrupted with 'Volunteer! I'm a regular or nothing!', and William Booth [...] paused, took the pen from Railton's hand, and stooping over his shoulder, crossed out the word 'volunteer' and wrote 'salvation'.[20]

'The Salvation Army' was first used as the movement's title in September 1878. Booth made it clear that he was creating a system modelled after Queen Victoria's imperial command:

---

[15] Phoebe Palmer, the American revivalist, was a key influence on the Salvation Army's teaching of holiness. She suggested that the experience of holiness was both an 'event in time' and 'a way of life'. It took place when a person gave her heart to Christ, and the way of life consisted of 'continued exercise of faith and obedience' to God. See L. Taiz, *Hallelujah Lads and Lasses: Remaking the Salvation Army in America, 1880–1930* (Chapel Hill, NC, 2001), pp. 14–15.

[16] Trinitarianism is the distinctively Christian doctrine that God exists in three persons, Father, Son and Holy Ghost.

[17] R. Hattersley, 'Shaw and the Salvation Army', in programme for National Theatre production of Shaw's *Major Barbara* (London, 2008), n.p.

[18] Sandall, *The History of the Salvation Army*, vol. 1, p. 181.

[19] For a fuller discussion of the constitutional issues, see Larsson, *1929*, pp. 15–20.

[20] C. B. Booth, *Bramwell Booth* (London, 1933), p. 97.

It is a remarkable fact that our system corresponds so closely to that of the Army and Navy of this country that we have been able to use even the very words of many of their regulations.[21]

Essentially William Booth was autocratic in his government of the Salvation Army, and this was to engender considerable tensions within the organisation, and more specifically with its musical direction as we shall see. It is difficult to overstate the extent of this dictatorial tendency which is encapsulated in the following comment contained within Booth's *Orders and Regulations for The Salvation Army* dating from 1880:

It is precisely under the absolute military system that it is possible to keep the greatest liberty for each one without losing the perfectly united action of all.[22]

Military nomenclature became *de rigeur*. The Christian Mission's *evangelists* eventually became known as *field officers* and the Christian Mission *station* became the Salvation Army *corps*. In January 1879 the *Christian Mission Magazine* changed its name to the *Salvationist*, and in February, Booth used the term *General* for the first time.[23] As for the place of women in the ranks, Booth held to his principles:

the Army refuses to make any difference between men and women as to rank, authority and duties, but opens the highest positions to women as well as to men.[24]

The following is a listing of some of the most important Salvation Army terms adapted for spiritual use:

Articles of War A statement of beliefs and promises signed by all Salvationists

Blood and Fire The motto of the Salvation Army referring to the blood of Christ and the fire of the Holy Spirit

Cadet Someone (male or female) in training to become a full-time officer in the Salvation Army

Citadel A hall used for worship

Colours The flag of the Salvation Army – blue for the purity of God; red for the blood of Christ; yellow for the fire of the Holy Spirit

Commission A document conferring authority upon officers and local leaders

Corps A ministering unit of the Salvation Army

[21] W. Booth, *Orders and Regulations for the Salvation Army* (London, 1880), p. 9.

[22] Ibid., p. 6.

[23] Murdoch, *Origins of the Salvation Army*, p. 104.

[24] W. Booth, *Orders and Regulations for the Salvation Army* (1880), p. iii.

'Fire a Volley' An instruction to shout 'Hallelujah' or 'Glory'

Firing a Cartridge Paying a tithe in the weekly collection

General The international leader of the Salvation Army

Junior Soldier A young person who has been converted and has signed the Pledge

Knee Drill Early morning prayer meeting

Officer A Salvationist who has left secular employment and has been 'commissioned' to serve within the Salvation Army – comparable to an ordained minister

Mercy Seat (or Penitent Form) A bench serving as a place of prayer placed at the front of the worship space

Promotion to Glory Description for the death of a Salvationist

Rank Based on years of service or special appointment. Today officers in the Salvation Army may be Captains, Majors, Colonels, and Commissioners, although previously there had been a plethora of ranks (e.g. Senior-Captain, Staff-Captain, Senior-Major, Brigadier etc.).

Soldier An enrolled member of the Salvation Army who has signed the Articles of War

Swearing in The public enrolment of a Salvation Army soldier

War Cry The weekly evangelical publication of the Salvation Army[25]

Norman Murdoch has pointed out that this Victorian love of militarism inspired the formation of such religiously based youth organisations as the Boys' Brigade (1883), the Church Lads' Brigade (1890), the Boys' Life Brigade (1899), and Boy Scouts (1908), not to mention the Church of England missions which merged to form the Church Army (1882).[26]

When we come to consider how William Booth's ideas were put into practice at the local level it is important to realise that the heart of the Salvationist evangelistic mission lay in the 'corps' of 'soldiers' based in a 'citadel' under the leadership of a 'commanding officer'. The corps officers were responsible for leading worship, and William Booth laid down strict regulations in 1886, as in the following timetable for Sundays to be followed by every corps:

7 a.m.	Knee-drill
10 a.m.	Procession and open-air meeting
11 a.m.	Holiness meeting
2 p.m.	Procession and open-air
3 p.m.	Free-and-Easy

[25] 'Salvation Army Terminology', in programme for National Theatre production of Shaw's *Major Barbara* (London, 2008), n.p.

[26] Murdoch, *Origins of the Salvation Army*, p. 111.

6 p.m.   Procession and open-air
7 p.m.   Indoor Salvation meeting
8 or 8.15 p.m.   Prayer-meeting begins.[27]

Some explanation is needed here. Open-Air meetings (in Salvationist parlance, 'open-airs') had the sole purpose of evangelical outreach. Usually held on street corners, they were populist in style, with music used as an element for attracting crowds. Traditionally they concluded with a march to the citadel. In the early days of the Army in addition to three 'open-airs' on a Sunday, there were frequently four such meetings held during the week. This emphasis on outdoor meetings was close to Booth's heart: 'It has from the beginning been the boast of the Salvation Army that its cathedral is the open-air.'[28] The Sunday morning Holiness Meeting was designed primarily for Christian believers especially the soldiers (lay members) of the corps, while the afternoon 'Free-and-Easy' (a term taken over from the early days of music hall)[29] was a Praise Meeting with often an emphasis on music and song, designed initially to attract those who had been drinking in public houses which were required to close at 3 p.m. The evening Salvation Meeting was designed primarily to reach unbelievers who may have been attracted as a result of an open-air meeting. In addition, Sunday would start with a prayer meeting (a 'knee-drill') and sometimes end with 'A Halle-lujah Finish', a kind of celebratory coda to the day.[30] Worship was not confined to Sundays, however; there was a great deal of weekly activity, as will become apparent in later chapters.

In spite of all this burgeoning activity, there is a view that because Booth eventually received little lasting success in reaching the casual poor through such evangelism, he turned to social reform as expounded in his classic text, *In Darkest England and the Way Out* (1890).[31] It had been on 30 November 1887 that Booth came across men sleeping rough on the Embankment by the side of the River Thames. He was adamant that something needed to be done.[32] Eventu-ally Booth identified that there were three million men, women and children 'in a condition nominally free, but really enslaved'.[33] This 'submerged tenth' of the population comprised the destitute, and Booth identified a number of schemes which might transform their lives, including plans for a city colony, a farm colony and overseas colonies, in addition to crusades aimed at criminals, drunkards, 'lost women', street children and 'moral lunatics'. Once the Darkest

---

[27] W. Booth, *Orders and Regulations for Field Officers of the Salvation Army* (London, 1886), p. 305.

[28] Ibid., p. 293.

[29] See D. Kift, *The Victorian Music Hall* (Cambridge, 1996), pp. 17–18.

[30] W. Booth, *Orders and Regulations for Field Officers* (1886), pp. 320–1.

[31] W. Booth, *In Darkest England and the Way Out* (London, 1890).

[32] Sandall, *The History of the Salvation Army*, vol. 3, p. 68.

[33] Booth, *In Darkest England*, p. 23.

England Scheme was launched, it altered the perception of the Army in the eyes of the public, and it caused Booth's work to come much more into the public domain, especially as he was asking for donations totalling one million pounds.

According to Anne Woodall, the scheme, although impressive in scope, did not succeed as a whole in terms of its original goals.[34] However, the Army's willingness to seek a solution to the problem of poverty made the organisation acceptable in the more tolerant climate at the end of the century. Possibly influenced by this change of direction, influential members of the Establishment lionised Booth in the early Edwardian years: he was received by Edward VII in 1904, and granted an honorary doctorate from Oxford University in 1907. For the historian E. P. Thompson, however, such official recognition was 'the kiss of death' for what might have been a socially radical movement.[35]

&. A Plebeian Musical Tradition

At this point I change my focus to consider the general musical context of the late 19th century in Great Britain, in order to appreciate some of the chief influences on the Salvation Army's musical mission.

It is a common view that the period after 1880 forms the English Musical Renaissance: a movement which gave new vitality and higher standards to national musical life.[36] In particular it wanted to escape from the domination of such German composers as Mendelssohn and Wagner, and to ensure that England would not be thought of as 'The Land without Music'.[37]

Pre-dating the English Musical Renaissance, but later contributing to it, was the mania for sight-singing that gripped the country as far back as the 1840s, leading the 19th century to be described as 'The Sight Singing Century'.[38] In many ways the establishment of sight-singing classes for adults and children became a moral crusade led by middle-class reformers seeking to use music as a force for social regeneration.[39] It was the dissenting minister John Curwen (1816–80) and his Tonic Sol-fa method that came to dominate most of this activity in schools and communities. The method provided an easy and effective introduction to singing at sight, based as it was on the 'movable doh', in which

---

[34] Woodall, *What Price the Poor?* p. 207.

[35] Thompson, 'Blood, Fire and Unction', pp. 25–6.

[36] See M. Hughes and R. Stradling, *The English Musical Renaissance 1840–1940: Constructing a National Music*, 2nd edn (Manchester, 2001).

[37] See B. Rainbow, *The Land without Music: Musical Education in England 1800–1860 and its Continental Antecedents* (London, 1967, r/1991).

[38] P. Scholes, *The Mirror of Music, 1844–1944: A Century of Musical Life in Britain as Reflected in the Pages of the 'Musical Times'* (London, 1947), vol. 1, p. 1.

[39] See Cox, *A History of Music Education in England.*

the tonic of the new key was always 'Doh'.[40] By John Curwen's death in 1880, he had introduced Tonic Sol-fa to the world, justified its existence, and made it self-sufficient.

What is of particular interest for this study, is McGuire's contention in *Music and Victorian Philanthropy*, that the Tonic Sol-fa movement was to play an indispensible role in some of the great moral philanthropic ventures of the period including temperance and missionary endeavour. He points out that fundamental to Tonic Sol-faists was the belief that music would greatly aid the moral improvement of men, women and children, although music was only a means to that end.[41] There are clear parallels in all this to Salvationist musical practice.

As a result of much of this musical activity the English Musical Renaissance witnessed a remarkable enthusiasm for amateur choral singing, evidenced in the great annual festivals at Birmingham and Leeds, and numerous competitive choral festivals and competitive musical festivals throughout the country. It is probable that one of the reasons why the choral movement in the Victorian era gained much of its popularity was because it was so suited to such an overtly religious society with its repertoire of cantatas and oratorios. In many ways 'the choral concert was the ideal musical vehicle of the age'.[42]

Alongside the sight-singing and choral traditions were equally important developments in popular music-making. Dave Russell has identified three key processes in this respect: expansion, diversification and nationalisation. Expansion of musical activity meant that more people purchased instruments. Connected to this expansion was a marked increase in the number of 'musicians and music masters': the figure of 19,000 in 1871 had risen to 47,000 by 1911.[43] The diversification of new styles, genres and institutions can be illustrated with the case of Bradford: by 1900 within 5 miles of the town there were almost 30 choral societies and some 20 brass bands, not to mention six concertina bands, an amateur orchestra, a team of handbell ringers, two music halls and a number of venues for popular concerts.[44] Finally, nationalisation was stimulated from the 1840s by the growth of cheap rail travel. This enabled such events to take place as the Belle Vue and Crystal Palace brass band championships, which involved the transportation of thousands of competitors and spectators over distances of up to 300 miles. Likewise the armies of music-hall performers, opera singers

---

[40] See C. E. McGuire, *Music and Victorian Philanthropy: The Tonic Sol-fa Movement* (Cambridge, 2009), p. 8.

[41] Ibid., p. 2. For a discussion of the distinctions between philanthropic and socialist thought in relation to music, see C. Waters, *British Socialists and the Politics of Popular Culture, 1884–1914* (Manchester, 1990), pp. 100–1.

[42] D. Russell, *Popular Music in England 1840–1914: A Social History*, 2nd edn (Manchester, 1997), p. 17.

[43] Ibid., p. 5.

[44] Ibid., pp. 5–6.

and concert artists were similarly dependent on the railway network.[45] It will become apparent in later chapters that Salvationist music-making reflected several of these developments.

Two of the key musical influences from popular culture on the Salvation Army, were the music hall, and the minstrel show. The principal source of musical entertainment initially for the working and lower-middle classes was the music hall. Stemming from the tavern concert rooms of the 1840s, it achieved 'respectability' as far as the middle classes were concerned from the 1890s.[46] Indeed, the so-called Golden Age of the halls spanned 1890 and 1914, with an audience firmly representative of all classes: what today we would call a mass audience.[47] Alongside music-hall songs and ballads the show would also include a selection of dances, dramatic sketches, and sometimes acrobats and trapeze artists.[48] Another essential feature of popular culture from the 1840s both in Britain and the United States was Blackface Minstrelsy. The comic blackface mask was as Michael Pickering has observed, 'a staple icon of British popular culture'[49] lasting well into the 1970s. Musically, minstrelsy drew on music hall and parlour songs, plantation melodies and comic ditties, alongside spirituals that had been introduced into the country by the black American university students, the Jubilee Singers from Fisk University, in their tour of Britain in 1873.[50] Scott makes the point that minstrelsy retained a cross-class appeal in Britain, in particular selling itself to the middle classes as wholesome entertainment.[51] Alongside the communal popular musical styles of the music hall and minstrel shows was the flourishing largely middle-class growth of the drawing-room ballad which catered for the needs of the bourgeois domestic market.[52]

With this general picture of popular music-making in view I now narrow the focus to look at civilian brass bands, volunteer bands and church bands, all

[45] Ibid.

[46] D. B. Scott, *Sounds of the Metropolis: The 19th Century Popular Music Revolution in London, New York, Paris and Vienna* (Oxford, 2008), p. 48.

[47] R. Middleton, 'Popular Music of the Lower Classes', in *The Romantic Age, 1800–1914*, ed. N. Temperley, The Athlone History of Music vol. 5 (London, 1981), pp. 63–91 (p. 81). Also, for a discussion of the relationship between music halls and working class life, and the growth of a second audience of sporting aristocrats, guards officers etc., see G. S. Jones, *Languages of Class: Studies in English Working Class History, 1832–1982* (Cambridge, 1983), pp. 224–36.

[48] Scott, *Sounds of the Metropolis*, p. 48.

[49] M. Pickering, *Blackface Minstrelsy in Britain* (Aldershot, 2008), p. xii.

[50] Scott, *Sounds of the Metropolis*, p. 165.

[51] Ibid., p. 147.

[52] D. B. Scott, *The Singing Bourgeois: Songs of the Victorian Drawing Room and Parlour*, 2nd edn (Milton Keynes, 2000), p. ix.

of which were the precursors of Salvationist bands.[53] The British brass band movement had its roots in the industrial North, although as Derek Scott points out the steel, ironworks and shipping companies of East London also had bands in the 1860s.[54] Underpinning the movement was the widespread sponsorship of works bands by factory owners. In many ways this was a reflection of the view that like choral singing, banding 'represented a force for the moral elevation of working people'.[55] From a technological point of view it was the invention of the piston valve system and its application to brass instruments in the mid-19th century that has been described 'as the principal reason why a large, working-class brass band movement came into existence'.[56] This enabled all instruments to be fully chromatic, and the valve principle could be applied to any brass instrument from the highest to the lowest.[57] The development of brass band contests from the 1840s set the seal on the arrival of the new form: 'The contest is the thing that has brought the brass band into the greatest prominence and has been its greatest glory.'[58] Contests became popular attractions. On 10 and 11 July 1860 the Crystal Palace, a huge glass conservatory in Sydenham built originally in Hyde Park for the Great Exhibition of 1851, held its first brass band contest with spectacular success. There was an estimated crowd in attendance of 29,000 over the two days.[59] As we shall see, however, Salvation Army bands during Richard Slater's lifetime were strictly segregated from the mainstream of brass band development and from contesting itself.[60]

Another strand in the brass band movement was the Volunteer Force, authorised in 1859, which comprised an army of home guards, replaced in 1908 by the Territorial Army.[61] The Volunteers were a popular part of Victorian life, with their uniforms and bands, embodying Victorian values of patriotism and self-help. Predominantly working-class, by the 1870s its membership reached 200,000 even though there was no material incentive, and its members were always out

---

[53] See Herbert, 'God's Perfect Minstrels'; R. Newsome, *Brass Roots: A Hundred Years of Brass Bands and their Music, 1836–1936* (Aldershot, 1998); J. F. Russell and J. H. Elliot, *The Brass Band Movement* (London, 1936).

[54] Scott, *Sounds of the Metropolis*, p. 62.

[55] T. Herbert, 'Nineteenth-Century Bands: Making a Movement', in *The British Brass Band*, ed. Herbert, pp. 10–67 (p. 32).

[56] Ibid., p. 25.

[57] Ibid., p. 29.

[58] Russell and Elliot, *The Brass Band Movement*, p. 77.

[59] Newsome, *Brass Roots*, p. 38. For details of the Crystal Palace, see *The London Encyclopaedia*, ed. B. Weinreb and C. Hibbert (London, 1995), pp. 221–2, and M. Musgrave, *The Musical Life of the Crystal Palace* (Cambridge, 2005).

[60] Russell and Elliot, *The Brass Band Movement*, p. 206.

[61] H. Cunningham, *The Volunteer Force: A Social and Political History* (London, 1975).

of pocket. From the beginning, bands were seen as a desirable and, for many, an essential part of the volunteer movement.[62] For our purposes, as Norman Murdoch observed, 'the volunteers furnished a model for the salvationists [...] Each army provided a cause in an era of causes; they attracted Victorian diligence while not neglecting a love of play.'[63]

Finally in looking at the plebeian precursors of Salvation Army bands we need to consider church bands. Vic Gammon has pointed out that from the mid-17th to the mid-19th century, musical services in rural Anglican churches were dominated by what he calls plebeian choirs and bands, described most famously by Thomas Hardy in *Under the Greenwood Tree* (1872).[64] Gammon found in his research on church bands in Sussex that in contemporary impressionistic accounts, such bands were described in phrases like 'an orchestra of farm labourers' whose members were 'of the peasant class', although in fact it was found that much strength was drawn from artisan tradesmen.[65] However, by the end of the 1860s very few of these mid-19th century old-style bands and choirs existed.[66] They were replaced by parish choirs and the organ or barrel organ, part of a movement led by the Tractarians in the Church of England to 'improve' church music by introducing surpliced choirs of men and boys.[67] For Gammon the employment of a single (usually middle-class) organist in place of a band or choir destroyed the potential for association through activity.[68] Furthermore, hymn books took the place of individually compiled manuscripts. This could be interpreted as symptomatic of the conflict between elite and popular cultural values, parallel to the suppression of traditional popular recreations. For E. P. Thompson such movements demonstrated that 'the Church lost command over the leisure of the poor'.[69]

In a later contribution to the discussion about the historical development of the brass band, Sheila and Vic Gammon maintain that it became an important

---

[62] Herbert, 'Nineteenth-Century Bands', p. 37. Henry Livings notes the relationship between the Dobcross Band and the local Rifle Volunteers between the mid-1870s and 1883 in *That the Medals and the Baton be Put in View* (Newton Abbott, 1975), pp. 12–15.

[63] Murdoch, *Origins of the Salvation Army*, pp. 102, 103.

[64] V. Gammon, '"Babylonian Performances": The Rise and Suppression of Popular Church Music, 1660–1887', in *Popular Culture and Class Conflict, 1590–1914: Exploration in the History of Labour and Leisure*, ed. E. and S. Yeo (Brighton, 1981), pp. 62–88.

[65] Ibid., p. 65.

[66] Ibid., p. 78.

[67] See B. Rainbow, *The Choral Revival in the Anglican Church, 1839–1872* (London, 1970, r/2001).

[68] Gammon, 'Babylonian Performances', p. 82.

[69] E. P. Thompson, 'Patrician Society, Plebeian Culture', *Journal of Social History* 7 (1974), pp. 382–403 (p. 391).

agent of change from the old plebeian musical tradition. Brass bands had used copied-out manuscripts, but with the development of cheaper printed music, print took over from manuscript. Performance became increasingly print based: 'as the pressure for excellence grew, the pressure to read well must also have grown'.[70] However, the Gammons maintain that something of the idiom and style of the old tradition found its way into music hall and then popular music, perhaps to be reabsorbed into pub singing. But, intriguingly for the purposes of this study, the Gammons state that 'something of the old tradition was retained in the populist evangelical music of the Salvation Army – brass instruments, anglo-concertinas, and all'.[71] This will become evident in some descriptions later in the book which relate to the performance styles, repertoire and background of early Salvationist musicians.

❧ 'Filling the world with Salvation by the means of Salvation Music'

By the turn of the century William Booth dreamt 'of filling the world with Salvation by the means of Salvation Music, and the agency of Salvation bandsmen'.[72] But he stressed that unlike cricket clubs or choral societies, Salvation Army bands had a much higher purpose, no less than promoting the Glory of God to a dying world. The barriers between 'inside' and 'outside' were erected: he made it clear that Salvationists had to abstain from alcohol and gambling, and from attending or taking part in cricket or football, theatres, music-halls, the circus, concert-halls, dancing halls and bazaars.[73] However, as Rapp has pointed out, the Salvation Army desired to appeal to the working classes on their own level by adapting certain elements of their culture for Salvationist purposes, thus making Christianity as accessible and attractive to them as possible.[74] Music was to play a vital role in this cultural adaptation.

In this section I shall discuss three aspects of early Salvationist musical culture. First Booth's thinking about the use of music in the service of religion

---

[70] V. and S. Gammon, 'The Musical Revolution of the Mid-Nineteenth Century: From "Repeat and Twiddle" to "Precision and Snap"', in *The British Brass Band*, ed. Herbert, pp. 122–54 (p. 131).

[71] Ibid., p. 152.

[72] W. Booth, 'The General Thanks his Bandsmen', *Field Officer*, Dec. 1900, p. 2.

[73] W. Booth, *Orders and Regulations for the Salvation Army* (1880), p. 20. Dominic Erdozain points out that such an emphasis by Booth upon separation from, and denunciation of secular recreation was a survival of a mentality that was normative for early evangelicals, but rare by the last quarter of the century. See D. Erdozain, *The Problem of Pleasure: Sport, Recreation and the Crisis of Victorian Religion* (Woodbridge, 2010), pp. 158–9.

[74] Rapp, 'The British Salvation Army', p. 163.

with particular attention to singing. Second, the implications of Booth's intention of 'robbing the devil of his choice tunes'. Third, the emergence of the Salvation Army's first brass band.

BOOTH'S THOUGHTS ON MUSIC IN THE SERVICE OF RELIGION

At one level William Booth appeared to relish music. His granddaughter, Catherine Bramwell Booth, paints a delightful picture of the musical life of the eight Booth children:

> And there were singing bouts! This whole flock of children was taught to sing and to love singing. William Booth loved music [...] though he played no music, his 'ear' was good; the music was in him. He sang as he went up and down stairs, he sang while dressing in the morning, and to the last days of his life he sang. And all the children sang too. What joyful shouting! Two or three of them on and around his knees, the rest at hand; all singing. [...] Of the eight, six wrote tunes, and all but one have written songs which are likely to be sung as long as hymn-singing constitutes a part of Christian worship.[75]

This picture is not quite the same when it came to Booth's somewhat cautious and guarded musical pronouncements about music in the service of religion. William Booth believed that music in itself had neither a moral nor a religious character. In an article entitled 'Music and the Fighting Spirit' published in the *Local Officer*, an unattributed quotation from Wesley reflects Booth's position:

> Listed into the cause of sin
> Why should a good be evil?
> Music, alas, too long has been
> Pressed to obey the devil.[76]

Likewise for Booth, if the Salvation Army could harness music for its own purposes he could embrace it. He used a striking image:

> Music acts on the soul as the wind on a ship, helping her forward in the direction in which she's steered. If she is sailing down the rapids of passion, direct for the falls of damnation, music will increase her speed and keep her merry on that awful course [...] But if steered along the track of Holiness straight for the port of glory, music will send her along more rapidly.[77]

---

[75] C. B. Booth, *Bramwell Booth*, p. 25.

[76] Quoted without details of source, *Local Officer* 4 (1900–1), p. 11.

[77] W. Booth, 'Singing', *Local Officer* 3 (1899–1900), p. 282. There are some resonances here between Booth's ambivalence towards music, and the debate going back to Plato and Boethius on the distinction between music's positive and negative influences. See B. Rainbow with G. Cox, *Music in Educational Thought and Practice*, 2nd edn (Woodbridge, 2006), p. 28.

We can find the practical implication of Booth's views on music in an address he gave at the last conference of the Christian Mission in 1877 on 'good singing'.[78] He believed singing in worship should be congregational, and poured scorn on the American practice in some churches of getting together 'a few people with fine voices by advertisement and pay[ing] them two, three or four hundred dollars per annum [...] they simply go in for sweet sound'.[79] On the contrary, Booth exclaimed, singing should be hearty, 'not a mincing, proper set of sounds given forth from a mere sense of duty and even pleasure'.[80] He believed merely professional music was always a curse, 'and should you ever find a choir in connection with any hall in this mission, I give you my authority to take a besom and sweep it out'.[81] Booth found choirs in general had three devils that were 'impossible to cast out': the quarrelling devil, the dressing devil, and the worst of the three, the courting devil. He declared to the assembly: 'We don't want, my brethren, and we are all agreed not, at any price, to have choirs.'[82]

He ended his address with five indispensable conditions for good singing. First, the singing should be heartfelt:

> The secret of cold, icy fishy singing is heartless formality. Fishy hearts can only make fishy music [...] Instead of a singing class or a musical machine, you want a penitent form, a hurricane of grace, a baptism of fire.[83]

Second, he wanted good songs, not sentimental rubbish. Third, was his most well-known requirement, good tunes. But in this respect he admitted to being a utilitarian, preferring the useful to the ornamental.[84] Booth's fourth requirement was for good pitch, and finally 'we must have good time [...] I always look upon slow singing as a sign of a low, backsliding spiritual condition in a society'.[85]

There was in all this a fear that his organisation could become like a church, and hence lose contact with that class of people alienated from formal religion. Booth's first lieutenant, George Scott Railton, put it like this:

> We shall never, we trust, so utterly mistake our path as to encourage anyone to try to ape the ministry. We trust the Christian Mission will never be crippled with a college, a theological seminary, a mutual improvement society, or a singing class.[86]

[78] W. Booth, 'Good Singing', *Christian Mission Magazine* 9 (1877), pp. 202–9.

[79] Ibid., p. 203.

[80] Ibid.

[81] Ibid., p. 204.

[82] Ibid.

[83] Ibid.

[84] Ibid., pp. 205–6.

[85] Ibid., p. 207.

[86] G. S. Railton, *Heathen England and What to do for it* (London, 1888), p. 184.

This was all consistent with Booth's suspicion of scholarship, and a certain anti-intellectualism.[87]

'ROBBING THE DEVIL OF HIS CHOICE TUNES'

William Booth's hunt for good tunes to sing involved him in taking his material from popular, secular traditions, including the music hall which as we have seen had become the staple of working-class culture. He led by example. As far back as 1866 in the days of the Christian Mission, James Dowdle, an early ally, recollected that he had heard William Booth sing 'Oh, how I love Jesus' to the tune of 'In and Out the Windows'.[88] Booth had no qualms about trespassing into the culture of secular entertainment, in fact he relished it:

> I rather enjoy robbing the devil of his choice tunes, and, after his subjects themselves, music is about the best commodity he possesses. It is like taking the enemy's guns and turning them against him.[89]

This reinforces Pamela Walker's view that Booth really wanted to convert working-class neighbourhoods, not through encouraging withdrawal from the world, but through a transformation of their urban culture.[90]

Salvationist song writers were encouraged to set sacred texts to popular, secular tunes. Gradually national melodies, jingoistic ones and popular sentimental ballads were all incorporated into the early Salvation Army repertoire. However, Booth was at first uncomfortable with comic music-hall songs. When he first heard the tune 'Champagne Charlie is my name' sung to verses by William Baugh, 'Oh, bless His Name', Booth exclaimed 'That's too wild!'[91] Booth's initial reservation is understandable. 'Champagne Charlie' was immensely popular with music hall audiences as a song of release and action. It was release from work, and action meant drinking.[92] It was a 'swell' song, in which the hero keeps the champagne industry afloat. Musically it comprised a simple and repetitive march theme, thereby appealing to Salvationist taste. On a subsequent occasion when he was in Bristol, Booth called upon a Captain

---

[87] See Murdoch, *Origins of the Salvation Army*, pp. 31–2.

[88] *Local Officer* 4 (1900–1), p. 11.

[89] W. Booth, 'Good Singing', p. 205.

[90] Walker, *Pulling the Devil's Kingdom Down*, p. 205. Walker also draws attention to the other side of the reciprocal relationship between the Salvation Army and music-halls, in which the music-halls parodied the uniformed preachers and ecstatic services of the Army, p. 175.

[91] 'Old Songs and Old Tunes: Brigadier Baugh and 'Champagne Charlie'', *Bandsman, Local Officer and Songster*, 8 Aug. 1914, p. 507.

[92] For an extended discussion of the song, see P. Bailey, *Popular Culture and Performance in the Victorian City* (Cambridge, 1998). Bailey points out that 'Champagne Charlie [...] received its ultimate accolade from the Salvation Army who appropriated it for a hymn tune' (p. 111).

Fielder, himself a fiddler, for a song. Fielder started off with 'Oh, bless His Name', and as its tune ('Champagne Charlie') was so well known particularly in the South of England, it 'was heartily taken up by the crowd, and especially by the unsaved in the gallery'.[93] This time Booth was won over. He commented, 'I never heard anything more sacred', whereupon he ordered it to be placed on the front page of the *War Cry*, although it had already appeared on the back page in the Christmas 1881 issue.[94]

However, not all of William Booth's influential financial backers agreed with such a policy, and some threatened to withdraw their support.[95] Booth decided to put the matter to the test on a most auspicious and public occasion, the opening of the Clapton Congress Hall in May 1882. This iconic Salvation Army building (now demolished) in the heart of London's East End had formerly been The London Orphan Asylum, and was acquired by the Army for use as a National Training Barracks and a Congress Hall.[96] We shall see later that its band had considerable prestige. At the opening the large congregation included a number of key non-Salvationist supporters. Gipsy Smith, a Salvation Army officer, who became well known as a revivalist, sang 'The blood of Jesus cleanses white as snow' to the tune 'I traced her little footsteps in the snow', followed by Adelaide Cox with 'If you want pardon if you want peace' to 'Pretty Louise'. Finally 'Sailor' Fielder sang 'the converted version' of 'Champagne Charlie':

> The large congregation was soon carried away. Choruses were repeated again and again and gradually public resentment weakened until everyone was clapping hands in rhythm with the songs and waving handkerchiefs. In this unexpected way hand-clapping was first introduced into Army meetings and the battle for the 'devil's tunes' was won.[97]

This wedding of popular secular tunes to sacred words became embedded in the Salvation Army's musical life, particularly pre-1914. If we take one example: the periodical *The Field Officer* published a series of 12 'Popular Songs to Popular Airs' between January and December 1906.[98] Of these, six belonged directly to the music hall tradition including 'In the shade of the old apple tree'[99] to the words, rather improbably of 'Gethsemane', 'I'll be your sweetheart'[100] to 'I'll be

---

93 'Old Songs and Old Tunes', p. 507.

94 Ibid.

95 Boon, *Sing the Happy Song!*, pp. 115–20.

96 Sandall, *The History of the Salvation Army*, vol. 2, p. 211.

97 Boon, *Sing the Happy Song!*, p. 116.

98 *Field Officer*, Jan.–Dec. 1906.

99 'In the shade of the old apple tree', by Harry Williams and Egbert Van Alstyne, 1905. See M. Kilgarriff, *Sing us one of the Old Songs: A Guide to Popular Song, 1860–1920* (Oxford, 1998), p. 535.

100 'I'll be your sweetheart', or 'Bluebells', by Harry Dacre 1899. See Kilgarriff, p. 176.

a soldier', 'Navaho'[101] to 'The Cleansing Stream', and 'I wouldn't leave my little wooden hut for you',[102] to 'I know a lot of funny things they do'. The remaining two music hall tunes had associations with the Salvation Army. Sir Harry Lauder, 'the first knight of the music hall', had wooed and won a Salvationist girl, and this led him to write 'I love a lassie',[103] first recorded in 1905, to which the text 'I love the story' was set. The second song with Salvation Army associations was by George Robey, billed as 'the Prime Minister of Mirth' whose song 'A thing he'd never done before' included the lines,

> When mama saw that papa was a-treading virtue's path,
> She said, Salvation Army-like
> 'Oh what a soul he hath'.[104]

The Salvationist text took over the song's title, but then related it to a convert's renunciation of drink and becoming 'a red-hot soldier' in the Salvation Army.

Of the rest of the songs in the collection, two were based upon tunes made popular in the American Civil War ('The Vacant Chair',[105] and 'The Girl I left behind me'),[106] another was sung by minstrel troupes ('Silver Threads').[107] Finally in this eclectic mix there was an American gospel melody ('Throw out the lifeline'),[108] a jingoistic tune ('Under the Union Jack') and a sentimental ballad ('My dear old mother I shall meet again').

In the *Orders and Regulations for Field Officers of The Salvation Army* (1886), Booth enumerated the advantages of singing such secular tunes. Because they were known by a large portion of the audience they could be sung 'right off, without any loss of time'.[109] As they pleased the ear of the people a ready entrance was gained 'for the sentiments which we want to convey to their

---

[101] 'Navaho', by Williams and Alstyne (1903), and in the repertoire of Peter Dawson, Louise Pounds and Ellanine Terriss. See Kilgarriff, pp. 313, 354, 355.

[102] 'I wouldn't leave my little wooden hut for you' by Tom Mellor and Charles Collins, 1896, sung by Daisy Dormer and Clarissa Talbot. See Kilgarriff, p. 49.

[103] 'I love a lassie', 1905, sung by Harry Lauder. See Kilgarriff, p. 42; Boon, *Sing the Happy Song!*, pp. 119–20.

[104] 'A thing he'd never done before' by C. W. Murphy 1911(?), sung by George Robey. See Kilgarriff, pp. 331, 495.

[105] 'The Vacant Chair', by Henry Washington and George F. Root, 1861. See Kilgarriff, p. 513.

[106] 'The Girl I left behind me', an English March – Eighteenth Century, in W. Chappell, *Old English Ditties from Popular Music of the Olden Time* (London, n.d.), vol. 1, pp. 172–3.

[107] 'Silver Threads' by Eben E. Rexford and H. P. Danks, 1873. 'Sung by sundry minstrel troupes'. See Kilgarriff, p. 83.

[108] 'Throw out the Lifeline' by Edwin S. Ufford, 1888. See www.nethymnal.org/htmt/h/throwout.htm.

[109] W. Booth, *Orders and Regulations for Field Officers*, p. 230.

hearts'.[110] Advantages appeared to outweigh 'any evils associated with the use of them'.[111] Booth addressed the moral character of music in relation to the employment of secular tunes:

> It has been objected that they are profane and ought not to be used for sacred work. To this we reply that there is no moral character in the music itself [...] The tune a man sings has no more moral character in it than the voice with which he sings it.[112]

He rejected the notion that using such tunes would stir up memories of sinful days: 'the so-called "roughs" in our buildings, even when in mocking mood, seldom or never sing the original words to these tunes'.[113] Finally Booth exhorted that his officers should seize upon every good tune they came across.

As far as congregational hymns or songs were concerned, William Booth compiled with the help of an early convert, Mary C. Billups, a collection of most of the hymns sung in the Christian Mission, including church hymns, American gospel songs, spirituals and songs set to national tunes. It was called *Revival Music* and was published in 1876.[114] It was enlarged to 533 tunes in 1880, and was renamed *Salvation Army Music*.[115] This in turn was supplemented by *Salvation Music Volume II* in 1883, which contained many of the earliest Army original compositions.[116] As Slater was to point out later, 'It was in this volume that this great stream of original music made its start.'[117]

THE FIRST BAND OF THE SALVATION ARMY

The first Salvation Army band came into existence in 1878 at Salisbury, and was a family affair consisting of Charles William Fry, and his three sons, Fred, Ernest and Bert playing two cornets, one slide trombone and one euphonium.[118] The history of the Fry family reveals a whole host of musical interconnections which are significant in a discussion of the rise of music in the Salvation Army,

[110] Ibid.

[111] Ibid.

[112] Ibid., pp. 230–1.

[113] Ibid., p. 231.

[114] *Revival Music: A Complete Compendium of Revival Music for Evangelistic Services, Open-Air Meetings, and the Home Circle*, compiled by William Booth for the use of the Christian Mission (London, [1876]).

[115] *Salvation Army Music (formerly published as 'Revival Music') with Supplementary Tunes*, compiled by William Booth for the use of The Salvation Army (London, 1880).

[116] *Salvation Music*, vol. 2: *Being a Collection of the Favourite Songs of the Salvation Army*, compiled by W. Booth (London, 1883).

[117] Slater, *Salvation Army Dictionary of Music*, p. 113.

[118] Ibid., p. 10.

involving self-help, church bands, volunteer bands, and chapel choirs.[119] Charles was a bricklayer, plasterer and slater (in this sense, an artisan) who became a builder, but above all was a keen musician, playing any valved instrument, the harmonium and piano, and string instruments. He had been a solo cornet player in the 1st Wiltshire Rifle Volunteer Band. Charles was the leader of the Wesleyan Chapel Choir, and under his direction the choir sang such staple works as 'Mozart's "Twelfth" Mass', Mendelssohn's *Elijah*, Haydn's *Creation*, and Handel's *Judas Maccabeus*.

He taught his sons to play both brass and string instruments, and they formed an ensemble comprising two violins, viola and cello. They played in the small orchestra (church band) at the Alderbury Wesleyan Chapel, which like many church bands became defunct and was replaced by a harmonium. The Fry family was drawn to attend the early meetings of the Christian Mission in Salisbury, and their playing attracted the crowds. Eventually William Booth heard them play at an open-air meeting in March 1878. He noted their drawing power, and they started to work for him full-time, in particular attending his Councils of War in different parts of the country and assisting at the opening of large halls for the Army's work. It was clear that the main duties of such bands could include heading a march, guiding the singing of a congregation and in quieting a noisy crowd. The hope was that every corps would in time have its own band.[120]

The Salvation Army became stirred up with respect to bands. The situation became chaotic and anarchic, as depicted in retrospect by Richard Slater:

> Every instrument that was available was pressed into service, forming in some cases, peculiar mixtures that certainly could not commend themselves to a trained Bandsman of the present day. Violins, flutes, banjos, guitars, concertinas, as well as various forms of brass and reed instruments were brought together. A joyful noise was attained, if the charms of harmony were absent on such occasions [...] Of course there was no music to play from, and every man did very much as his fancy led him, with what results the imagination of the musical will scarcely dare to seek to realise. This state of things could not but be preliminary.[121]

---

[119] See Fry Family Papers, The Salvation Army International Heritage Centre.

[120] F. W. Fry, 'Leaves from the Diary of an Early-Day Musical Composer', *Bandsman and Songster*, 13 Jan. 1934, pp. 9–10.

[121] Slater, *Salvation Army Dictionary of Music*, p. 11. There was considerable opposition to the Salvation Army's early musical efforts, particularly from the pages of the *Musical Times*: 1 Feb. 1881 (pp. 73–4), 1 Apr. 1881 (p. 178); 1 June 1881 (p. 296); 1 Feb. 1882 (p. 76); 1 Oct. 1884 (pp. 576–7); 1 July 1889 (p. 400).

❧ *Summary*

The soldiers of Booth's Army had no doubt that they were engaged in a quest which could transform the lives of the poor and the society in which they lived. George Kendall's troops in Exeter were reminded forcefully of the task before them:

> We are engaged in a terrific battle; against sin and vice of every description. Every person on being enrolled as a soldier, soon finds out that God and the Army expects them to do their share in the fighting, which as a rule is joyfully undertaken; and with the indispensable strength of unity, a mighty effort is being made daily to suppress the Nineteenth Century evils, which are so apparent all around us.[122]

Music came to be seen as an appropriate weapon in such warfare. However, there were many different ideas about the part that music could play in these early years of the Salvation Army, some of them contradictory: a puritanical distaste for performance and display; a desire to incorporate popular culture into worship and to create a parallel working-class culture; a requirement to develop militaristic musical genres and styles to reinforce the Army's aggressive mission often in the open air; a view of music as being morally neutral; the development of a centralised and autocratic control over the lives of adherents; an ambivalent relationship with plebeian musical traditions. Much of the success in facing up to the musical implications of these seemingly oppositional ideas and forging a distinctive Salvationist musical world, was largely due to one man, Richard Slater, to whose story we now turn.

---

[122] Kendall, *The Salvation Army, Exeter Corps*, p. 7.

CHAPTER 2

Who was Richard Slater?

I N this chapter and the next I shall investigate the life of Richard Slater from his birth in 1854 until his retirement in 1913. I shall maintain that because of his achievements as the 'Father of Salvation Army Music'[1] he should be regarded as an outstanding figure in the history of working-class music-making in the service of religion in Great Britain in the late 19th and early 20th centuries. The most important fact about him is that he was the lynch-pin of the Musical Department of the Salvation Army between 1883 and 1913, responsible for shaping the rapid musical development of the movement in its formative years.[2] Although Slater is still remembered within the Salvation Army, elsewhere he is ignored or forgotten.

In considering how to organise Slater's life story, much of it drawn from his diaries, it became apparent to me that it would be best to present it in two halves. In this chapter I shall focus upon Slater's earliest years up to his conversion at the age of 28. This will be followed in Chapter 3 by an account of his subsequent career in the Salvation Army and his crucial influence upon its music-making, principally in the years between 1883 and 1913, the year of his retirement. However, Slater will be a constant presence throughout the book, as he continued to take a lively interest in the Salvation Army's musical life until his death in 1939. I shall discuss his musical legacy in the book's final chapter.

Slater is a fine example of a Victorian working-class autodidact, brought up in poverty, for whom learning was lifelong.[3] His self-education up until 1882 engaged him with amateur and professional musicians, with religious and temperance organisations, and with sceptics and free-thinkers. He eventually managed to establish himself, albeit somewhat precariously, as a lecturer in phrenology and music in Working Men's Clubs, and as a teacher of violin, piano and voice. His story during these years presents a fascinating portrayal of the Victorian working-class intellectual and musical worlds. It is my intention to reveal something of the educational, religious, social and cultural contexts within which Slater was to develop new ways of thinking and being, which culminated in him joining William Booth's Salvation Army.

---

[1] See Wiggins, *Father of Salvation Army Music*.

[2] For autobiographical details, see R. Slater, 'Life of Staff-Captain Slater of the Training Home', *War Cry*, 7 May 1887; R. Slater, 'My Twenty-Six Years Service', *Bandsman and Songster*, 24 Apr. 1909, pp. 3–4.

[3] P. Gardner, '"The Life-long Draught"; From Learning to Teaching and Back', *History of Education*, 36:4–5 (2007), pp. 465–82.

🙜 *Early Years, 1854–70*

Richard Slater was born on 7 June, 1854, in 6 Oldham Place in the district of Clerkenwell, adjoining the City of London.[4] His father was Alfred Richard Slater, a brass founder, married to Mary Ann Suich, of Italian extraction. The next time we encounter Slater in official documents is in the 1861 census, where we read that Mary Ann Slater was now a widow whose occupation was a laundress. She was living at 27 Brighton Street, King's Cross, a house which contained 11 inhabitants including herself and her two children, Richard, aged 6, and Eliza, his younger sister.[5]

Slater himself provides some detail about his grandparents in his account of his early life, from which the data in this section are drawn. On his paternal side his grandfather came to London from Christmas Common in Oxfordshire, and settled in business as a coal merchant and greengrocer on the Blackfriars Road. Slater remembered him vividly:

> He became fond of drink, but not so as to ruin his business, and his love of women was more than platonic. He was a robust, healthy, full-bodied man of about medium height, of a cheerful disposition and fond of society where he soon made friends. He had little or no education, and more than once gave forth the opinion that most of what is in books are lies. (RSd, 'Early Memories', v. 1, p. 158)

Slater's maternal grandmother had become acquainted with her future husband when he was working as a gentleman's servant in London. He had come originally from Naples at the time of the Napoleonic Wars. As the result of a crisis he had put to sea with his brother in order to escape to England. Slater's mother, Mary Ann Suich, was the oldest of three sisters. She also had five brothers. Her own mother died in very poor circumstances, receiving bread and money from the parish.

Slater's parents were married in 1853. They had met at Kew where Alfred was playing cricket. Mary Ann happened to be there, and 'an intimacy sprang up from this chance meeting which ultimately ended in marriage'. According to Slater, Alfred was an engineer who had served his apprenticeship with a City firm, working with success on ships' pumps. He had also produced some inventions of his own: 'his ingenuity was never exhausted'. The plan was that Richard would undertake employment in the same firm. Alfred had learned to play the violin as a boy, and the currency for payment was a bag of coal from his father's business. He eventually played as an amateur in the Orchestra of the Sacred Harmonic Society at the Exeter Hall under Sir Michael

---

4 Richard Slater birth certificate, General Register Office.
5 1861 Census, The National Archives.

Costa.[6] Alfred was also an able singer, particularly fond of the songs of Henry Russell.[7] Tragically, he died from consumption at the age of 28. Richard recollected 'I have some memory of the last struggle, and this motionless form of my father on the bed, and all was over' (RSd, 'Early Memories', v. 1, p. 156).

Mary Ann had helped to bring up her brothers and sisters when she was only a girl, and then worked as a cook and for a while also served in a public house. Like Alfred, she was a singer, she was fond of reading, and knew by heart almost all of *Hamlet*:

> She was dark, had an abundance of black hair, and in her early years had some signs of her Italian ancestry. She could be the life of a social gathering, by wit, song, and untiring effort to meet the needs of others [...] In her later years she sought comfort in religion, reading her Bible [...] and attending the Cromer St. Mission Hall meetings [...] Moral worth seemed to her more important than profession of a creed or performance of ceremonies. (RSd, 'Early Memories', v. 1, pp. 173–4)

Slater was devoted to his mother. Sadly, two of her four children died soon after Alfred's death when they were both very young. Slater succinctly itemised the disadvantages he encountered in his early years: 'bad sight, great poverty, narrow circumstances; and, being fatherless' (RSd, 'Early Memories', v. 1, p. x).

For the next 17 years the family lived in Cromer Street in the heart of the King's Cross district of London. It was an area dominated by the railway: King's Cross station opened in 1852 as the terminus for the Great Northern Railway, and the adjoining St Pancras Station opened as the terminus for the Midland Railway in 1868.[8] King's Cross had a bad reputation, long notorious for poverty and prostitution.[9] Charles Booth, the social reformer, observed in his classic study of the poor in London undertaken in the 1880s and 1890s, that 'the lowest of women used to live in the vile quarter off Cromer Street'.[10] The mean streets of King's Cross and its immediate surroundings comprised the focal point of Slater's life until he was 28, and in fact for some years before he retired, his office was located in Judd Street, situated right beside Cromer Street.

Today there is little evidence of the buildings in which Slater lived; Cromer

---

[6] The Sacred Harmonic Society was London's outstanding large-scale choral society, whose home was the Exeter Hall, 1832–89. The Society had its own orchestra. See Scholes, *The Mirror of Music*, vol. 1, pp. 24–8.

[7] Henry Russell (1812–1890), whose songs include 'Cheer Boys, Cheer', 'A Life on the Ocean Wave', and 'Oh! Woodman Spare that Tree'. See Scholes, *The Mirror of Music*, vol. 1, p. 511; Scott, *Sounds of the Metropolis*, pp. 66–7.

[8] L. Picard, *Victorian London: The Life of a City, 1840–1870* (London, 2006), pp. 43–4.

[9] M. Hunter and R. Thorne (eds), *King's Cross* (London, 1990).

[10] C. Booth, *Life and Labour of the People in London. Third Series: Religious Influences*, vol. 2: *London: North of the Thames: The Inner Ring* (London, 1902), p. 174.

Street is now a mixture of modern high-rise flats, and tenements built by 'East End Dwellings' between 1892 and 1904. A prominent feature is the Holy Cross Church, built in 1887 – a fine example of the Tractarian tradition – which today includes a refugee centre. Its sign proclaims it 'the church in the heart of King's Cross'. There is no sign now of the Cromer Street Mission Hall which figured prominently in Slater's life. However, the Boot Tavern, which Dickens immortalised in *Barnaby Rudge* (1841) is still there, although it does not figure in Slater's story.

At first the family lived in a kitchen below a shop; later they progressed to a front kitchen. Mary Ann's main occupation was mangling, a job which allowed women to earn at home, even if there were no facilities for washing. The mangle took up space often in cramped conditions. Anna Davin quotes an observer of a house in Stepney, writing in 1892, 'The Mangle half fills the kitchen, while the parlour and the passage from the front door are often blocked with bundles of clothes.'[11] It was the heaviest job associated with laundry work. Even so, as we shall see, it was a task that was often carried out by children

Richard Slater described the occupation vividly:

> At least mother's main earnings were by taking in clothes for mangling which was done by what was called a box mangle, as the body of it was of [a] long box form filled with stones to give pressure to the rollers that were under it. At one side in the centre was a handle which worked a top roller to which was attached a chain of just length to allow the box to go to and fro over the under-rollers. I used to turn the handle as well as fetch and return clothes for mangling. (RSd, Early Memories, v. 1c, p. 26)

He later recollected the contents of the one-room kitchen where he lived with his sister and mother: a box mangle, a [shut-up] bedstead, a fireplace, a washstand, two boxes one over the other serving as a table, a small round table, a window, chairs, a large cupboard, coal cellars, steps leading up to the street, a clock with a swinging pendulum (RSd, Early Memories, v. 1c, p. 27). For sleeping he made his bed on the box mangle with a few chairs added to extend the length, while his mother and sister slept on a shut-up bedstead pulled down from the wall (RSd, Early Memories, v. 1, p. 177). Such descriptions of the working-class interior are, as Steedman observes, 'an extraordinary rarity'.[12]

Slater mentioned little about his schooling. He attended an infants' school in a house near the Regent's Canal; after his father's death he moved to Dutton Street School, off Cromer Street, and then for some unremembered reason he went to the nearby Woburn Place School, off Marchmont Street. In retrospect he felt he had been disadvantaged at school because he could not see the blackboard due to his poor sight. For this reason he was often excused writing work, which

---

[11] A. Davin, *Growing Up Poor: Home, School and Street in London* (London, 1996), p. 47.

[12] C. Steedman, *Dust* (Manchester, 2001), p. 117.

he thought one of the reasons for his bad handwriting later in life. In his later school days he only attended three days a week, as he had to help his mother at home to fetch or take back clothes for mangling: 'As a boy I had some very heavy loads of clothes to carry at times. I used to carry these clothes baskets on my shoulder and have thought some evil results did arise at the time' (RSd, 'Early Memories', v. 1, p. 190). He also had to turn the mangle on Fridays and Saturdays. Undoubtedly times were hard. Slater reflected in his account that

> I have no idea how much mother earned by mangling, but beyond doubt we were in deep poverty. How she managed to pay rent, buy food and clothes I cannot imagine. It was a hard brave fight. She never applied for or received parish relief. Yet I have no memories of shortage of food or clothes. (RSd, 'Early Memories, v. 1c, pp. 26–7)

The Cromer Street Mission Hall was a significant place for Slater. Established in 1854, it was a Baptist Chapel, run in Slater's day by the London City Mission.[13] It provided Slater with his first start in music, which was through his membership of the drum and fife band of the mission's Band of Hope, a leading temperance organisation.[14] Slater became an excellent B♭ flute player, and as a result was invited on numerous occasions to play with other bands. Sometimes he received a fee. Slater was a member of the Cromer Street Sunday School, where he eventually taught. The Sunday School Superintendent was a Mr Woolacot, 'a man of education and worldly means', who was a significant influence on Slater, encouraging him in his wide reading.

A continual fear for Slater, which lasted well into adulthood, was that he would go blind, as there were inherited problems with cataracts in the family. It was for this reason that both his mother, and her brother, Frank, were keen that the boy received violin and musical tuition of various sorts. They believed that violin playing, maybe in the streets, might serve to be a good source of income when blindness finally struck. Indeed, it was his uncle Frank who took him onto Hampstead Heath in order that he might play 'here and there' on his violin. He introduced the boy to an old violinist busker, and also purchased a book of popular tunes in order to encourage Slater to acquire such a repertoire. Eventually in 1908 Slater underwent a successful operation which removed the cataracts (RSd, v. 10, 14 Nov. 1908).

Slater had a variety of teachers, but perhaps the most significant was J. Sidney Jones (1838–1914), who taught him the violin. The two met through the Cromer Street Mission's drum and fife band. In fact Jones had been bandmaster of the

---

[13] The London City Mission was founded in 1835 and was the largest and most successful of the interdenominational city missions. It financed evangelists who were normally attached to particular congregations. See Bebbington, *Evangelicalism in Modern Britain*, p. 119.

[14] See J. F. C. Harrison, *Drink and the Victorians: The Temperance Question in England, 1815–1872* (London, 1971), pp. 192–4.

5th Dragoon Guards, and was one of the leading military bandmasters of his day, finally becoming conductor of the Harrogate Municipal Orchestra.[15] Slater used to practise the violin for hours as a boy, in the front-room kitchen in Cromer Street, as well as reading voraciously:

> My memory lingers over that poor room, recalling the many happy hours I enjoyed there in the days of the opening out of my mind. (RSd, 'Early Memories', v. 1, p. 177)

Slater also undertook a little work for pocket money as a delivery boy for a harmonium bellows maker, called Mr Bath, who was a concertina player. With the proceeds Slater made many of his early purchases of music and books. He listed some of the musical scores he purchased when he was 15 (in 1869), including Haydn's *Creation*, and Handel's *Samson* and *Jephtha*. One of his chief friends at this time was Alfred Edwards, with whom he shared an interest in music and reading. Alfred eventually became, like his brothers, a piano maker.

On a later occasion Slater recalled his musical progress:

> As I grew up my mother decided that I should try music as a profession, and at much self-sacrifice – as she was really poor – I was put under different masters [...] Apart from my set studies I pushed on in other directions, such as the study of harmony, counterpoint and composition for in my teens I felt an impulse towards making music.[16]

𝄢 *The Autodidact, 1871–82*

In his diary entries between 1871 and 1882, from when he was 17 until he was 28, Richard Slater charted his personal search for a cause to which he could devote his energies and talents. At the start he was living with his mother at 66 Cromer Street, and listed as 'unemployed'[17] although he was kept busy helping his mother with her mangling. Eleven years later in 1882 he made the momentous decision to join the Salvation Army and to enter it as a full-time officer. He approached his search during these years with great seriousness of purpose, demonstrating his qualities as an ardent autodidact.

Much of my interpretation of Slater's life will be grounded in this autodidact culture, which Jonathan Rose has traced back as far as the Middle Ages, and particularly relevant for this study, has documented its surge in the 19th

---

[15] For further details on Jones, see T. Herbert and J. Wallace, 'Aspects of Performance Practices: The Brass Band and its Influence on other Brass-Playing Styles', in *The British Brass Band*, ed. Herbert, pp. 278–305 (p. 281); Newsome, *Brass Roots*, pp. 21, 96, 115; A. Lamb, 'Jones (James) Sidney', in *New Grove 2*, vol. 13, p. 199.

[16] Slater, 'My Twenty-Six Years Service', p. 3.

[17] 1871 Census, The National Archives.

century.[18] The mission of the autodidact was 'to be more than passive consumers of literature, to be active thinkers and writers'.[19] Gardner argues that the autodidact's passion for education was 'a process of individual self-discovery';[20] the engagement with learning was lifelong. Indeed, it was 'an inherently emancipatory exercise, and therefore a deeply moral one'.[21] As we shall discover, Slater's life was underpinned by such a passion.

In this account of Slater's life between 1871 and 1882, I shall consider five crucial stages in his overall development as a thinker, a musician and a teacher: first, coming to terms with ideas which eventually were to result in a rejection of the Christian faith; second, some discouraging attempts at musical composition; third, a fascination with phrenology, and its connections to music teaching; fourth, participation in amateur music-making, and a passion for Wagner; fifth, making a living as an itinerant lecturer in London's Working Men's Clubs.

Although there is inevitably some overlap between the sections, I have attempted for the most part to treat Slater's progress chronologically through these years.

THE ADVANCEMENT OF LEARNING

Throughout his life Slater listed his reading in his diaries. At the age of 17 he was relishing the great poets, notably Tennyson, Goethe, Scott, Browning and Spenser. A couple of years later he was engrossed in psychology and philosophy, reading John Locke's *Essay Concerning Human Understanding*, the essays of Jeremy Bentham, Dugald Stewart's *Elements of the Philosophy of the Human Mind* and Francis Bacon's *Essays*.

He recalled his excitement on finally purchasing a copy of Francis Bacon's *Novum Organum*:

> I have a clear recollection of my buying this work, making many attempts to get it, going in shop after shop in vain […] After our mangling work was done on March 14, 1874, I remembered hurrying off to Hollowell [sic] Street, Strand, at the shop at the corner of the west end of the street expecting to get a copy, as I had called sometime before […] I found they now had a copy, which I received with intense excitement and interest, and wondered with some anxiety if after all it was in Latin and not English […] On reaching home my joy was great to find *Novum Organum* was in English and with notes, and that unexpectedly *The Advancement of Learning* was in the same volume […] on mother's return, she asked me if I was satisfied

---

[18] J. Rose, *The Intellectual Life of the British Working Classes* (New Haven, CT, 2001). See also E. P. Thompson, *The Making of the English Working Class* (Harmondsworth, 1968), pp. 781–820.

[19] Rose, *Intellectual Life*, p. 57.

[20] Gardner, 'The Life-long Draught', p. 467.

[21] Ibid., p. 468.

with my book [...] My reply was of the brightest character and I said I had much more than I expected. (RSd, v. 7, 1881, annual review)

In *Novum Organum*, published in 1621, Bacon put forward the idea that in building a true model of the world in the human understanding, it was necessary to dissect its anatomy.[22] Slater understood from this that there were three stages in the growth of the individual mind: the grasp of the actual, the perception of the possible, and the extraction from the possible of the proper and sustained endeavour for its accomplishment (RSd, v. 1, 1877, annual review). He elaborated on the extent of Bacon's influence upon him in a letter to Sir George MacFarren, the distinguished blind composer and Principal of the Royal Academy of Music:[23]

> My mind eagerly desires to be such as Bacon – a true teacher and guide of men as to what they are, and what their surroundings are, and what therefore they should seek. (RSd, v. 5, 13 July 1876)

Meanwhile Slater was avidly acquiring knowledge and devouring ideas. His reading was now encompassing Kant, Goethe, Schlegel and Swedenborg (RSd, v. 6, 5 Sept. 1877). In 1874 he attended the Latin class held in Mr Woolacot's house, Slater being provided with the necessary books by his Sunday School Superintendant. Two years later we learn that he would rise at 5.30 a.m. and work from 6 until 7 on mastering Book 2 of Euclid, and then from 7 until 8 on Algebra. He confided in his diary, that he had been led to examine the nature and extent of his knowledge, opinions and beliefs:

> The results have been painfully disappointing. Instead of building on rock, I find, in many cases I have been building on sand. False notions and misconceptions have been leading me in erroneous paths. Most often those I look to for guidance have failed me, and they have given chaff in place of wheat. They have taken me into the dreary desert instead of into the green pastures and by the still waters of truth. (RSd, v. 5, 2 July 1876)

Slater began to associate himself with freethinkers. His interest preceded by a couple of years, what Royle has identified as the golden age of secularism 1877–86.[24] The Euston and St Pancras area was something of a hotbed for the propagation of these ideas: the Midland Arches of St Pancras provided a popular

---

[22] See G. H. Bantock, *Studies in the History of Educational Thought and Practice*, vol. 1: *Artifice and Nature, 1350–1765* (London, 1980), pp. 292–3.

[23] Sir George MacFarren (1813–87), described by Scholes as 'this heroic man'. See Scholes, *The Mirror of Music*, vol. 1, p. 101; N. Temperley, 'Sir George (Alexander) MacFarren', in *New Grove 2*, vol. 15, pp. 471–3. Slater's diaries contain two letters sent by Slater to MacFarren, but I have been unable to trace MacFarren's letters to Slater.

[24] E. Royle, *Radicals, Secularists and Republicans: Popular Freethought in Britain, 1866–1915* (Manchester, 1980).

platform for secular lecturers. Slater became a regular visitor, as he noted on 14 June 1874:

> After the service I went to the Arches in the St Pancras Road where so many combats between infidels and Bible defenders take place. Here are opportunities for my carrying on some of my important studies. (RSd, v. 5, 14 June 1874)

Part of Slater's desire to understand the world resulted in a rejection of Chrisianity, and an alliance with freethinkers or sceptics. He had been a Sunday School teacher at the Cromer Street Mission since he was 17. However, in his 21st year he announced, 'I've finished with Christian teaching; there's nothing in it!'[25] He resigned from the Sunday School on 2 July 1876. Slater's letter to Woolacot on his resignation is apologetic, yet firm:

> It is with great reluctance that I make this communication to you, because of its unpleasant nature to myself, but duty requires that it should be made. You will not be surprised to learn that I have been engaged for some years past in serious and diligent analysis of my mind [...] but I am sorry that it may be an unpleasant surprise for you to learn that my advance in my task has been remarkable for the divergence in religious thought which my acquisitions have necessitated [...] My divergence on several religious subjects is now so considerable that it is quite impossible for me to obey demands of trust and duty and continue in connection with you as a teacher in the school, or as a helper in the services at the Hall [...] From this communication you will see the cause of my reserve and non-participation in many doings at the Hall in which you may have thought I should have joined. I do sincerely thank you for your many acts of kindness and regard and I am happy to be able to state that my remembrance of the school both as a scholar and as a teacher, is unmarred by unpleasant occurrences, but I have pleasure in many tokens of friendship and esteem. (RSd, v. 5, 2 July 1876)

In a subsequent discussion with Woolacot, Slater emphasised his doubts about the historical basis of the gospels, and ventured his opinion that the first verse of St John's Gospel, 'In the beginning was the Word, and the Word was with God, and the Word was God', was 'an absurdity' (RSd, v. 5, 2 July 1876). Writing over 30 years later, Slater put the matter succinctly:

> During my early manhood I became a sceptic, and lost all belief in the reality of the objects about which religion is concerned.[26]

---

[25] Wiggins, *Father of Salvation Army Music*, p. 9.
[26] Slater, 'My Twenty-Six Years Service', p. 3.

LABOURING WITH MUSICAL COMPOSITION

While many working-class autodidacts looked to literature for enlightenment, others regarded music as 'the high road to a better world'.[27] Slater had access to both highways. In his diary entry for 1871, he itemised the musical scores he had purchased which included Bach's Mass in B minor, and Mozart's *Idomeneo*. He was keen to develop as a composer, and was hard at work tackling Cherubini's *Treatise on Counterpoint and Fugue* (1835). On 1 August he was commencing the study of four-part counterpoint, and two months later he was writing fugues. Slater's first composition in definite form was a setting of words taken from a Band of Hope source, followed by a hymn tune. By the February of the following year he was composing the first part of an Allegro for two violins, a setting of Psalm 100 for four voices with solo parts, a trio for violin, viola and cello, 12 hymn tunes, and a further psalm setting. But he was dissatisfied with his progress: 'when I see how little I have composed in spite of all my opportunities I feel disgusted with myself' (RSd, v. 4, 13 Feb 1872). These early compositions do not appear to have survived.

In another entry Slater itemises the difficulties he had come across in trying to master the art of composition. His first attempts had been spontaneous, but although he then studied books on the subject, and lots of scores, he was working in isolation without an overall plan, so that he failed to consider gaining a qualification. Furthermore,

> While living at Cromer St. my conditions of study were not good [...] I see I have been under a disadvantage in having to work so much by the eye in place of the ear [...] I heard little good music in my boyhood, and cannot remember having been deeply moved by anything in that period; I have laboured in composition without aid and sympathy from others, and little in my circumstances had any stimulating effect on me. (RSd, v. 6, 1877, annual review)

Meanwhile a welcome change occurred in his material circumstances due to the generosity of a Mrs Rees, a retired cutler, for whom Slater's mother had undertaken some domestic work. Mrs Rees decided to take the family under her wing. She offered Mary Ann the chance to move to a small house nearby in Claremont Place, to take responsibility for it at a comparatively small rent, which could be supplemented by taking in lodgers. Mrs Rees also believed that through this move, Richard could be given opportunities to see what he could do as a teacher of music. A piano was provided for him. Slater was still expected to do the household chores for his mother, and guiltily admitted to his diary, 'I have felt disposed to complain because of having to do so much housework, but I feel it is wrong to be under such a feeling' (RSd, v. 6, 3 Oct. 1877).

Before this move, in order to gain some professional advice as to whether his

---

[27] Rose, *Intellectual Life*, p. 200.

compositions might find a publisher Slater wrote to Sir George MacFarren on 13 July 1876, 'with considerable uneasiness' (RSd, v. 5, 13 July 1876). First of all Slater told of his upbringing, his problems with his cataracts, and his musical development:

> [a]lthough I have never had conversation with anyone who had any knowledge of harmony or composition, I have gained some little knowledge of the subject through reading. All the pence I have been able to earn by carrying baskets of linen for persons we have worked for, or going on their errands, have been spent in the acquisition of books, chief of which are Cherubini's Treatise of counterpoint and fugue, Albrechtsberger's writings, Callcott's Grammer [sic], and the works of Bach, Beethoven and Wagner. I have laboured hard on these books, but without anyone to guide or correct, but I have often thought of writing to you when I thought I had some things upon which judgement might be formed, as to whether I should be able to accomplish anything as a composer. I think this has now come. (RSd, v. 5, 13 July 1876)

Slater sent seven of his songs to MacFarren, who then provided a letter of recommendation which Slater could use in his negotiation with publishers. He submitted some of his work to six well-known music publishers, including Ashdown, Novello, and Joseph Williams. Disappointingly, he received only rejection notices from them, one of them implying that what was wanted were pieces more in sympathy with modern styles. He unburdened himself in a further letter to MacFarren:

> If so little is possible in the direction of musical composition, as the recent experiments seem to indicate, I cannot deem it to form anything like the principal part of my life's plan. (RSd, v. 5, 22 Jan. 1877)

In a key passage, Slater reflected that his future work

> lies in the direction of teaching, and in changing persons and things, I have to teach others what ends should be for them, and what plans they should use to gain them [...] composition should be thought of rather as of a secondary character, to be taken up when freedom from teaching will permit, but it then stands as a subject to be weighed with another course, viz. the philosophy of the mind, chiefly in its relation to art, and although my desire to engage in musical invention is strong, I must confess that my mind is more inclined to the latter of the two courses. (RSd, v. 5, 22 Jan. 1877)

His priorities therefore became teaching, investigating the philosophy of mind, and composing, in that order. For the next six years, however, until he began his work for the Salvation Army, there is scarcely any mention of composition in his diaries.

PHRENOLOGY AND MUSIC TEACHING

By 1878 it was apparent that Slater was becoming passionate about phrenology:

> For gaining a living I am to try Phrenology and teaching music; if the former means turns out successful I should drop teaching music, as it is more interesting to me and more in harmony with my other intellectual tasks than the latter. (RSd, v. 6, 13 Mar. 1878)

What is fascinating about Slater, is that rather than pursuing a radical atheism, or socialism, characteristic of the time, he put his energies into propagating phrenology, 'a conjoining of the Greek words for mind and discourse'.[28] Slater's interest in phrenology had been stimulated by reading his father's copy of the *International Journal of Art and Science*. Subsequently he gathered together a number of friends to hold regular discussions with them about phrenology. What intrigued him was the possibility of mapping clearly and fully the world of the mind.

A. N. Wilson's succinct description of phrenology is hard to improve upon:

> Its various proponents divided up the skull into areas – twenty-six in one scheme, forty-three or more in another – in which it was purported that organs could be discovered explanatory of human behaviour. The lumps and bumps of the human cranium were seriously supposed to relate to propensities and characteristics such as amativeness, hope, wonder, wit and so on. The fact that no relation between brain functions and cranial formation could be demonstrated did not prevent serious people, many of them scientists, being wholly convinced by it.[29]

Phrenology's golden age in Britain was in the first half of the 19th century, emerging from the work of Franz Joseph Gall (1758–1828) in Vienna.[30] It entered Britain as a new strain from seeds brought by Gall's 'wayward disciple', J. G. Spurzheim, who in turn influenced George Combe. It was Combe who popularised the subject in England.[31] Phrenology was faithfully preserved and pursued in popular working-class culture in the second half of the century, mainly due to the popularising of the subject through the tours of England from 1860 onwards of the American phrenologist L. N. Fowler.[32] Significantly as regards Slater, early

[28] D. Stack, *Queen Victoria's Skull: George Combe and the Mid-Victorian Mind* (London, 2008), p. xi.

[29] A. N. Wilson, *The Victorians* (London, 2007), p. 54.

[30] See J. van Wyhe, *Phrenology and the Origins of Victorian Scientific Naturalism* (Aldershot, 2004), p. 3.

[31] See J. F. C. Harrison, *Learning and Living, 1790–1960: A Study in the History of the English Adult Education Movement* (London, 1961). For a biography of Combe, see Staff, *Queen Victoria's Skull*.

[32] See R. Cooter, *The Cultural Meanings of Popular Science: Phrenology and the Organisation of Consent in Nineteenth-Century Britain* (Cambridge, 1984), p. 282.

phrenologists thought of themselves as following in the footsteps of Francis Bacon, emphasising observation, absolutising 'objective facts', and stressing accessibility, practicality and progress.[33]

Slater was attracted to phrenology as if to a religion, and by 1878 was in the thick of it, evangelising through lecturing on the subject, often for well over an hour at open-air venues all within a couple of miles' radius of King's Cross. Table 1 lists his open-air phrenology venues (with the exception of the St Pancras Club which was an indoor venue) between April to August 1878 (RSd, v. 6, 19 Aug. 1878).

Slater itemised his spendings on phrenology: the phrenological bust 8s. 6d., 1,000 handbills 2s., Charts 5s., Professional cards 1s. 6d., Window Card 1s. 3d., a second 1,000 bills, 2s. 6d. He charged individuals 2s. for a personal delineation, and up to 27 July had examined in all about 60 persons (RSd, v. 6, 27 July 1878).

What is particularly revealing is the phrenological examination given to Slater by L. N. Fowler on 7 June 1879, revealing in the sense of outlining Slater's character and personality. In presenting Slater's account I have italicised the phrenological organs which he mentions, and where necessary have clarified which organ is being referred to, by enclosing it within square brackets:

> My love [*Amativeness*] is not strong. There is little regard for fashions, forms, ceremonies. There is strong attachment to home, also to children [*Philoprogenitiveness*]. *Continuity* is small. My affection is as much outside as inside the family circle. There is a marked condition of *Combativeness*. *Self-esteem* is large, no fear of responsibility, can speak heroically to heroic men, have manliness, a feeling of superiority. *Firm*[*ness*] was large, have a tendency to hold fast to my views and purposes. *Conscientiousness* is an active organ, I desire to know the right and wrong of everything, but I lack circumspection, 'likely that I do, or will, strain a point'. *Hope* is good, active, giving tendency to look on the bright side [...] *Spirituality* was stated to be good, but no other remark on it was made. *Benevolence* was an active organ, likely to work [more] in home relations than in external institutions. I did not put things unwisely, but my blunt plainspeaking way was apt to tell people just what I thought of them. Wit [*Mirthfulness*] is large, I am disposed to see and enjoy the comic and to be lively. There is a vein of poetry in my nature, *Ideality* being a prominent organ, and there is a love of, a taste for the perfect, the finished, the beautiful. Acquisition [*Acquisitiveness*] is an active condition so far as gaining money goes, but

Slater possessed in his own library at least one of Fowler's books, *How to Read Character: A New Illustrated Hand-Book of Phrenology and Physiognomy for Students & Examiners; with a Descriptive Chart* (New York, 1881). I am indebted to Gordon Taylor for this information. Slater's own copy is held in The Salvation Army International Heritage Centre.

[33] Cooter, *The Cultural Meanings of Popular Science*, p. 73.

Table 1 Slater's open-air phrenology venues

Date	Time	Place	Subject
6 April	evening	Cobden Statue	Nature of phrenology
2 June	morning	Midland Arches	Phrenology and self-education
2 June	evening	St Pancras Club	Character and teachings of phrenology
9 June	morning	Midland Arches	Reasons for belief in phrenology
23 June	morning	Midland Arches	Value as well as truth of phrenology
30 June	morning	Midland Arches	Discovery and truth of phrenology
3 July	evening	Cobden Statue	Discovery and truth of phrenology
4 July	evening	Claremont Square	Discovery and truth of phrenology
6 July	evening	Hampstead Road	Discovery and truth of phrenology
7 July	morning	Midland Arches	Man's nature and empire
7 July	evening	Regent's Park	Man's nature and empire
14 July	morning	Midland Arches	Phrenology and perfection of character
14 July	evening	Regent's Park	Discovery of phrenology
21 July	morning	Midland Arches	Teachings of phrenology
21 July	evening	Park Street	Teachings of phrenology
28 July	morning	Midland Arches	The science of character
28 July	evening	Park Street	Phrenology and self-culture
31 July	evening	Claremont Square	Character and teachings of phrenology
18 August	morning	Midland Arches	Phrenology and its moral influence
18 August	evening	Park Street	Phrenology and its moral influence

not for its own sake. *Tune* is large, and it takes a high [position?] in my head, the organ being high up works with *Ideality* [...] *Causality* is large, and I want to know all about the reasons, principles, the basis of things. There is sufficient *Cautiousness* so as to keep me safe, but not enough to cause timidity or procrastination. *Order* is large, giving fondness for system, ability to work by method. *Form* and *Size* both large, fitting me for mechanical work, so I could put things together with success [...] *Individuality* is well exercised, and with sight could give great delight in physical phenomena. *Destructiveness* low, so I am not disposed to be cruel or harsh (RSd, v. 15, 7 June 1879).

In order to clarify some of these phrenological terms, Table 2 lists them side by side with a description of each, and their numbering, taken from the Fowlers' *New Illustrated Self-Instructor in Phrenology and Physiology* (1860).[34]

---

34 O. S. and L. N. Fowler, *New Illustrated Self-Instructor in Phrenology and Physiology* (London, 1860), p. vi.

Table 2 Phrenological organs

Phrenological Organs	Description
1 Amativeness	Love between the sexes
2 Philoprogenitiveness, Parental love	Regard for offspring, pets, etc.
5 Continuity	One thing at a time
6 Combativeness	Resistance – defense
7 Destructiveness	Executiveness – force
9 Acquisitiveness	Accumulation
11 Cautiousness	Prudence – provision
13 Self-esteem	Self-respect – dignity
14 Firmness	Decision – perseverance
15 Conscientiousness	Justice – equity
16 Hope	Expectation – enterprise
17 Spirituality	Intuition – faith – credulity
19 Benevolence	Kindness – goodness
21 Ideality	Refinement – taste – purity
23 Mirthfulness	Jocoseness – wit – fun
24 Individuality	Observation
25 Form	Recollection of shapes
26 Size	Measuring by the eye
29 Order	Method – system – arrangement
34 Tune	Sense of harmony and melody
36 Causality	Applying causes to effect

Fowler credited Slater, in his phrenological assessment, with considerable musical power and musical taste, 'not for the common ditty style, but "Mozart music" rather' (RSd, v. 15, 7 June 1879). He advised him to take a course of philosophy, and saw that public speaking might be his line in life. Then Slater confided to Fowler that he had no belief and religion. Quite the contrary, he held to Kant's view of religion, backed up by Huxley. Fowler, however, did not think such men as Huxley were proper moral guides, and advised Slater to reason out the question of God's existence.

It will be apparent that in most of this examination Slater comes out positively, although we do not know how selective he was being in his report. Perhaps the listing is helpful in pointing out at least what Slater himself thought of as significant.

The different fields of phrenology and music did come together in Slater's teaching, which was becoming quite extensive, so that by the end of the first quarter of 1877 he had managed to build up a teaching practice comprising 34 pupils each of whom received one or two lessons weekly on the violin or piano or the voice (in that order). The average quarterly rate was 12s. (RSd, v. 6, 13 Apr. 1877).

One of the phrenological organs was Tune, which was also associated with the faculty of Time. J. M. Severn devotes a whole chapter in his life story as a phrenologist to the problems associated with locating Tune, but he concludes:

> A good phrenologist would be able to tell in the space of a few moments, the amount of musical capacity a person may possess, and whether it would be worth while to learn music.[35]

Slater described his practice in this regard:

> Upon receiving a new pupil I have sketched his character as declared by the formation of his head, then I have watched the character as it has unfolded itself and have found my prediction to answer to actual facts. I have made experiments in my teaching and have had positive results of the development of certain characteristics in the head by calling into activity certain faculties. (RSd, v. 6, 22 Nov. 1878)

He was many years later to record in his diary a conversation with a colleague about his views on musical intelligence and ability, demonstrating the continuing influence that phrenological thinking had upon him:

> The chief line was taken by my contention that capacity, ability, conditions and character of success are determined by natural possessions we start life with more than on training, education, or will to be or do this or that [...] We start life with a certain momentum as to bodily and mental capacity and force, and as we can only by great effort and long use make an increase of an inch or so in height or length of limb, so it was with our powers of minds, and that energy could be better used on the lines of our naturally predominating faculties, than by will or forced activity of those that were weak. (RSd, v. 13, 1912, annual review)

MUSICAL PERFORMANCE AND WAGNER STUDIES

Throughout these years Slater played the violin in a number of amateur orchestras. He and his friend Alfred Edwards had joined the Royal Albert Hall Amateur Orchestral Society when it began in 1872,[36] adding somewhat characteristically,

---

[35] J. M. Severn, *The Life Story and Experiences of a Phrenologist* (Brighton, 1929), p. 319.

[36] For further details of the Royal Amateur Orchestral Society, see Scholes, *The Mirror of Music*, vol. 1, p. 405. The orchestra, led by the Duke of Edinburgh, was reported to be 'the pre-eminent amateur orchestra in this country', in P. Gillett, 'Ambivalent Friendships: Music-Lovers, Amateurs and Professional Musicians in the Late Nineteenth Century', in *Music and British Culture, 1785–1914: Essays in Honour of Cyril Ehrlich*, ed. C. Bashford and L. Langley (Oxford, 2000), pp. 321–40 (p. 335).

'I being placed on examination among the 1st violins, and he among the 2nd' (RSd, v. 1, 'Early Memories', p. 192). Slater was invited in 1874 to join a new such group which was to rehearse in the schoolrooms of St Anne's Church, Soho, under the management of Oliver King who according to Slater had been a pupil of Joseph Barnby, and who was to become an established composer of church music.[37] Slater often played in orchestras for oratorio performances. For example, *Messiah* at the Alexandra Palace on 17 December 1881. On several occasions Slater played the violin with the Isledon Orchestral Society which rehearsed in a schoolroom in Hornsey. On one such occasion in 1881 he records there were only nine of the band present, two violins, a cello, a clarinet, two bassoons, a flute, a double bass and a side drum (RSd, v. 13, 1881, annual review). He volunteered to play 'The Cuckoo', a favourite solo piece of his, and an unidentified Air from Verdi's *I Lombardi*. At another rehearsal the cellist brought the parts he had purchased of a number of Haydn Quartets, in which Slater was to play the first violin part.

Sometimes there would be domestic music-making, frequently with Alfred Edwards on cello. Their repertoire included parts of Donizetti's *Lucia di Lammermoor*, Wallace's *Maritana*, and Flotow's *Stradella*. As a soloist Slater played at various institutes and schools, for example presenting one of de Bériot's 12 *Airs Variés* at a concert at Holborn Town Hall, where, after a minstrel troupe had finished performing, he also acted as the piano accompanist for two vocalists at the last minute, for which he received the sum of 5s. (RSd, v. 7, 12 Dec. 1881). There are numerous references peppered throughout the diaries of his involvement as a violinist with mostly amateur orchestras, with choral societies, and playing Beethoven Sonatas and Haydn Quartets. In addition to his orchestral playing, Slater was also involved in playing the flute in drum and fife bands.

But undoubtedly the most profound musical influence on Slater was Wagner. Years later, he even went to the length of calling his two daughters after Wagner's heroines, Brunnhilde and Elsa. Back in 1872, his first purchases of the vocal scores of Wagner, included *Tannhäuser* and *Lohengrin* (RSd, v. 1, 1872, annual review). He became caught up in the arguments vis-à-vis Wagner's protest against the evils and abuses of Italian opera. The following year he was present at a Wagner night at the Promenade Concerts at Covent Garden Theatre, and in 1877 he wrote his judgement of the music based on his knowledge of the scores of *Tannhäuser* and *Lohengrin*:

> On getting them [...] my study of them straightway convinced me he was one of the greatest of composers [...] impressed me, for I saw therein evidence of his great intellectual power [...] Without a doubt one of the chief things in my life has been becoming acquainted with his works from which I have had some of the deepest pleasures I have ever experienced, and also one of the main forces determining the lines of my mind's

---

[37] See Scholes, *The Mirror of Music*, vol. 2, p. 557.

activity [...] The more I study him, the more wonderful does he appear to me [...] I think he stands alone among musicians in having consciously an intellectual aim to the scheme as the basis of his artist labours. (RSd, v. 6, 26 June 1877)

In the same entry he noted that he had brought ten or so individuals to an appreciation of Wagner.

Perhaps Slater's Wagnerian fervour stemmed from the relationship of Wagner's music to religious feelings and sensibilities. In his discussion of music and religion in the 19th century, Obelkevich makes the following point:

Wagner [...] gives the religion of music its most grandiose expression [...] The aim was not only to entertain his audiences, but to save their souls, the message [...] being of love and self-renunciation.[38]

Slater's passion for Wagner was lifelong, and serious. In 1882 he submitted a manuscript to the *Musical Times* on Wagner. The article related to the number of bars in *Parsifal*, and how they functioned, including an analysis of the amount and frequency of different time signatures, and the number of bars which were purely vocal, purely instrumental, or mixed. There was an analysis of the amount and frequency of different time signatures. Slater's findings were published in 'Comments from the Editor of the *Musical Times* about data sent from "Richard Slater" concerning his study of Wagner's works'.[39] The editor went on to say that while accepting 'this enthusiastic calculator['s] document as a unique specimen of industry and perseverance, it was to be hoped that it may not lead the admirers of other composers [...] to count up and classify the bars contained in the numerous works bequeathed to us'.[40] Unfortunately the details were printed with errors, and Slater wrote to the editor asking that corrections be published. The editor apologised saying 'we take the earliest opportunity of correcting them, in justice to the energy and earnestness of our correspondent'.[41]

CLUB LECTURER

Slater gradually began to see that he could combine his interests in phrenology and music by becoming an itinerant lecturer in Working Men's Clubs. The Working Men's Club movement had been founded in 1862 by Henry Solly, a Unitarian minister. He was keen that the clubs provided opportunities for social intercourse, and rational amusement and opportunities for instruction and

---

[38] J. Obelkevich, 'Music and Religion in the Nineteenth Century', in *Disciplines of Faith: Studies in Religion, Politics and Patriarchy*, ed. J. O. and L. Roper and R. Samuel (London, 1987), pp. 550–65 (p. 562).

[39] ['Comments from the Editor of the *Musical Times* about data sent from 'Richard Slater' concerning his study of Wagner's works'], *Musical Times* 24 (1883), p. 601.

[40] Ibid.

[41] *Musical Times* 24 (1883), p. 658.

study.[42] The instruction came from lectures, given by educated friends of the movement. In his study of six clubs in mid-Victorian London, Shipley found that in most the cornerstone was the Sunday-evening meeting, in which visiting lecturers were expected to be coherent in speech and well armed with facts, which would then lead to debate. Lectures on political economy, history or religion were the staple fare. The fact that Sunday was the Club day tended to be seen as a rebellion against the church and the Christian Sabbath. However, with the 1870 Education Act coming into force, by the 1880s the lectures were on the wane, and declined further with the new Board Schools offering evening classes for adults from the 1890s.[43]

From 1878 Slater was establishing himself in a number of Working Men's Clubs as a lecturer in phrenology and music. He worked in this way across the eastern, northern, south-western and western areas of London. Some of the clubs Slater worked in included: Clifden Club (Hackney), Cobden Working Men's Club (Kensal Road), Commonwealth Club (Bethnal Green), Eleusis Club (Chelsea), Hammersmith Club, London Tailors' Club (Golden Square), North London Club (Pentonville), Progressive Club (Notting Hill Gate), St Pancras Working Men's Club, Westminster Democratic Club.

Historically, phrenology had been one of the most popular activities of the mechanics' institutes; 'the phrenologists' motto "Know Thyself" had in it the germ of self-culture and self-improvement'.[44] Slater was devoted to the cause: 'The work of a practical phrenologist seems one of the highest forms of individual activity for the good of humanity' (RSd, v. 4, 4 Sep. 1878). The subjects of his phrenology lectures included 'Is Phrenology a Science?', 'The Body and its Manifestations of Character', 'Teachings of Phrenology', 'The Utility of Phrenology', 'The Discovery of Phrenology'. In a sketch of one of his lectures his plan was as follows: a general introduction, followed by the chief doctrines of phrenology, followed by personal application of tests and results (RSd, v. 6, 22 Nov. 1877). The detail included the following important points

the brain is the organ of the mind

the brain is an assemblage of organs and each faculty has a special part of the brain allocated to it and its organ

the brain is dual, so that the organs are in pairs

the size of the brain, other things being equal, is a sign of power

[42] H. Solly, 'On Working Men's Clubs and Institutes', *Transactions of the National Association for the Promotion of Social Service* (Edinburgh, 1881), pp. 504–5.

[43] S. Shipley, *Club Life and Socialism in Mid-Victorian London*, 2nd edn (London, 1983), pp. 26–7, 33.

[44] Harrison, *Learning and Living*, p. 117. David Stack also makes the point that with demonstration being crucial, 'phrenological knowledge was peculiarly suited to the lecture format' (Stack, *Queen Victoria's Skull*, p. 51).

each faculty in its proper place is essential to man's well-being and perfection

Slater was mostly pleased with his lectures, but sometimes he had to cope with challenging situations:

> In the evening I gave a lecture on the Discovery of Phrenology at the London Tailors' Club. I did not commence till about 9.30, and had only a small audience at first, but later the room was quite full. I had good attention on the whole, but some present were the worse for drink, and one was actually sick in the room. I spoke easily, with energy, and steadily, though not in a systematic way in some parts. (RSd, v. 8, 3 Apr. 1881)

After his lecture on this occasion, he examined four adults, and in addition a boy of 13 and two little children. But in a later diary entry he bemoaned the fact that in spite of four very successful deliveries at the clubs on phrenology, not one single person had come forward for examination. Slater wondered if it was a deficiency on his part (RSd, v. 7, 14 Dec. 1881). Ten years later, after his conversion to the Salvation Army, he declared in relation to phrenology, 'my interest has declined' (RSd, v. 7, 16 June 1891).

Music played a prominent role in the early Working Men's Clubs, some had their own brass bands; others had string bands and glee clubs.[45] Slater limited himself for the most part to lectures on the life and works of composers. He was excited at the prospect:

> There is a unique work possible before me I believe in this direction. My past efforts show it to be work by which important and valuable influences can be exercised upon my hearers. I am fitted for such work by [...] vocal and instrumental skill, impressiveness of manner, enthusiasm in the great composers. It opens up chances of original work for my mind [...] bringing me money, pupils, friends, helpers [...] It is work that is likely to smooth the way in work as a music teacher, leading me to more skill, to more reputation [...] I see in this work one of my best tasks in which ability and circumstances unite. (RSd, v. 6, 24 May 1878)

In January and February 1880 his subjects included Beethoven (at the Eleusis Club, and the Cobden Club), and Wagner (at the Hammersmith Club and the London Tailors' Club). He later branched out to include Handel, Haydn, Mendelssohn and Schubert.

Slater always illustrated his lectures with musical examples played by himself, and sometimes with guests. For example, his Haydn lecture included several movements from a quartet in which he played first violin, while Miss A. White sang the canzonet 'My mother bids me bind my hair' and an extract from *The Seasons*, both accompanied by Slater on the harmonium. At his second lecture

---

45 J. Taylor, *From Self-Help to Glamour: Working Man's Club, 1860–1972* (Oxford, 1972), p. 41.

on Wagner at the Cobden Club in 1881, on Wagner's birthday, 22 May, the musical illustrations included the March from *Tannhäuser*, 'Elizabeth's Prayer', 'Elsa's Vision', 'Say dost thou breathe', and 'Lohengrin's Farewell'. Interestingly, one individual who attended Slater's Wagner lecture at the North London Club on 22 January 1882 was J. M. Wheeler, a prominent secularist, and subeditor of the *Freethinker*. Subsequently he and Slater talked about Wagner's theories (RSd, v. 8, 23 Jan. 1882) and Slater lent him his copy of *Lohengrin* (RSd, v. 8, 27 Jan. 1882). Their conversations were broad, encompassing phrenology, mesmerism, spiritualism, the place and nature of psychology, and Wagner's *Der fliegende Holländer* (*The Flying Dutchman*) (RSd, v. 8, 31 Jan. 1882).

At the end of one of the lectures on Haydn at the Cromer Street Mission, the chairman, Mr Bridge, a London City Missionary, gave an impassioned panegyric on Slater's achievements:

> He said there was very much in my own case worthy of attention and imitation. I had risen in spite of many difficulties [...] He had known me in years gone by scraping on my own fiddle, and had heard people in the house on more than one occasion wish me and my fiddle further [...] I had risen in spite of many difficulties, having almost lost my sight, but [through] my determination as in dealing with other difficulties, I gained the victory. (RSd, v. 8, 23 Jan. 1881)

At least three of Slater's subjects were wider than the works of a single composer, namely Shakespeare and the music connected with his plays, national songs, and sea songs. With regard to his lecture on national songs, he wanted to mark clearly the national characteristics of each nation. He also wanted to remove prejudices, so that he could 'make citizens of the world of my hearers' (RSd, v. 7, 11 Aug. 1881). Because of his Italian blood, he looked forward to the forthcoming publication of Boosey's *Songs of Italy*.[46] He supposed there would be Venetian boat songs, many love songs, serenades, and sacred songs to the Virgin Mary. Among the other nations he investigated, he found that songs of England rose in his estimation in comparison with other countries, songs of Scandinavia did not rouse his interest, whilst songs of France did not quite satisfy his interest.[47] He envisaged that in a lecture on songs of Germany, songs by the great composers would find a place, 'without a doubt, Germany for its songs is ahead of all other nations' (RSd, v. 7, 11 Aug. 1881). It was on 17 September 1882 that he gave his first lecture on sea songs at the North London Club. He observed that 'the subject seems opportune as the war is on in Egypt. Patriotic songs would be

---

[46] *Songs of Italy: Containing 54 canti populari of Naples, Florence, Milan and Venice, Including some Popular Modern Songs* (London, [c. 1890]).

[47] Slater was to continue his interest in national songs in his musical arrangements for Salvation Army bands, including *Songs of Germany* (Band Journal (hereafter BJ) 694), *Hebrew Melodies* (BJ 491), *Songs of Holland* (BJ 497), *Songs of Scotland* (BJ 428, 429), *Swiss Melodies* (BJ 514, 515).

in favour with my hearers' (RSd, v. 8, 10 Sept. 1882).[48] Slater clearly identified with such patriotic sentiments: 'My own mind is all aglow with the work of the songs with which I have to deal, with the noble characteristics of the English people, the greatness of England' (RSd, v. 8, 16 Sept. 1882).

Slater ideally wanted both the lectures and his musical examples to be delivered without notes. This was not always possible:

> I have not had much time to impress my memory with my particulars so must use notes, but I shall not take music, as I have mastered them [*sic*]. (RSd, v. 8, 16 Sept. 1882).

Nevertheless, on this occasion he expected his lecture to be, 'in popular sense', a success. He was critical of himself when he went on too long. His lectures generally lasted 1 hour and 10 minutes, although he records on one occasion at the St Pancras Club when lecturing on Wagner, 'I commenced at 9.10 p.m. and went on until 11.10 p.m' (RSd, v. 8, 26 Feb. 1882).

Slater's fees for his lectures were mostly 2s. 6d., although there were exceptions. He was keen to impress at the North London Club which paid 5s., 'as it is only about ten minutes walk it costs me nothing to go, to and from, so that is a reason for seeking to get the place on my list' (RSd, v. 7, 1881, annual review). Later he stated that his terms for a lecture were generally 5s. (RSd, v. 8, 19 Sept. 1882). But although he was pleased that his musical lectures were affording him a good position at the clubs, he was worried about the falling-off of his teaching work and his phrenological examinations (RSd, v. 7, 1881, annual review). By 1883 he was teaching only 11 pupils per week (RSd, v. 1, 26 May 1883).

The previous year had seen him disillusioned with the club scene, especially as he had just discovered the Salvation Army:

> my labours so far in gaining support have been met with very poor success by the means I have used. It is somewhat depressing to think that the moral tone I have sought to maintain in my Club lecturing has been as it were by permission, for such audiences do not gather with a moral end as the chief one in view. It is also depressing to think how my moral efforts have had to be done in the midst of the drinking of the Clubs, and the lax moral tone there compared with what is to be found in the Army [...] I feel eager to reach something better. (RSd, v. 8, 18 Sept. 1882)

---

[48] The war in Egypt mentioned by Slater refers to the invasion and occupation of Egypt by Britain on behalf of the creditors of the Suez Canal in 1882. See H. C. G. Matthew, 'The Liberal Age (1851–1914)', in *The Oxford Popular History of Britain*, ed. K. O. Morgan (Oxford, 1993), pp. 518–82 (p. 563).

❧ *Conclusion*

In this chapter I have focused upon Slater as a representative of a relatively late flowering of the Victorian working-class autodidact tradition, which was to change fundamentally around the end of the 19th century with the impact of compulsory education.[49] Slater reflected many of the characteristic traits of the self-educated man. He had a passion for education and through it for self-discovery. The engagement with lifelong learning defined itself as an 'art of living', rather than a preparation for a life of work. Slater's pursuit of knowledge was ambitious in its range, but the ambition was for knowledge itself, summed up in Gardner's phrase, 'to live was to learn, and to learn was truly to live'.[50]

It becomes apparent that Slater's idea of lifelong education carried with it a dual meaning of not only transforming the life of the learner, but also the life of society itself, touching the educational lives of all. Slater's sense of purpose was rooted in his engagement with the 'pseudo-science' of phrenology, with music teaching, and with Working Men's Clubs. In all of these contexts he had the desire to become 'a true teacher and guide of men' (RSd, v. 3, 22 Jan. 1877).

[49] Gardner, 'The Life-long Draught', pp. 469–71.
[50] Ibid., p. 468.

CHAPTER 3

Richard Slater: The Musical Salvationist

As will become apparent, Slater's encounter with the Salvation Army proved a turning point in his life. It seems he found his destiny within it, although as the narrative will show this was not to be achieved without considerable amounts of tension and battles. Stated briefly, after his conversion Slater commenced work in the Musical Department of the Army in October 1883, and retired from it as head of the department in 1913.

The focus of this chapter is upon Slater's working life in the Salvation Army. After describing his entry into the organisation and his initial informal apprenticeship within the Musical Department I discuss his early attempts to provide a vocal and instrumental repertoire for the Salvation Army within the requirements that William Booth laid down. Next I concentrate upon his years as head of the Musical Department from 1893 until 1913, including a discussion of a significant Memorandum in 1901 which ostensibly granted a measure of musical freedom for composers to include some original matter in their compositions. Four years later George Bernard Shaw made a well-publicised visit to an Army musical festival in 1905, and I examine the subsequent furore which served to open up Salvationist music-making to public scrutiny. I then consider Slater's influence as a musical liberaliser often in the face of considerable opposition. Finally I focus upon his ongoing studies of Wagner, his relationship with William Booth, and his battle over copyright issues with the Salvation Army authorities immediately before his retirement.

✍ *Entry into the Salvation Army, 1882–3*

In his quest for self-knowledge Slater systematically visited places of worship on Sunday evenings, partly to learn something of oratory, and also to resolve questions about religion. He had read in newspaper reports of the doings of the Salvation Army. Curious, he attended his first meeting at Hampstead in July 1882. He was impressed by the hearty sincerity of the people, but particularly by the testimony of a young servant girl, who exclaimed, 'My missus says she believes I am saved, because I sweep beneath the mats now, and I didn't before.'[1] These words made a more profound impression on Slater's mind 'than all the sermons I had ever heard'.[2] He felt deeply disturbed at the moral defeats he had known, and 'how vain and disappointing had been the vaunted moral impetus which freethought could give a man in the crisis of

---

[1] Quoted in Slater, 'Life of Staff-Captain Slater of the Training Home'.

[2] Ibid.

temptation'.[3] Slater desired to get into contact with the Jesus of the gospels, so that he might accomplish moral victories over himself, similar in spirit to that expressed in the servant girl's testimony. He visited other London corps (centres) such as Chalk Farm (near Hackney) and the Regent Hall (in London's West End). Coincidentally, both of these corps became centres of musical excellence headed by two distinguished bandmasters who will figure prominently in this history, A. W. Punchard and Herbert Twitchin.[4] Slater started to reflect on whether or not the Army might well offer him a chance to use his gifts:

> I am more inclined towards the Salvation Army because of the earnest-ness and progressive nature of the movement, and its dealing so success-fully with the people [...] I am impressed with the fact that the extravagant aspects of the movement are not essential conditions of its life, and I need not adopt all or defend all I see in this direction [...] It is probable that there is much direct work in the Training Homes for teaching music, and so here is another chance by which I might gain a living. (RSd, v. 8, 18 Sept. 1882)

Here we see a coming together of the idealist and pragmatic aspects of Slater's personality, together with a perception that he could detach himself from some of the Salvation Army's ways and methods.

After eight weeks of inward conflict since his first contact with the Salva-tion Army, and coinciding with preparation for one of his lectures on sea songs, he decided to attend the Salvation Army's Regent Hall in Oxford Street for a meeting on Friday evening, 22 September 1882. He had to decide whether or not he was willing to face the consequences of becoming a Christian:

> While sitting in the meeting several times the idea arose, now of having a conviction of the reality of Christ's life on earth and the declaration of a life beyond the grave, should I not go out to their penitent form to make a public acknowledgement of submission to Jesus. Towards the close the hymn 'Just as I am' was sung, the stimulus to go out became stronger. In the last verse, because of its giving so unexpected expression of my expe-rience, I was melted to tears, and I went to the form, with my eyes filled with tears and my throat thick with strong emotion as I viewed myself like another Peter, the beauty and charm of Christ in the meanwhile sinking into my heart. (RSd, v. 8, 22 Sept. 1882)[5]

As a result of his conversion, Slater decided to give up his lecturing, and wrote

---

3 Ibid.

4 See Chalk Farm Band, *A.W.P.* [A. W. Punchard], *1894–1938* (London, [1938]), and J. Atkins, *Always in Step: Herbert Twitchin* (London, 1956).

5 The last verse of 'Just as I am' is 'Just as I am – Thy love I own / Has broken every barrier down: / Now to be Thine, yea Thine alone, / O Lamb of God I come.' From W. Booth, *The Salvation Army Music* (London, 1900), p. 131.

the next day to the Hammersmith Club, cancelling his appointment in October, 'because of changes which have taken place in me of an unlooked-for nature' (RSd, v. 8, 23 Sept. 1882).

It was agreed that Slater could use his musical talents to good effect at the Grecian Corps, on the City Road. This had been formerly a long-established music hall known as the Grecian Theatre and Eagle Tavern, believed by Salvationists to be 'in the service of evil'.[6] William Booth decided to purchase the buildings, and in an announcement on 29 June 1882 proclaimed that both the Eagle and the Grecian had been 'captured' by the Army.[7] On his first visit to the Grecian Corps, Slater admired the conscientiousness of the leaders but noted the difficulty of keeping the attention of much of the audience, particularly those in the gallery. These were mostly between the ages of 12 and 18, 'appearing to be of the lower classes. Their clothes, voices, language, as well as phrenological conditions […] told plainly of poverty, ignorance, coarseness, vulgarity, and evil tendencies' (RSd, v. 9, 4 Oct. 1882).

Slater's description of what he encountered musically on this visit provides an apt example of the somewhat chaotic arrangements of the time:

> There were 4 brass instruments and a big drum on the stage, a few tambourines, a triangle and a violin. The playing was only just passable. A young man with a thin voice sang a hymn to the tune – 'Hiding in Thee', and a female sang a song about heaven. To the last there was no accompaniment and as she started in a high key, the gallery folks made forms of bet of her difficulty in reaching the high notes. To the first song the violinist made an attempt at a sort of <u>pizzicato</u> as accompaniment, a few notes vamped, and a note or two given by the cornet. Another song by a Bass Singer was given, but it was quite a failure. (RSd, v. 9, 4 Oct. 1882)

Later he joined in the scratch band, playing violin alongside two other violinists and four brass instruments. It was not long before he was appointed bandmaster. In February 1883 he estimated that he had paid 47 visits to the Grecian Corps, and had given 28 addresses and 11 testimonies (RSd, v. 1, 24 Feb. 1883). Notwithstanding, Slater felt a lack of emotional satisfaction, and had thought of severing his ties with the Army (RSd, v. 1, 6 Mar. 1883). But he was impressed with the potential of addressing 400 people in the Sunday night congregation – 'from a moral standpoint the position here for me is almost perfection' (RSd, v. 1, 6 Mar. 1883) – but he could not bring himself to agree with many of the ordinary views of Christianity and the Army. At this time Slater was still teaching 11 pupils the piano and violin, and earning £6 16s. per quarter. His earnings from phrenology had virtually dried up (RSd, v. 1, 26 May 1883).

Gradually the idea of serving in the Army as a full-time officer grew in him

---

[6] Sandall, *The History of the Salvation Army*, vol. 2, p. 21.

[7] See H. Scott, *The Early Doors: Origins of the Music Hall* (London, 1946), p. 70; Walker, *Pulling the Devil's Kingdom Down*, pp. 188–90.

as he renewed contact with the Regent Hall Corps, despite some ambivalence: 'the nature of their meetings seems adverse to any manifestation of liberty of thought or theology' (RSd, v. 1, 10 Sept. 1883). However, a lieutenant's salary in the Army would have been an improvement on his own financial position. He resolved to give it a 12-month trial. Coincidentally at this time he met his future wife, Eliza Archer, at the Regent Hall (RSd, v. 1, 11 July 1883).

The matter was finalised by General Booth, who called for Slater to speak to him after a meeting at the Regent Hall.

> 'Draw that chair up; I want to speak to you. Where do you live?'
> I told him my address.
> 'You have been gaining your living by teaching?'
> 'Yes'
> 'What do you teach?'
> 'Violin and piano'
> 'Do you know anything of the Brass?'
> 'Yes, but not sufficient to teach'
> 'You have also been working as a lecturer; on what subject?'
> 'The lives of great composers and different aspects of human character'
> 'Can you transpose, and do you know Thoroughbass?'
> 'Yes, have had letters from MacFarren'
> 'You write shorthand'
> 'Yes, Pitman's system […] as to transposition, I could do it in any key'
> 'Are you married?'
> 'No, but I entertained the idea for the future.' (RSd, v. 1, 14 Oct. 1883)

The next day Slater met Herbert Booth (1862–1926) who was the third son of William and Catherine. He had oversight of the musical side of the Salvation Army, and was a natural musician, playing several instruments, and composing a good number of songs.[8] It was agreed that Slater should undertake musical duties and that his wage was to be 25s. per week (RSd, v. 1, 15 Oct. 1883). With the entrance of Slater on to the scene, the ground was laid for the institution of a Musical Department on 22 October 1883. This replaced the previously rather *ad hoc* arrangements, and Slater was given full scope, under the general supervision

---

[8] One of Herbert Booth's best-known vocal selections was his *Songs of Peace and War* (London, 1890), published on the occasion of his marriage in September 1890. Slater later in *Salvation Army Song Writers* (London, [1929]) accorded Herbert Booth first place amongst the poets and composers of the Army (p. 10). Herbert Booth resigned in 1902 accusing his father of undermining his leadership of the Army in Australia. William took four months to reply to his son's resignation, his time having been taken up 'in European tours'. As Hattersley perceptively notes in *Blood and Fire*, for William Booth 'his only family was the Salvation Army' (p. 421).

of Herbert Booth. Some time later Slater expressed his excitement about the possibilities of the job,

> It is a fact that the position of chief writer of Army music is within my reach. I should be stirred by the possibility of writing for so large a number of people throughout the world. Also that it is upon the noblest of subjects that I have to write music. (RSd, v. 8, 25 July 1884)

His mother was less pleased. In fact she was greatly distressed and thought he was throwing away his prospects.[9]

Slater married Eliza Archer, at the Regent Hall, on 17 September, 1884. It was witnessed by a crowd of 2,000. Eliza worked in an Oxford Street store, she had an attractive voice and was frequently used as a soloist in Army meetings. According to Wiggins she was impressed by Slater's musicianship, but rather embarrassed by his somewhat eccentric manner.[10] The couple were to have two daughters, named after Wagnerian operatic characters, Elsa and Brunnhilde. For most of Slater's working life within the Salvation Army, he lived with his family in the Wood Green area of London, travelling daily into the Musical Department which was located in turn at the Clapton Training Home in the East End; New Barnet; Clerkenwell Road; Queen Victoria Street, and Judd Street (in the same neighbourhood as Cromer Street, where Slater had spent his boyhood and adolescence).[11]

❧ Apprenticeship, 1883–92

We may call the years spanning 1883 until 1892, Slater's apprenticeship years with the Army's Musical Department, as they provided him with the opportunity to find his feet within the organisation.

Back in September 1881 Fred Fry, a member of the Fry Family Band, had been appointed to produce music to meet the growing needs of bands. To aid him the Army purchased a second-hand printing press, some letter type, and two founts of pied music type which no printer would put in order. Fry taught himself how to set up the press ready for printing Salvation Army music and song, both in staff and tonic sol-fa notation.[12]

Thus commenced, rather uncertainly, the Musical Department of the Salvation Army. Slater took over the responsibility of managing the everyday running of the department, assisted by Fred Fry and Henry Hill (Bandmaster of the Clapton Congress Hall Band), and under the general supervision of Herbert Booth. As was his custom, Slater shrewdly summed up his main rival:

---

[9] *War Cry*, 30 Dec. 1939.

[10] Wiggins, *Father of Salvation Army Music*, p. 17.

[11] Ibid.

[12] Ibid., pp. 26–7.

The chief person I think in the Musical Department at present is Mr Fry. I see clearly that his character is such that he is not likely by the natural bearing of things to keep a chief place when my influence comes into play. His technical knowledge is less than mine, and I have more varied ability to carry me beyond him [...] I think I shall be able to make a friend of Fry, and this will prove useful. (RSd, v. 1, 18 Oct. 1883)

In considering these apprenticeship years I shall focus first on Slater's contribution to vocal music, and then to music for bands.

MUSIC FOR VOICES

One of Slater's early tasks in 1883 was to find individuals with suitable voices to form The Salvation Songsters. Members were recruited from the Training Homes where they were preparing to become Salvation Army officers. It was then Slater's job to teach them the vocal parts of the song repertoire. The Salvation Songsters had three aims: to win souls for Christ, to enlist the interest of young people in full-time work for the Salvation Army, and to raise money for the training of cadets through a regular series of national tours.[13] Altogether between 1883 and 1885 Herbert Booth led this group, with its regularly changing personnel, on six national tours of six weeks each. Many of the songs in the repertoire were specially written by Slater and Herbert Booth, and instrumental accompaniment was provided by Slater on violin, Fry on the harp, and Hill on the double bass. The Salvation Songsters were disbanded in 1885, and were succeeded in the following year by the Singing, Speaking and Praying Brigade. Again Slater and Herbert Booth wrote many of the songs, and some of these were then issued as *Favourite Songs of the Singing, Speaking and Praying Brigade* in eight numbers, later published in one volume.[14] According to Slater, this was the first time that original Salvation Army music was published.[15]

In July 1886 Slater produced the first number of what was to become a regular monthly magazine, the *Musical Salvationist*, which he edited as well as providing much of the material. Subsequent numbers contained songs for solo voices and mixed voices, arrangements of Army pieces for various instruments, including the piano, violin, string bands, concertina bands, and drum and fife bands, as well as concerted pieces for brass instruments. In addition there were articles on all kinds of musical subjects.

Slater outlined his preparation for the task before him as a composer for the Army, particularly of vocal music:

[13] Boon, *Sing the Happy Song!*, p. 8.

[14] *The Favorite Songs from the Singing, Speaking and Praying Brigade* (London, [1886]).

[15] Slater, *Salvation Army Dictionary of Music*, p. 79.

Lyrical poetry giving the forms in which I should endeavour to write, the poets who are noted for this kind of work should be read by me. I should finish off songs I have sketched. Musical stimulation to aid me can be got from the works of the great composers I possess and books of songs. I should consider the subjects of my songs so to get variety in future efforts. I should consider the nature of the opportunities the Army offers me as a composer. I should collect tunes likely to be of use in the Army. I should take thought to find out means to induce the mood most favourable for song writing. I should make a list of music and poetry of most value to aid my efforts in composition. I have felt it somewhat difficult to get new musical ideas in recent efforts, but that may result from having so little musical exercise by which to keep in a musical mood. (RSd, v. 1, 4 Dec. 1885)

Interestingly, as an example of Slater's musical taste, the very first song in the first issue of the *Musical Salvationist* was entitled 'While in my Lord confiding'.[16] It comprised words by Slater set to an unattributed tune, which Steadman-Allen has identified as 'On yonder rock reclining' ('Voyez sur cette roche') from Auber's opera *Fra Diavolo* (1830).[17] In all, Slater was to publish 587 songs, of which he wrote the words of 127, the music of 166, and the words and music of 294.[18] In addition, Wiggins reckoned there remained another 264 songs in manuscript by the time of Slater's passing.[19]

Whilst most of Slater's songs were single pieces, he developed the form of what he called a 'Song Service' or 'Service of Song', which he defined as 'a treatment of a connected story by means of readings and songs [...] It is the simplest form of what is more elaborately realised in the Cantata and Oratorio'.[20] The first of these was *The Life Story of a Salvationist*, composed between 1–3 December 1888, and first published in the *Musical Salvationist* in February 1889.[21] It was followed by *The History of the Army*,[22] *The Story of a Song*,[23] *The Life of Christ in*

---

[16] Originally published in *Musical Salvationist*, July 1886, reprinted in *Musical Salvationist Vols. 1–3 with Favorite Songs Supplement* (London, 1893), p. 1.

[17] Steadman-Allen, 'The Evolution of Salvation Army Music', *The Musician*, 26 June 1965, p. 406.

[18] Slater, *Salvation Army Song Writers*, p. 68.

[19] Wiggins, *Father of Salvation Army Music*, p. 32.

[20] Slater, *Salvation Army Dictionary of Music*, p. 117.

[21] R. Slater, *The Life Story of a Salvationist* (Song Service), *Musical Salvationist* 3 (Feb. 1889), pp. 65–72.

[22] R. Slater, *The History of the Army* (Song Service), *Musical Salvationist* 7 (Apr. 1893), pp. 121–32. [Also arranged for band, *Band Journal*, 253–6].

[23] R. Slater, *The Story of a Song* (Song Service), *Musical Salvationist* 9 (Nov. 1894), pp. 49–60.

Song.[24] Some of the song services were unabashed propaganda. For example, *The Salvation Army's Social Scheme*[25] celebrated William Booth's plans for social regeneration that he had outlined, as we have seen, in his book *In Darkest England* (1890). Slater's medley of songs included, 'The Reason for the Scheme', 'The Enquiry Department', 'The Labour Bureau', 'The Slum Work', 'The Shelters', 'The Rescue Work', 'The Farm Colony', and 'The Future of the Scheme'. Most of these items were in four parts, but there was also a solo, a solo with chorus, and a duet. Slater wrote both words and music for these song services.

The *Life Story of a Salvationist* offers a good example of his vocal settings. (See Example 1.) In all there are eight separate 'scenes' using eight songs. Six are in unison with piano accompaniment, and two are in four parts with no independent accompaniment. There is no indication of whether or not verses might be sung as solos.

Slater introduces us to the main character in the first scene, 'The Salvation Army Hall'. This happened to be a drunkard whose thoughts had previously turned to suicide. But on hearing a Salvation Army Band on the march he decided to enter the Army hall. The bible reading from the Captain made him weep in penitence. Writing for unison voices with piano accompaniment, Slater sets the verses to a lyrical and gentle melodic line, but contrasts this with a rousing *fortissimo* chorus in march style, with the Salvationists entreating, 'O drunkard, drunkard, with us will you go along?' Appropriately at this point the piano plays an elaborate and energetic 'running bass' accompaniment in octaves in imitation of so many early Salvation Army marches.

In contrast is Slater's musical cameo of the drunkard's contrition, and his gaining of a sense of peace, whilst he kneels at 'The Penitent Form'. There is no denying the sense of fervour which is engendered by this *adagio* movement in a gently rocking 6/8 time, with an insistent refrain, 'Oh hear the sinner praying Lord'. Slater underlines the pathos of the scene with a restrained use of some major and minor seventh chords in the harmony. In other contexts, this setting could well be imagined as a basis for an operatic ensemble piece.

In returning to 'The Workshop' after his conversion, the penitent tells his family and his workmates of the joy he has experienced. Slater suggests a palpable feeling of excitement in this unison *vivace* setting, with an effective contrast between the musical 'patter' of the verse, and the solemn emphatic refrain 'Oh, 'tis true. Oh, 'tis true'. The second part of the refrain acts as a bridge to lead into the following verses, and does so in a dramatic fashion with the voices accompanied by bare octaves in the piano part.

The next step for the new convert was to take his place on 'The March', and

---

[24] R. Slater, *The Life of Christ in Song* (Song Service), *Musical Salvationist* 10 (Aug. 1895), pp. 13–24.

[25] R. Slater, *The Salvation Army's Social Scheme* (Song Service), *Musical Salvationist* 11 (Feb. 1897), pp. 85–96.

Example 1 Richard Slater, 'The Salvation Army Hall',

from *The Life Story of a Salvationist* (1889)

Slater here provides an exemplary vocal march for four parts, with a character-istic A1–A2–B1–B2 form. With its dotted rhythms throughout, and its triplet figures in the chorus, the song swings along with straightforward harmonies enlivened by the occasional accented diminished seventh resolving onto the tonic chord.

In 'The Open-Air Ring', the convert bears witness, and here Slater effectively contrasts the 4/4 *moderato* verse telling of the man's experience, with a waltz-time chorus, *allegro moderato*, expressing the personal assurance that 'I'm saved, this I know'. The rhythmic momentum is nicely propelled along by alternating tonic harmony with a diminished seventh chord, leading to a *fortissimo* climax, itself also upon a diminished seventh, emphasising 'I've had a great find'. The song ends back on the tonic with a sense of serenity, 'I've cause to be free and easy'.

But the sense of serenity is soon dissipated by 'The Riot', reminding us that the Salvation Army had been, in its early days, the butt of much vocal oppo-sition. Slater paints a dramatic picture of the rage of the mob, *presto, ma non troppo*, with the voices and piano at times in unison at the octave. A feature of the second half of the refrain is an independent melodic line played on the piano, something unique in this song service.

Slater sets 'The Death-Bed', in the form of a funeral march, *andante con espress* in A♭ major. The phrase, 'A conqueror will he depart' prompts Slater to utilise some chromatic harmonic colouring which eventually resolves on the dominant (E♭) with a suspended fourth, itself resolving on to a diminished seventh chord and then cadencing in the tonic.The chorus is a *molto tranquillo* dotted rhythmic march which bids farewell on the penitent's departure to 'the better land'.

The final scene, appropriately enough, is 'Heaven'. Here, a lovely fresh melodic line has a relatively elaborate arppeggiated accompaniment. One can sense in the *vivace* setting a personal commitment in Slater's writing. The lyrical verse changes into a catchy revival-type song setting, 'Hallelujah to the Lamb that once was slain', which gives an appropriately triumphant conclusion to this life story of a Salvationist.

The Life Story of a Salvationist proved so popular, not only in England but also in Holland and Norway, that in his retirement Slater prepared an edition in which each song was set for four-part voices with connected readings written by himself. Slater instructed,

> The last reading is to serve the purpose of a final appeal to the unsaved among the audience [...] The whole service is of such a character as to justify a belief for penitent-form results, by the blessing of God, so as to give it the desired spiritual success, which was the aim for which the story was written.[26]

[26] R. Slater, *The Life Story of a Salvationist* (London, n.d.), Foreword, n.p.

To sum up, Ray Steadman-Allen describes Slater's song-writing idiom as relating to the mid-19th-century Italian tradition, rather than to any Wagnerian influence.[27] But it is also reminiscent in style of the Victorian drawing-room ballad, and occasionally of Gilbert and Sullivan. Certainly *The Life Story of a Salvationist* demonstrated Slater's versatility as a song writer, composing attractive settings for often inexperienced singers and singing brigades, within the requirement that such songs were essentially functional, primarily for the purpose of spreading the evangelical message of the Salvation Army.

DEVELOPING POLICY FOR BANDS

It is necessary at this point to provide some contextual detail regarding the Army's regulations vis-à-vis instrumental music, in order to understand the situation in which Slater was placed. Two Orders for bands had been promulgated in the Salvation Army prior to Slater's involvement. The first, 'Musical Instruments from the General' on 27 March 1880, encouraged a mass movement of musical engagement, certainly not confined to brass instruments, nor to males:

> We do here express our desire that as many of our officers and soldiers generally, *male and female*, as have the ability for so doing, shall learn to play on some instrument [...] This includes violins, bass viols, concertinas, cornets, or any brass instrument, drums, or anything else that will make a pleasant sound for the Lord.[28]

The second, 'General Order: Brass Bands', was published on 24 February 1881, this time focusing specifically upon brass bands. The following extracts provide a flavour of these directives, which emphasise the discipline and control exerted upon the membership:

> No one will be admitted or retained a member of any Band who is not a member of The Army.

> All the instruments in every Band are to be the property of The Army, no matter by whom they may be purchased, or through whom they may be presented [...]

> In no case are instruments to be used to play anything but Salvation music, or on any but Salvation Army service.

> In no case will any committee be allowed in connection with any Band.

> In no case will any Band, or any member of any Band, be allowed to go into debt, either for instruments, or anything else connected with the Band.

27 Steadman-Allen, 'The Evolution of Salvation Army Music', *The Musician*, 14 Aug. 1965, p. 519.

28 'Musical Instruments from the General', *War Cry*, 27 Mar. 1880.

In no case is the practice of the Band, or any member of it to interfere with the meetings of the Corps.

Any Band [...] which does not carry out this Order will not be recognised as a Salvation Army Band, and [...] must at once be disbanded.[29]

These two Orders were followed on 27 May 1885 by a Third Order, which was to have an influence on the musical life of the Army that would endure for over a century:

From this date no Band will be allowed to play from music excepting 'The Salvation Army General Band Book' – the Journals published by us from time to time and other music issued from Headquarters. Quicksteps and Introductions are strictly prohibited.[30]

Holz provides a judicious estimate of this order's significance: 'That this order created difficulties would be a gross understatement. By this edict, Booth was to gain absolute autocratic control.'[31] Holz relays a well-sourced opinion that publishers did not want Salvation Army music sold to 'outside' bands, particularly if Booth was to continue his embargo against the music of 'outside' bands being played by Salvation Army bands. Booth apparently reached such an agreement with the band publisher and instrument manufacturer Boosey & Hawkes.[32] Dave Russell points out that 'the publishers found the Army's self-sufficiency a further source of annoyance and took their revenge in the trade press gleefully reporting salvationist 'defections' to the enemy'.[33]

The Third Order had the effect of causing a long rift in British brass band culture world-wide. From this point the Salvation Army published all of its own materials, including its music. Its imprint was various in the early years, including The Salvation Army Book Stores, The Salvation Army Trade Headquarters etc. From 1917 it became Salvationist Publishing and Supplies (SP&S).[34] The exclusiveness of the Salvation Army with respect to its musical life meant that 'in no sense were Salvation Army bands part of the orthodox band

---

[29] 'General Order: Brass Bands', War Cry, 24 Feb. 1881. These appear to be the initial set of rules which were to be expanded considerably. It was announced in the War Cry on 2 July 1887 that 'Every Bandsman should have a copy of the new Band Rules, eighteen pages [...] price one penny' (p. 2). It would appear that this 18-page list was later published as Orders and Regulations for Bands as a supplement to Orders and Regulations for Field Officers of the Salvation Army (London, 1889). I am indebted to Gordon Taylor for this information.

[30] 'General Order Respect Brass Bands', War Cry, 27 May 1885.

[31] Holz, Brass Bands of the Salvation Army, vol. 1, p. 89.

[32] Ibid., p. 108, fn. 27.

[33] Russell, Popular Music in England, p. 213.

[34] See R. Steadman-Allen, 'One Hundred Years of Music Publishing', in The Salvation Army Yearbook 1976 (London, 1976), pp. 15–18.

tradition'.[35] This separation would be strengthened by the development of its own instrument-making factory, beginning in a small way in May 1889.[36] There were severe practical implications of this musical exclusivity for the work of the Army's Musical Department, whose job it became to supply the voracious appetite for new music from the rapidly growing number of musical troops.

As far as writing for bands was concerned in these years, the situation Slater came into was chaotic, because there was no unified plan. No such thing as Salvation Army Music existed. There were few teachers and unless a local man could be found there was little that could be achieved. Many combinations had teachers who were not Salvationists, and some of these arranged music for the bands they taught and formed, while others bought music that was often far from suitable. Slater recollected William Booth commenting that the early musical arrangements originated from diverse sources – 'Some from Liverpool, some from Hull, and perhaps from Hell'.[37] Moreover, bands were not built on any common plan of instrumentation. No two bands could play together unless taught by the same man.[38] Slater realised at once that unity of labour as well as a plan of instrumentation became a necessity, so that all bands should be units in a great musical movement.[39] The development of a musical repertoire became of prime importance, and challenging the musical demands made on bandsmen became the basis for developing the skills and abilities of Salvationist musicians.

In 1882 Fred Fry had organised the publication of 13 sets of cards containing eight tunes each, and sold for 6*d.* per instrumental part. The venture was not a success; in fact after the seventh card had been produced, there was a total loss of £100.[40] According to Wiggins some of the bands were already playing more advanced music, and were not attracted to such simple arrangements of straight-forward hymn tunes.[41]

In these apprenticeship years Richard Slater's scope was severely limited. One of his first tasks was to produce brass arrangements of hymn tunes, in particular revising and correcting the work of Fry and Hill, and 'for seeing the harmony is according to the rule, though not for the choice of chords or tunes worked on by Hill and Fry' (RSd, v. 8, 28 Jan. 1884). These arrangements eventually comprised the first band tune-book for accompanying congregational singing, *Band Music for the Salvation Army* (1884). It comprised 88 tunes in total. The purpose was to

[35] Russell, *Popular Music in England*, p. 212.

[36] Slater, *Salvation Army Dictionary of Music*, p. 57.

[37] R. Slater, 'The First Bandmasters' Council', *Bandsman and Songster*, 18 Sept. 1926, p. 290.

[38] Slater, 'My Twenty-Six Years Service', pp. 3–4.

[39] Ibid.

[40] Sandall, *History of the Salvation Army*, vol. 2, p. 122.

[41] A. R. Wiggins, 'The Music Editorial Department [...] The Beginnings of Things', *Bandsman and Songster*, 26 Apr. 1930, p. 131.

supply music that all Army bands could use, so that amalgamated playing could take place. It can be regarded as the first true Salvation Army band music, the purpose of which was to assist the singing. In the 'general order' from William Booth printed in the book, his ambivalence about bands is apparent: 'The playing of any notes to which no words are sung [...] is quite contrary to our wishes.' However, an exception was allowed on large united marches, where 'it may be tolerated for bands to play our tunes (but only our tunes) one after the other without any attempt at singing'.[42]

Whilst William Booth appreciated the power of brass bands to attract outsiders into the Salvation Army he was concerned about the tendency of the same bands to overpower the congregational singing in indoor meetings. He had addressed his Field Officers (F.O.) as follows in the 1880 *Orders and Regulations for the Salvation Army*:

> The FO must never allow the singing of his people to be drowned by the accompanying music. The bandsmen like to hear themselves, and consequently they will not be overmuch concerned about drowning the voices of everybody else [...] the FO must insist upon the band playing softly [...] if not, the band will be a curse rather than a blessing.[43]

It is important to realise that the earliest repertoire of approved music for band between 1880 and 1900 consisted of transcriptions from the songs and medleys published in the *Musical Salvationist*, thus ensuring that Salvation Army instrumental music be directly referential, with a precise textual message. These arrangements were published in the *Band Journal* which had been established in August 1884. It appeared irregularly in the early days, then at a variety of intervals: once monthly, once every quarter; bimonthly. In addition at that time the journal included simple settings of well-known hymn tunes/gospel songs, and popular songs or classical airs to which Salvationists had added new words.[44] The majority of the works for brass mentioned in this present study were published by the Salvation Army in the Ordinary Series of the Band Journal (hereinafter BJ), apart from a small number appearing in the Festival Series (hereinafter FS) begun in 1923 for more advanced bands, and the Second Series (hereinafter SS) introduced in 1921 for smaller less proficient bands.

While providing a vocal and instrumental repertoire for the Army prompted by Booth's Third Order, Slater was also working hard on meeting the educational needs of Salvationist musicians. He pointed this out in a letter to Bramwell Booth: 'The department set itself to meet the music educational needs of the Army, not waiting for any instruction to do so, but went on at its own initiative' (RSd, v. 10,

---

[42] *Band Music for the Salvation Army* (London, 1884), n.p.

[43] W. Booth, *Orders and Regulations for the Salvation Army* (1880), p. 233. Indeed, Booth advocated the use of string bands in every corps, which he believed would be far more suitable for indoor meetings (pp. 233–4).

[44] See Holz, *Brass Bands of the Salvation Army*, vol. 1, p. 91.

6 Feb. 1909). By 1890 Slater was checking the proofs of instrumental tutors for the cornet, the euphonium, and the bombardon (E♭ Bass). The completed series was eventually to also include manuals for clarinet, concertina, autoharp, piano, drums and fifes, soprano cornet, tenor horn, baritone [horn], B♭ trombone, bass trombone, and drums.[45]

SLATER was generally muted about these years. He thought the Musical Department did not have much merit (RSd, v. 7, 12 Apr. 1886). He later observed that there was considerable dissatisfaction amongst some bands about the musical arrangements of his colleague Fred Fry (RSd, v. 4, 10 July 1890). Approaching seven years in the Department, Slater admitted to his diary, 'there has been little musical practice, culture, and little pleasure' (RSd, v. 7, 31 Dec. 1888). In spite of this, his financial situation was more secure. Ever his own severest critic, Slater concluded, 'Life has grown smooth for me, perhaps too much so for my mental and spiritual good' (RSd, v. 7, 31 Dec. 1888).

In 1892 Herbert Booth, Slater's boss, sailed for Canada to take control of the Salvation Army in that country. Slater wrote, 'This makes a new start in a sense of the Music Department as he will cease to exercise any direct control over it in any way' (RSd, v. 1, 1892, annual review). It so happened that Fred Fry also went to Canada, so in his place was appointed Frederick G. Hawkes. Before joining the Army, Hawkes had had little musical experience or training.[46] He happened to apply to a request in the *War Cry* of 12 March 1887 for Army bandsmen to offer themselves for service in a band which was to travel the country and hold musical meetings. This was to be the Household Troops Band, and for four years Hawkes was one of its most valued members. He was particularly intrigued by how music worked from the inside, and he set out to study the various branches of the art of music. He was in contact with Slater, and it was on Slater's recommendation that Hawkes received his appointment in the department.

Mention should also be made of the later appointment of Arthur Goldsmith to the Musical Department in 1908.[47] He came from a Salvationist family and had been a bandsman at the Poplar Corps in East London. On leaving school he worked for the Salvation Army at its International Headquarters and was one of the original members of the Junior Staff Band, and later the International Staff

45 According to Slater, *Salvation Army Dictionary of Music*, the first tutor produced was for the cornet, which appeared 'as one of the novelties at The Army's Anniversary celebration on July 15th, 1890' (p. 79).

46 [A. R. Wiggins,] 'The Music Editorial Department: A Review of its History [...] Discovery of Lieut.-Col. Hawkes', *Bandsman and Songster*, 10 May 1930, p. 147.

47 [A. R. Wiggins,] 'The Music Editorial Department: A Review of its History [...] Lieut. Colonel Goldsmith: The Poplar Boy who became a Front-Rank Army Composer', *Bandsman and Songster*, 24 May 1930, p. 165. Also see Henry Hall's affectionate remembrance of Goldsmith in *'Here's to the Next Time!': The Autobiography of Henry Hall* (London, 1955), pp. 22–4.

Band. He achieved some renown as an able exponent on the soprano cornet, and in addition had contributed several songs for publication in the *Musical Salvationist*. He undertook part-time studies at the Guildhall School of Music, and gained one of its diplomas, as well as first prize in the Army's Musical Selection Competition. Slater was particularly taken with Goldsmith's prize selection, and consequently recommended him for a music appointment.

Both Hawkes and Goldsmith were to become major figures within the musical world of the Salvation Army. Hawkes was a most able administrator, and a competent composer and arranger. Goldsmith was to contribute some influential works for band, which maintained for a considerable period their place in the repertoire. He also later developed a fine reputation as Bandmaster of the Men's Social Work Headquarters Band in the 1930s. On the retirement of Slater in 1913 the two men were appointed as joint heads of the Musical Department, an arrangement which lasted until 1921, when Goldsmith became the Financial Secretary of Salvationist Publishing and Supplies, whilst Hawkes shouldered the leadership of what became known as the Music Editorial Department until 1936.[48]

⊱ *In Command, 1893–1913*

With Herbert Booth away in Canada, Richard Slater could now take full command of the Musical Department. Much of the Department's work in the years leading up to the new century was concerned with William Booth's project of compiling a suitable Salvation Army song book, which eventually contained 870 songs and 216 choruses. *The Salvation Army Songs* was published in 1899.[49] It was the Musical Department's job to supply as companions, *Band Book No. 1* (1900) which contained 303 tunes,[50] and for vocal purposes the keyboard edition, *Salvation Army Music* (1900).[51] It was a heavy task, and caused 'a serious strain for the Department'.[52] In retrospect, however, Slater called the assembling of the Song Book, the Tune Book and the Band Book, 'by far the greatest and the most important task undertaken by The Army in connection with songs and music'.[53]

What dominated his day-to-day life as head of the department in the new century, was his often fraught relationship with what became known as the

---

[48] Holz, *Brass Bands of the Salvation Army*, vol. 1, pp. 140–1.

[49] *The Salvation Army Songs* (London, 1899).

[50] *Band Book No. 1* (London, 1900).

[51] *Salvation Army Music* (London, 1900). Both *Band Book No. 1* and *Salvation Army Music* provided 303 tunes for *The Salvation Army Songs*. Tunes for the other 567 songs in that volume were indicated by reference to other Salvation Army sources, including the *Musical Salvationist*, and *Salvation Army Music*.

[52] Slater, *Salvation Army Dictionary of Music*, p. 124.

[53] Ibid.

International Headquarters Music Board. In this section I shall describe first the genesis of this Board that attempted to prescribe the musical limits within which Slater and his department had to work. I shall then focus on the 1901 memorandum that ensured a greater sense of musical freedom, but always kept in check by the Music Board. The heart of this section comprises my account of the widely reported visit of George Bernard Shaw, the playwright, to a musical festival at the Clapton Congress Hall on 9 December 1905. It was a visit that was to have important repercussions for Slater. I shall then assess Slater's contribution as a composer to the liberalising trend following the 1901 memorandum. Finally I shall discuss his preoccupations in the years immediately preceding his retirement, including his continuing project on Wagner, his thoughts on politics, and the attempt to own the copyright of his compositions, which brought him into some conflict with William Booth.

THE INTERNATIONAL HEADQUARTERS MUSIC BOARD

There is no doubt that Slater's room for manœuvre in his early work in the Salvation Army was extremely limited. A few years after entering the Army's Musical Department Slater outlined the musical aesthetic of those years, which has also permeated Salvationist musical life to the extent that traces still remain:

> We make no endeavour to meet the tastes of the cultured few. Our appeal is to the masses. Those who have any acquaintance with our operations are fully aware how inappropriate would be music of a complicated nature in Army meetings. To reach the masses the music called for is that which goes direct to the souls of men, not such as demands a measure of culture and an intellectual process for its comprehension. The Army music is therefore popular in style, depending more upon melody than harmony, simplicity of style and structure characterizes it, and it is thus universal in its scope and direct in its effect.[54]

It was within these limits that Slater carried out his work.

A couple of years after his appointment as head of department, the International Headquarters Music Board was instituted to which the Musical Department was responsible. In many ways the Board was to be Slater's *bête noir*. It came into being through the following circumstance. In August 1896 the Salvation Army held its first international exhibition at the Royal Agricultural Hall, Islington, which hosted such popular events as Sanger's Circus, and the Grand Military Tournament.[55] Two bands were on duty – the International Staff Band and the Trade Headquarters Band. Both featured programmes of the latest music so that bandmasters might be persuaded to purchase the current band

---

[54] R. Slater, 'Music in the Salvation Army', *All the World*, Apr. 1891, p. 287.

[55] Boon, *ISB*, pp. 18–19. For Royal Agricultural Hall, see *The London Encyclopaedia*, ed. Weinreb and Hibbert, p. 681.

journals. On the final day both bands participated in the finale. It was agreed at the last minute that the Trade Headquarters Band, conducted by Hawkes, would end the day with two rousing pieces, an unpublished march by Hawkes and *Rule Britannia*. It was generally thought that William Booth would not be present at such a late hour:

> The band played [...] the crowd went wild with excitement. This was something new. No other band had access to this music. There had to be an encore – and more applause. When the cheering was at its height William Booth appeared. He had been resting in an ante-room, and the stirring music and subsequent sounds of enthusiastic acceptance had not met with his approval.[56]

It was as a result of this 'outrage', with its apparent showmanship and lack of an explicit religious message, that William Booth insisted that an International Musical Board (later known as the International Headquarters Music Board), be formed as a controlling body to ensure that music selected for publication was only that which had received a stamp of approval from the Board. The Board was to be answerable to William Booth himself.[57] It was this body that Slater had to deal with as Head of the Musical Department. He was required to sing the songs that he felt should be published to the Board, accompanied by himself on the harmonium, and the International Staff Band similarly had to play band compositions for the Board's approval. The Board was to comprise some of the leading officers of the Army, and was first chaired by Commissioner John Carleton.[58]

Trevor Herbert has this to say about the Board:

> The function of the Music Board has been quite unique in British musical life. No other agency, from the Church of England to the British military establishment, has sought to centralize the control of its repertoire by vesting authority in a single office, and imposing a total restriction on any repertoire which does not pass through it.[59]

It undoubtedly served to rationalise and standardise Army music, thus almost completely controlling its production and consumption, and more insidiously 'it is hard to avoid the impression that control and censorship were almost in the foreground'.[60]

The Board at once made it clear to Slater, in reaction to the débâcle at the Royal Agricultural Hall, that it wanted a return to the musical style of the

---

[56] Boon, *ISB*, p. 19.

[57] See F. G. Hawkes, 'Fifty Years of Army Music', *The Officer* 11:1 (Jan.–Feb. 1951), pp. 15–20.

[58] Apparently John Carleton was a capable musician, and served as songster leader at Penge for 28 years. See *Bandsman and Songster*, 30 Oct. 1926, p. 348.

[59] Herbert, 'God's Perfect Minstrels', p. 209.

[60] Ibid., p. 204.

early Army. It was felt that the music played at the international exhibition was undesirable and dangerous to the interests of the Salvation Army. But Slater disagreed. The idea had been that the music would represent the international character of the exhibition, after all 'the tunes have as much right to appeal as national flags, dresses, customs [...] of the people' (RSd, v. 3, 8 Feb. 1897). Most of the tunes had been national anthems, so the musical elaboration was characteristic of them. Carleton questioned whether or not bands were as spiritual as they had been, as 'a degenerating influence had been exercised by the recent Band music upon them' (RSd, v. 3, 16 Feb. 1897). This was to become a familiar theme.

As a footnote, in spite of the continued criticism Slater was to make of the Board, he was in fact a supporter of it in principle. In 1904 he expressed himself disappointed that other countries did not seem to be bound by the regulation that only Salvationist music as printed or approved by Headquarters could be played (RSd, v. 9, 1904, annual review). From a friend in Australia he had heard that the two territorial bands there were actually playing operatic and contest selections, purchased from 'outside' publishers, and included works by Verdi, Rossini, Weber and Meyerbeer (RSd, v. 9, 19 Aug. 1904). As for the New York [Staff] Band, it played no Salvation Army music, 'but plays chiefly Sousa's marches and also other pieces that have no religious aim in them whatever [...] I raised a protest' (RSd, v. 9, 1904, annual review). Slater was keen that musical boards be established in other countries, to ensure there was 'one band life' (RSd, v. 2, 19 Aug. 1903).

THE 1901 MEMORANDUM AND ITS MUSICAL IMPACT

On 4 September 1901 the Musical Department had submitted a memorandum for consideration through the Music Board to William Booth requesting certain changes in music publication policy.[61] This occurred partly as a result of a perceived need to provide more challenging music for bands, and also to keep the bandsmen from straying elsewhere. Somewhat surprisingly, William Booth acceded to the request, principally that band music might be allowed to contain original material for which no words had been composed or intended. It was the job of the Musical Department to provide exemplars for such music.

This was indeed a momentous step in the struggle between those who, like Slater, wanted to expand the musical horizons for Salvationist composers and bandsmen, and those who regarded instrumental music with deep suspicion, and who were antagonistic to new forms of expression. The latter I call musical Calvinists. (Originally Calvinists had attempted to curtail the opportunities for musical abuse by restricting the use of music in worship to simple and pure singing.)[62] Slater's musical opponents within the Army wanted to restrict instrumental music solely to the accompaniment of singing. There is no doubt

---

[61] Holz, *Brass Bands of the Salvation Army*, vol. 1, p. 94.

[62] See Rainbow with Cox, *Music in Educational Thought and Practice*, pp. 60–1.

that he saw himself as a musical liberal and reformer within the Salvation Army, attempting to push the musical and hence the educational boundaries of the repertoire.

Slater was pleased, but others, particularly senior figures, were somewhat fearful. Commissioner T. Henry Howard,[63] who was to become the Army's second-in-command, had put the case for reform to William Booth, but he admitted to Slater, that he

> feared he had put the advanced view in so good a light as to have led the General to have taken so much of what the Musical Department had been contending for as to have gone beyond what the Commr. Thought to be prudent. (RSd, v. 4, 15 Sept. 1901)

Commissioner Thomas Coombs,[64] who led the Army in Great Britain, said to Slater, 'You have gained a victory this time'. Slater commented in his diary that

> the unexpected siding of the General on our suggestions for a larger policy led the Commr. to fear many dangers in our opening out in the way we could now claim to do by the General's permission. He dwelt upon the dangers of educational advance in the Army, and the regrettable movement in the Army in the direction of entertainment. (RSd, v. 4, 30 Oct. 1901)

It was Slater's job to provide exemplars of this new musical style. He wrote three specimen marches, *The Festival March* (BJ 422) (which was fully original), *Our Battalions* (BJ 415) (which 'gives existing matter for the whole except introduction and links etc.'), and *The Morning Hymn March* (BJ 411) (which 'gives a well-known piece for the trio, the rest being original') (RSd, v. 4, 18 Nov. 1901).

It so happened that the International Staff Band was due to play at a festival at the Clapton Congress Hall, a week after Slater had completed these marches. Pressure was placed on Commissioner Howard, by now the chair of the Music Board, to allow these pieces to be played. In fact, Slater put it more strongly: 'Almost a demand was made for the pieces, and hints at a sort of rebellion if there was a refusal. Commissioner Howard was in a fix' (RSd, v. 4, 25 Nov. 1901). Permission was given for *Our Battalions* and *The Morning Hymn* marches to be played. Howard made a statement that these pieces were experiments as a result of the General's new ruling on music. This 'met with much applause from the musicians who were present' (RSd, v. 4, 25 Nov. 1901).

It was also Slater's job to provide exemplars of other musical genres. The first example of a 'selection' was written by him in 1901, *Old Song Memories*

---

[63] For details of T. Henry Howard, see Sandall, *The History of the Salvation Army*, vol. 2, p. 61.

[64] Thomas Coombs was responsible for forming the Headquarters Brass Band in Melbourne in 1890, later to become the Territorial Staff Band. See Wiggins, *The History of the Salvation Army*, vol. 4, p. 94.

(BJ 407–10, Supplement), described by Holz, 'in all but name a long medley of 11 songs'.[65] But Slater considered his *Songs of Scotland* (BJ 428, 429) published in 1902 as the first true selection, containing as it did an introduction, and short links between some of the 11 songs.[66] Selections thereafter comprised the following types: national melodies, praise, seasonal, or devotional. Eventually the unique Salvationist genre, the 'meditation', was established, which gave rise to freely composed materials as episodes between the verse of the hymn tune that was the subject of the work, rather like a chorale prelude. Again it was Slater who wrote the prototype (although he did not call it a meditation) in 1902, entitled *Jesus Hope of Souls Repentant* (BJ 412): it was, according to Holz, 'the first SA composition for band in which the composer attempts to portray the separate verses of a song through instrumental music'.[67]

In 1904 a great International Congress was held, which coincided with William Booth's 75th birthday. Music played a key role in the event. Over 200 bands involving 7,000 bandsmen from various parts of the world took part, including France, Sweden, Norway, Germany, Bermuda, Canada and the USA. There were huge demonstrations at the Crystal Palace and the Strand. It was speculated that there were 17,000 Salvationist bandsmen worldwide.[68]

Slater had contributed a number of items for the *Band Journal*, to be used on this occasion. The Music Board heard the Staff Band play his *All Nations* (BJ 456, 457) and *Crown Him* (BJ 462) selections. However, it felt that the Musical Department had gone too far with respect to advanced music. Introductions and episodes were not wanted; all that was needed were links to bring about changes of key and to join together pieces in different styles (RSd, v. 4, 16 Feb. 1904). Slater was instructed to cut out introductions, episodes and finales of the selections he had put forward, and return to the old style of band journals, at least for three or four issues (RSd, v. 5, 3 Mar. 1904).

Slater was suspicious that the Board's decision was a reflection of their fear of what William Booth might think of the new musical developments,

> There's great anxiety, hesitation, lack of straightforwardness in the Musical Board as to the new English Band music coming to the General's ears, for the feeling they has [*sic*] is <u>that he will not like it, may probably condemn it</u>, and so against their own opinions and sanction would make his desire supreme and <u>keep away from his knowledge</u> the facts of the recent music. Is there not here one of the results of autocracy? It leads to weakness of personal judgement, principle, and <u>to please the whims of the top man</u> takes the place of doing one's duty according to one's own convictions and experience. The lack of policy and principles on the part of the Board is

[65] Holz, *Brass Bands of the Salvation Army*, vol. 1, p. 95.

[66] Ibid.

[67] Ibid.

[68] Ibid., pp. 100–4.

very demeaning [...] it indicates weakness at the foundation. (RSd, v. 9, 1904, annual review)

GEORGE BERNARD SHAW: WHAT THE CRITIC HAD TO SAY

So far in this account of Slater's work within the Salvation Army much of the evidence has been from his own points of view as expressed in the diaries. For a brief period in December 1905, however, Salvationist music-making came under considerable scrutiny from the national press, prompted by a visit to a Salvation Army festival by George Bernard Shaw. In many ways this event and its aftermath can be seen as something of a turning point in the public recognition and acceptance of the quality and potential of Salvation Army music. The following account provides a welcome opportunity to view the achievements of Slater in a wider, and at times critical perspective.

Although Bernard Shaw's reputation rests chiefly on his plays, he was a man of many reputations. Indeed, he claimed to be the victim of 12 to 15 of them according to his biographer, Michael Holroyd, whilst in religion he described himself as a Creative-Evolutionist, and in politics as a Fabian.[69] One of his reputations was as a professional music critic, principally in the years between 1888 and 1894. Although he had received little formal education in music, and in many ways was self-taught, he became one of the most brilliant music critics in London. In Charles Osborne's opinion, 'Shaw's unique value as a critic of music is due to the fact that he wrote an incomparably fine prose, and that he was completely uninfluenced by fashion.'[70]

Shaw's biographer St John Ervine has pointed out that few religious bodies could have been more antipathetic in belief to Shaw than the Salvation Army: early Salvationists tended towards fundamentalism and a literal understanding of the Bible. But what drew him (rather like Slater) was described by St John Ervine as 'the simple beauty of the average Salvationist's life or the greater power for good the Army is'.[71]

In a discussion with Slater, Shaw told him that he had seen the Army at work in the past when he used to speak in the open air as a socialistic advocate. Moreover he often listened to a girl officer who could sing well, and he had put a shilling in the tambourine when it was sent round (RSd, v. 2, 12 Dec. 1905). Allan Chappelow describes how Shaw was impressed by the way in which certain Salvation Army ladies exhibited great dramatic talent in the singing of a certain type of song, 'in which they secured an extraordinary effect'. Chappelow explains that:

---

[69] M. Holroyd, 'Introduction', in *The Genius of Shaw: A Symposium*, ed. M. Holroyd (New York, 1979), pp. 9–11 (p. 9).

[70] C. Osborne, 'The Music Critic', in *The Genius of Shaw*, ed. Holroyd, pp. 70–1.

[71] St J. Ervine, *Bernard Shaw* (London, 1956), p. 398.

The song was usually about an unfortunate woman who was saved, but was married to a terrible scoundrel, who drank terribly and jumped on her with hob-nailed boots, and nothing but the woman's faith sustained her. The climax of the song was when the woman was at home praying and dreading her husband's return. She heard his hob-nailed boots coming along the corridor, and was expecting to feel them on her as usual, when the door opened, and she saw his face shining – he had been saved.[72]

Such experiences likely influenced Shaw in writing his play, *Major Barbara*, first performed in 1905, which centred upon the work of the Army, and specifically focused in the plot on the dilemma of the Salvationists in discovering that their good work had been subsidised by a brewer and an arms manufacturer.[73] Act Three of the play in which the idealists surrender to the armaments industry was problematic for Shaw, he needed to rewrite the final scene in order to end the play convincingly. To encourage himself he attended the Salvation Festival at the Royal Albert Hall in early [2nd] October 1905.[74] It happened to be a special memorial meeting 'to commemorate dead comrades' and was presided over by William Booth. Shaw captured the scene in a letter to J. E. Vedrenne:

> When the roll-ll-ll is called up yon-der
> When the roll-ll-ll is called up yon-der
> When the roll-ll-ll is called up yon-der
> When the roll is called up yonder I'LL BE THERE.

I stood in the middle of the centre grand tier box, in the front row, and sang it as it has never been sung before. The Times will announce my conversion tomorrow [...] Glory Hallelujah!

GBS

P.S. I now doubt whether Major B. will be ready [...] The last act is a total Failure: I must sit down and write it absolutely afresh.[75]

The audience at the first performance of *Major Barbara* on 28 November 1905 at the Court Theatre included a box of uniformed Salvation Army Commissioners, 'who for the first time in their lives had passed through the gates of hell into a theatre'.[76] There was a whisper in the air that the play was blasphemous. Some theatre critics took the play to be a withering attack on the Salvation Army,

[72] A. Chappelow, *Shaw – 'The Chucker-Out': A Biographical Exposition and Critique and a Companion to and Commentary on 'Shaw the Villager'* (London, 1969), p. 46.

[73] G. B. Shaw, *Major Barbara* (London, 1907/2000).

[74] M. Holroyd, *Bernard Shaw: The Pursuit of Power* (London, 1989), p. 108.

[75] G. B. Shaw, *Collected Letters (1898–1910)*, ed. D. Laurence (London, 1972), pp. 564–5.

[76] Holroyd, *Bernard Shaw*, p. 116.

but Shaw refuted such a claim in his preface to the play. In Shaw's opinion the Army was right in his play 'to take the money because it cannot exist without money and there was no other money to be had'.[77]

Certainly *Major Barbara* received mixed reviews, and the critic in *The Standard* was particularly scathing, commenting 'when it is dull then it is monstrous tedious'.[78] He went on to talk of 'the ill-tuned bands and poke bonnets and big drums' associated with the Army. The next day a letter appeared in the paper from Shaw, headlined 'A Gross Libel'. It is worth quoting in full:

> I thought that nothing could provoke me to reply to a criticism of one of my plays; but there is a passage in your notice of 'Major Barbara' which I simply will not submit to. Your critic speaks of the 'ill-tuned bands of the Salvation Army'. Never was a greater libel penned. From the early days of the Army, when I first heard a Salvation band play as a march, that wedding chorus from Donizetti's 'Lucia di Lammermoor' which I have introduced into my play, to the great meeting two months ago when the Salvation band played 'Dead March from "Saul"' as I verily believe it has never been played in the world since Handel was alive to conduct it. I have never heard a Salvation band that deserved your critic's reproach. I have heard Handel's great march snivelled through by experienced professional bands until the thought of death becomes intolerable. The Salvationists quite instinctively, and probably knowing as little of Handel as they do Donizetti, made it a magnificent paean of glory that sent me – a seasoned music critic of many years' standing – almost out of my senses with enthusiasm. After that, your critic may say what he pleases about my plays; but he should not slander the Salvation bands whilst my hand can wield a pen in their defence.[79]

It was not surprising that all this went down very well with William Booth. Chappelow noted that Shaw's letter 'produced an extraordinary effect on General Booth who had never received a compliment on his bands before'.[80] On 1 December Slater wrote to Shaw:

> Dear Sir, As the officer who has been in charge of the Army's Musical Department for the last 22 years, and who has had more to do than any other individual in the guidance and development of the Army's musical activities, I want to express my thanks for the rigourous [*sic*] defence of the music of the Army from your pen, which took the form of a letter in the Standard on Wednesday's date. As you evidently take an interest in our music allow me to send you the latest issue of our Full Score [...] On the

---

[77] Shaw, Preface to *Major Barbara*, p. 27.

[78] *The Standard*, 29 Nov. 1905.

[79] Ibid., 30 Nov. 1905.

[80] Chappelow, *Shaw – 'The Chucker-Out'*, p. 47.

9th (tomorrow week) at the Congress Hall, Clapton, 5 of our best London bands will give a musical meeting at which the level of our playing will be demonstrated. Yours faithfully, Richard Slater, Brig. (RSd, v. 2, 1 Dec. 1905)

Shaw did accept the invitation. The occasion was the opening meeting of the Bandmasters' Councils at the Clapton Congress Hall. For Slater it was to be 'the Army's greatest musical festival' (RSd, v. 2, 9 Dec. 1905). Much was at stake, and the newspapers made the most of it. *The Standard* reported that 'it would be a direct challenge to the musical unbelievers, and the Army leaders declare their performers will come out of the ordeal without a stain on their characters'.[81]

Meanwhile the *Westminster Gazette* entered the fray, asking, 'Has the Salvation Army band quite deserved all the evil that has been said of it?' Its reporter visited Richard Slater, who sturdily defended his bands. He admitted that 20 years before the standard might have been low, but now many of the musical Salvationists 'with the scarlet jersey' had won local fame as musicians, and were in demand for concerts and for mayoral processions. He cited the Worthing Band, which occupied the town's bandstand four or five times a year. Slater estimated there were now 800–900 Salvationist bands and nearly 18,000 instrumentalists. He emphasised that all the instruments came from the Army's own instrument works in St Albans, where the music was also printed.[82]

Slater proudly recorded the details of the evening in his diary:

Some 270 Bandmasters and Songster Leaders were on the slope of the left side of the Hall from the platform. A large table was put at the right side of the main stairway into the Hall, and several seats on the slope above were kept besides for press representatives [...] Mr Shaw was there himself and sat about 4 seats up from the table. Representatives were at the table from the Brass Band News, British Bandsman, the Morning Leader, Daily Express, Daily News and The Standard. I was in charge of the table and had arranged 5 sets of the 5 Full Scores from which the Band pieces were drawn [...] for the use of the press people. (RSd, v. 2, 9 Dec. 1905)

Besides the International Staff Band, there were bands from the Clapton Congress Hall, Chalk Farm, Highgate and the Regent Hall. In addition, vocal items were presented by the Staff Songsters and a male quartet from the Regent Hall.

The *Daily Express* described the audience of several thousand. The Salvation 'soldiers and lassies' included working men and their wives and children, factory girls with smiling faces and youths 'from the desk and the counter. Babies in arms frequently announced their presence with unauthorised solos'.[83] As the

---

[81] *The Standard*, 2 Dec. 1905.

[82] *Westminster Gazette*, 7 Dec. 1905.

[83] *Daily Express*, 11 Dec. 1905.

audience gathered it was soon being whispered, 'Is Bernard Shaw here?'[84] All eyes naturally were on him sitting in the body of the audience 'between a young man who looked like a grocer's assistant and an older one who bore the stamp of a gas stoker'.[85] Shaw concentrated his attention on

> the wide platform, where in a blaze of light, the massed brass bands [...] poured out 'Salvation' marches and 'songs' through a couple of hundred powerful instruments [...] Each band played a resounding march, and Mr Shaw paper and pencil in hand made notes rapidly about each piece.[86]

The critic of the *Daily News* on his first visit to a Salvation Army gathering, confessed he had no idea that the Salvation Army had such good material. For him, the International Staff Band 'could well compete with the pot-hunting bands of the North', and its bandmaster, George Mitchell, 'might easily become a second Sousa'. Above all it was the singing of the hymns by the congregation that made the greatest impression; 'if a British tourist had heard that singing in Germany he would have written to "The Times" to prove how inferior are British musical gifts by comparison'.[87]

Slater found more weak spots in the playing than he had anticipated, but there were many good places. The Clapton Congress Hall Band was the only band in his opinion that really advanced its reputation; Chalk Farm sustained its good name, and Highgate and Regent Hall were below their best. The Staff Songsters were 'only passable' (RSd, v. 2, 9 Dec. 1905). But for the *British Bandsman* the festival was a vindication: 'the time of the ill-tuned band and ill-timed drum is practically over'.[88]

The following Tuesday Slater met Shaw, and thanked him for his interest. He also confided with the author of *The Perfect Wagnerite* (1898) about his own 30-year study of Wagner and that Shaw's treatment of Wagner's works and theories had always interested him. But straight to the point Slater told Shaw he did not hold with his socialism. Perhaps this was an awkward moment, so Commissioner Nichol intervened by commenting 'Perhaps Mr Shaw does not hold with your salvationism.' At this meeting Shaw promised to write a full critical account of the festival for internal use within the Army's headquarters as had been requested by Bramwell Booth (RSd, v. 2, 12 Dec. 1905).

In that report, which was not published until 55 years later, Shaw found that all the bands that he had heard at the festival were first-rate.[89] For skill the International Staff Band was 'beyond criticism'. But skill in execution was not enough.

---

[84] *British Bandsman*, 16 Dec. 1905, p. 697.

[85] *Daily Express*, 11 Dec. 1905.

[86] Ibid.

[87] *Daily News*, 11 Dec. 1905.

[88] *British Bandsman*, 9 Dec. 1905, p. 681.

[89] [G. B. Shaw,] 'What the Critic had to Say', *The Musician*, 3 Dec. 1960, pp. 776–7.

Shaw argued that even a blindfold critic should be able to tell which was a Salvation Army band, and which was the professional. Only one band at the festival for him achieved that quality, this was the Clapton Congress Hall Band which possessed 'a joyous vivacity of style and clear jubilant tone which stamped it as *the* Salvation Army Band *par excellence*'.[90]

Shaw was critical of the secular quality of the marches. He had sat next to a labourer at the festival, weary from heavy physical toil. On waking from his fatigue his neighbour was pleased as the Chalk Farm Band 'played a piece of empty but exciting circus music for him in the most violently spirited way'.[91] For Shaw this was counterproductive, as it served to switch off the current of religious enthusiasm and switch on the current of circus excitement: 'it woke him up very much as a tablespoon of brandy would have woken him up'.[92] Shaw was concerned that even marches should have a religious character, rather than being 'rowdy and empty'. Nevertheless, Shaw expressed his unqualified admiration for what had been achieved within the music of the Salvation Army.

Shaw also criticised the arranging skills of the composers whose work he had heard:

> They do not make half enough use of the individual character of the instruments and the way in which they can be made to relieve and contrast each other [...] and the scorers seem to have no idea of the effect of a unison passage for a mass of wind instruments [...] They harmonise all the time in the same way, using all the instruments indiscriminately. In a word they neglect variety.[93]

Slater provided his own take on the comments in his diaries:

> [Shaw's] criticisms on the music were severe and mostly condemning it, being he thought too monotonous in harmony, too continuously full, bad in the figuration to so great an extent of the euphonium part, and of a circus and empty showy character. (RSd, v. 3, 10 Apr. 1906)

But he felt personally criticised:

> He made many of such remarks in speaking of Chalk Farm's rendering of my Italian March [BJ 490], and as I think this among my best, his remarks have had a depressing effect on me. (RSd, v. 3, 10 Apr. 1906)

Certainly Slater had earlier expressed a great affection for his piece:

> Finished my Italian March, one of my best, and into which I sought to put something over the ordinary in memory of my mother's father who was an Italian. (RSd, v. 2, 18 Feb. 1905)

90 Ibid., p. 776.

91 Ibid., p. 777.

92 Ibid.

93 Ibid.

For this musical tribute to his maternal grandfather, Slater used 'Garibaldi's Hymn', 'which played so prominent a part in the making of modern Italy',[94] as the theme of the march's Trio section. (See Example 2.)

Slater countered Shaw's critique of his scoring by comparing it with the favourable opinions of other critics, such as Mr E. Baughan:

> His adverse remark on the scoring must be set over against Mr Baughan's statement that Army musicians know how to score for a Brass Band and the praise of the Morning Leader of the Japanese March [BJ 479] and the Songs of Holland [BJ 497]. I took a shorthand copy of Mr Shaw's criticisms on Army Music and scoring and shall copy them to preserve them with care. The over-elaboration of the euphonium part is a fault with Hawkes, but that want of variety in the use of instruments is a fault in his or my scores I do not think to be the case. These criticisms are likely to come up again, I believe, as the General, the Chief and the Musical Board are likely to read them and consider if any steps should be taken. My Swiss Melodies [BJ 514, 515] are in the hands of the Staff Band at a fitting time to support my reputation for scoring, the band thinks this selection the best done so far. (RSd, v. 3, 10 Apr. 1906)

Slater realised Shaw's criticisms might come back to haunt him once the Booths and the members of the Music Board had read them, adding somewhat ominously 'and consider if any steps should be taken' (RSd, v. 3, 10 Apr. 1906). However, whatever sensitivities Shaw's comments understandably stirred up in Slater, the overall critique stands as a considerable tribute to the musical progress that had been made within the Salvation Army since its inception in 1878.

RICHARD SLATER, THE MUSICAL LIBERALISER

Just before Bernard Shaw's visit, on 7 December 1905, Slater was called in to the Chief of the Staff, Bramwell Booth, who informed him that he was to be appointed as Secretary for Musical Affairs, a post that gave responsibility for the development of bands and songster brigades within the Army. This would entail a good deal of travelling in order to visit the chief bands once a year, and smaller bands once in 18 months. Slater's role would be advisory. At first Slater was flattered, but later after much heart-searching decided he would not be the right man for the job. Fundamentally he realised he would have had to make

---

94 Slater in *Local Officer*, 9 July 1905, p. 460. He had already used the tune of 'Garibaldi's Hymn', for a song entitled 'Fight for God and Souls', *Musical Salvationist* 3 (1888–9), p. 47. Garibaldi had commissioned a hymn for his volunteers in 1858. According to Trevelyan it was 'destined in the coming years to resound on the battlefields of Italy from the Alps to the Sicilian mountains, and to become in effect the National Anthem'. See G. M. Trevelyan, *Garibaldi and the Thousand* (London, 1909), p. 82.

Example 2 Richard Slater, *The Italian March* (1905), solo cornet part.
Note 'Garibaldi's Hymn' at Letter F.

the sacrifice of leaving the composing world (RSd, v. 2, 5 Jan. 1906). In point of fact an appointment was made in 1907 of the Army's first Band Inspector for the British Territory, Edward H. Hill, whose job included some of the tasks that Slater might have been allocated.[95]

Slater's decision to focus on his composing activities meant that he could continue to push forward the musical boundaries. By 1908 Slater had regained his musical confidence after Shaw's critique, and the uncertainty regarding the new post he had been offered:

> At the office during the week almost all my time has been spent in setting words from Song books, and my flow of ideas has continued for over 14 days, so that I only have to look at a set of verses to get ideas for what seem to be appropriate musical settings. I believe this period of my life has been in the given time the most fruitful of my life. (RSd, v. 9, 11 Apr. 1908)

Between 23 March and 20 August 1908 he composed 139 vocal settings mostly to well-known words from various hymn books, a series of marches including *The Drum March* (BJ 569), *The Cornet March* (BJ 577), *The Horn March* (BJ 617), *The Bass March* (BJ 650) as well as transcribing and scoring marches by the great composers, including Handel's March from *The Occasional Overture*, the march from Mozart's *Die Zauberflöte*, Rossini's march from *Tancredi*, the march from Act 3 of Wagner's *Lohengrin* (RSd, v. 10, 22 Oct. 1908 and 31 Dec. 1908).

Another crisis occurred with William Booth and the Music Board at the Salvation Army's Crystal Palace Musical Festival held in July 1908. On this occasion, none of the music that was presented was more than 12 months old. The Staff Band gave the premiere of Klaus Østby's meditation, *Princethorpe* (FS 2), which was reckoned to be 'the severest ordeal to all-round testing music that it has experienced' – it was 'a little too long for some listeners'.[96] But in his diary Slater confides that the whole festival had displeased William and Bramwell Booth. Indeed, Bramwell had been so upset 'as to leave the platform more than once in great disturbance of mind' (RSd, v. 8, 31 July 1908). William Booth blamed Commissioner Howard who was responsible for managing the event. It had been Howard who had presented the need for musical reform to take place in 1901. Booth felt that no soul could have been moved by such a festival, which focused on performances of the latest musical scores. Indeed, Howard

---

[95] For further details of the Band Inspector's appointment and tasks, see Wiggins, *The History of the Salvation Army*, vol. 5, p. 208; Holz, *Brass Bands of the Salvation Army*, vol. 1, p. 129.

[96] Boon, *ISB*, p. 36. For discussions regarding the significance of Østby's *Princethorpe*, see Holz, *Brass Bands of the Salvation Army*, vol. 1, pp. 155–6, and Steadman-Allen, 'The Evolution of Salvation Army Music', *The Musician*, 7 Aug. 1965, p. 503; 6 Nov. 1965, p. 731. Also for Østby, see T. Hanson, 'Sweden', in Holz, *Brass Bands of the Salvation Army*, vol. 1, pp. 255–72.

was accused of destroying the General's work built up over 45 years. But in his defence, Howard pointed out that Booth's sanctioning of the 1901 Memorandum had led to this kind of musical expression.

As a result, Howard insisted there would need to be a return to simpler music, with a clear straightforward melody: episodes and finales would have to be dropped. Slater vented his exasperation in his diary. After all, he pointed out, it was the Music Board that had passed all the music: 'Is he [William Booth] alone right and they are wrong?' Furthermore, there was general acceptance of the modern musical style by officers, bands, soldiers and the public: 'can it be that the Army has so seriously gone astray, as the statements from the General would have one think?' The problem was that William Booth 'acts on personal whims, uncontrolled desires, and not on all-round and soundly reasoned principles' (RSd, v. 8, 31 July 1908).

Finally Slater betrayed his own insecurity:

> After my 25 years of continuous service in the direction of musical labour in the Army, will he focus his wrath on me as being the source and main strength of all this so called musical liberalisation in the Army? [...] If I am the chief culprit in the eyes of the General or the Chief then I have little to hope as to favour peace or safety in future consideration [...] Efforts may be made to get rid of me, so to free the Army from a supposed so subtle foe [...] Or I may be so placed as sent on foreign service [...] personally I have no regrets for my work and influence on Army music. (RSd, v. 8, 31 July 1908)

Slater's most vocal critic was actually a man he admired, Commissioner George Railton, an early ally of William Booth, although the two men later became estranged from one another.[97] Railton entered Slater's office where Slater was talking with George Mitchell, Bandmaster of The International Staff Band. Railton said:

> 'You are just the two fellows I want to see. If you only saw the country' (the Army, he meant, in different parts) 'as I see it, you would see all the harm the new music is doing. It is killing, or has done so, the open air singing and is doing spiritual harm to the Bandsmen, so that they do not pray or speak'. (RSd, v. 1, 30 Dec. 1909)

Slater asked him what he would suggest and summarised his reply:

> he would go back to the early style regardless of consequences; there should be no note but was connected with a word, and the side and bass drums with 6 or 8 instruments were all that were needed in a Band. So he considered all the musical progress and development of the Army a great and regrettable mistake. He said the General never allows modern Band

---

[97] See B. Watson, *Soldier Saint: George Scott Railton, William Booth's First Lieu-tenant* (London, 1970).

music in his meetings [...] Commr. Railton considered a sort of condemnation was virtually passed on such pieces. (RSd, v. 1, 30 Dec. 1909)

This was a classic restatement of the Calvinist view, which seemed to reflect the overall position of the Board.

Nevertheless Slater continued to write music that broke through the rigid constraints erected by William Booth and the Music Board. Perhaps the most notable of these was his set of six *Bible Pictures*, which he considered his best band pieces (RSd, v. 11, 31 Dec. 1909). Four of these were published: *The Stilling of the Storm* (BJ 601), *The Widow of Nain* (BJ 616), *Abraham's Offering* (BJ 695), and *The Death of Stephen* (BJ 745). The last two of these contain wholly original music with no reference to Salvation Army songs.

The first of these bible pictures, *The Stilling of the Storm* was published in 1910 and represents the first Salvationist programmatic work.[98] At its first performance, the International Staff Band performed it to Slater's satisfaction:

A great impression was made, and the demand for me to acknowledge the appreciation which was given to the piece was a most flattering affair for me, one of the great things in my public life[...] my reputation has been considerably increased by it from tonight's performance. (RSd, v. 11, 15 Jan. 1910)

Characteristically, four months later, he was questioning himself on one of his walks:

My *Bible Pictures* – are they outside the range of Army Bands? Do they aim to do more than music can satisfactorily accomplish even with the programme known to the hearers? Do they really give me a standing as a composer? (RSd, v. 11, 9 Apr. 1910)

It is worth examining *The Stilling of the Storm*, as it presents one of Slater's most ambitious scores. He planned to write a descriptive work, 'a bible picture', of a key biblical story told in Mark 4: 35–41, in which Christ stills a storm that was provoking terror amongst his disciples. There are eight sections to the piece. Significantly Slater provided descriptive notes in the full score, with additional song, poetic or paraphrased biblical texts as appropriate.[99]

---

[98] Holz, *Brass Bands of the Salvation Army*, vol. 1, p. 143.

[99] The score layout of *The Stilling of the Storm* is representative of Salvationist practice. This differs slightly from standard band score formats as follows: Salvationist band scores include parts for solo, 1st and 2nd cornets, whilst secular band score layouts include solo, repiano, 2nd and 3rd cornets. The flugel horn in Salvationist scores has an independent part, whilst it is often linked in standard band formats with the repiano. 'Repiano' is the brass band adaption of the Italian term, *ripieno*. See R. Steadman-Allen, *Colour and Texture in the Brass Band* (London, 2005), p. 11.

The opening depicts 'The calm sea' with a swaying 6/8 rhythm accompanying a gentle undulating theme in D major, with some individual phrases emphasised by repetition (Example 3). This leads into 'The Voyage', represented by the well-known Salvationist version of a children's hymn,

> A little ship was on the sea,
> It was a pretty sight;
> It sailed along so pleasantly,
> And all was calm and bright.[100]

Introduced by the flugel horn and tenor horn, the tune is then taken over by the cornets. At the same time the euphonium plays a delicate filigree accompaniment, and the trombones provide a secure harmonic anchor. However, with the onset of 'The sudden storm' Slater ratchets up the tension, and introduces an energetic rising motif marked *furioso*, which is played three times sequentially on the euphoniums and basses, followed by an insistent rhythmic figure comprising a quaver, two semiquavers and a quaver, before the scene changes into 'Jesus asleep in the storm'. There is a brief respite in B minor, *poco tranquillo*, with a rising figure on the solo cornet against some harmonic suspensions, but after five bars the *furioso* section returns, and leads into 'the fury of the tempest' where Slater takes the opportunity to make dramatic musical gestures, characterised by extreme changes in dynamics, leading eventually to a grand climax with the full band. 'The terror of the disciples' is represented by a gradual crescendo of secondary and diminished sevenths in a chordal passage given to cornets and horns alone. This sense of panic, leads to a *fortissimo* diminished seventh chord, before subsiding into the 'The storm is stilled'. A theme marked *placido* emerges on the first cornets and solo horn characterised by a descending melody concluding with a semiquaver triplet figure which connects to the next sequence. Slater underlines the emotional resonance of this moment by effective use of the flattened submediant chord (B♭) within D major. The final section, 'Jesus is Omnipotent Lord', consists of the whole band playing the old gospel song 'Peace be Still' in a straightforward setting, but with some ornamental passages from the euphonium and baritone. The final bars reflect the song text:

> The winds and the waves shall obey My will!
> Peace! … be still.[101]

---

[100] 'A little ship' was a popular children's hymn written by Doroth Thrupp. The tune used by Salvationists and Slater is an adaptation of the Cheshire hunting song, 'Let Bucks A-Hunting Go', in F. Kidson and A. Moffat, *A Garland of English Folk-Songs* (London, 1926). See G. Avery, 'Companion to our Tune Book', vol. 1, tune 59 (typescript, 1972, held in The Salvation Army International Heritage Centre).

[101] 'Peace be Still', in I. D. Sankey, *Sacred Songs and Solos with Standard Hymns: 750 Pieces* (London, n.d.), song no. 395.

Example 3 Richard Slater, *The Stilling of the Storm* (1910), full score, p. 1

As Holz observes, 'This type of descriptive piece called for a new kind of imagination on the part of the performers and congregation.'[102] Steadman-Allen helpfully summarises the musical design of Slater's Bible Pictures as

> short, sharply contrasted sections with dramatic incident and sudden climaxes. Aside from the lyrical portions, much of the musical development is on the principle of a single bar repeated, a new bar repeated and so on.[103]

To appreciate the impact the piece had upon the audience, we should recollect that at the time there was nothing quite like it in the Salvation Army repertoire, as at least two-thirds of the score contained original material, while the rest comprised two hymn or song tunes. Moreover, in the contesting brass band world, test pieces consisted of selections from an opera or a choral work, or from the works of a particular composer of the past, rather than original compositions. It was not until 1913, three years after *The Stilling of the Storm*, that Percy Fletcher's *Labour and Love* marked a transition in the repertoire of secular bands from contest selections to more creative pieces, in this case a work based upon a programme and using thematic transformation techniques.[104] Certainly Slater's work lacked such musical sophistication, but his musical pioneering qualities should be acknowledged. The gradual opening up of opportunities for composers in the Salvation Army which had been signalled since the 1901 memorandum, meant that increasingly there was some scope for originality. Salvationist audiences, or at least the bandsmen, appeared to appreciate such developments. Without his efforts it is doubtful that the ground would have been prepared to receive such fine programmatic works as the Salvationist tone poems of Eric Ball from the 1930s, notably *Exodus* (FS 117) and *The Triumph of Peace* (FS 130).

We have already noted that Slater wrote the first 'Selection', the prototype for the 'Meditation', and the first example of programme music. To these should be added the first 'festival arrangement' (that is a work for concert rather than devotional use), *Lead Kindly Light* (BJ 436), whose florid cornet solo playing semiquaver decoration aroused controversy and comment.[105]

Although Slater's music did not betray any great originality, in many ways it was derivative, he did successfully demonstrate ways in which the formal structures of musical compositions could be expanded upon, most notably in the use

---

[102] Holz, *Brass Bands of the Salvation Army*, vol. 1, p. 144.

[103] Steadman-Allen, 'The Evolution of Salvation Army Music', *The Musician*, 5 Feb. 1966, p. 95.

[104] For an assessment of Fletcher's *Labour and Love*, see P. Hindmarsh, 'Building a Repertoire: Original Compositions for the British Brass Band, 1913–1998', in *The British Brass Band*, ed. Herbert, pp. 245–77 (pp. 246–9).

[105] Steadman-Allen, 'The Evolution of Salvation Army Music', *The Musician*, 5 Feb. 1966, p. 95.

of more extended original passages linking song references, while remaining true to the spirit of the Salvation Army. In such ways Richard Slater proved himself to be the source and strength of musical liberalisation within the movement he actively served for 31 years.

TOWARDS RETIREMENT

As retirement approached, Slater started to focus ever more intensely on his studies of Wagner whose life and music continued to fuel his intellectual curiosity and admiration. He went to the British Museum and looked at Wagner's letter to Wesendonck, and the full score of *Tristan* (RSd, v. 10, 11 Jan. 1909). He bought himself the full scores of *Parsifal* and *Die Meistersinger* (RSd, v. 10, 31 Dec. 1909). By 1909 he was making a trial index of his guide to Wagner's Ring cycle. He wondered whether to approach such publishers as Schott, or Breitkopf & Härtel, or whether he should seek the views of eminent musical authorities as Corder, Ellis, Shaw or Costa,[106] as to the value of his work (RSd, v. 10, 20 Nov. 1909).

The sinking of the *Titanic* on 15 April 1912 caused Slater considerable distress: '[it] has had a staggering bewildering effect on me as on many more. Such a disaster to a ship seems most inexplicable' (RSd, v. 13, 17 Apr. 1912). On 24 May 1912 he attended a memorial concert for the victims, and was impressed that four of the eight items were by Wagner; 'how great has become his reputation' (RSd, v. 13, 22 May 1912).

Slater's plan was to publish his studies in 1913, the centenary of Wagner's birth. Slater sent to Novello's his 514 pages of manuscript on *Die Meistersinger*:

I have in MSS an exhaustive study of Wagner's Mastersingers. The copy extends to 514 small 8ve passages of text and 22 of index. The work is one of several results of over 40 years study of Wagner on quite unique lines [...] The work is in two parts [...] In the first part there is a historical table, then chapters on an estimate of the Work, the Drama, the characters, the Psychology of the Work, the music, and lastly a group of analytical tables. In the second part, the study of each scene is divided into a survey, analysis, the Drama, and the music. Methods of investigation quite novel have resulted in the attainment of facts and conclusions which I claim are largely unique. (RSd, v. 13, 25 Apr. 1912)

Just over a month later he received a rejection note: 'I was really depressed by the rejection of the work on which I had spent so much thought and labour' (RSd, v. 13, 22 May 1912). He consoled himself by recollecting that Wagner had suffered numerous disappointments in his own life. Slater's next step was to submit

---

[106] Michael Costa (1808–84) was one of the outstanding conductors of the age. Frederick Corder (1852–1932) was a composer and conductor. W. Ashton Ellis (1852–1919) was an eminent authority on the works of Wagner. Bernard Shaw was author of *The Perfect Wagnerite*.

his collection of 100 hitherto unpublished hymns to Novello, and his Wagner studies to other publishers (RSd, v. 13, 14 June 1912). Unfortunately all this was to no avail. The songs were not accepted by Novello. As far as the Wagner study was concerned, the publisher regretted it was not typewritten; 'the labour involved in reading the MS is sometimes too trying and pressing' (RSd, v. 13, 30 Aug. 1912). Slater turned down the offer made by the editor of the *Musical Times* to issue a condensation of the work, as the original was much too long (RSd, v. 13, 17 Dec. 1912). Slater was not willing for a summary or extracts to appear. A further rejection was received from the editor of the *Musical Standard*, and Slater confided in his diary, 'It seems as if I have no outlet for my facts on Wagner, and as if my toils are in vain, but for my own pleasure and profit' (RSd, v. 13, 27 Jan. 1913). In spite of this considerable setback, Slater accorded his musical hero a paean of praise on the occasion of Wagner's centenary:

> What a marvel is his place today in the history of our time! He is now in a place among the greatest men, one of the most dominating minds of the present age, a man whose works seem as if they will take their place beside Shakespeare's in future ages [...] He is the man who has had most of my time and energy as a student. I do not regret this, although it is disheartening that I find no outlet for the results of my labours on his works. (RSd, v. 13, 21 May 1913)

In the diaries covering the years immediately leading up to his retirement, Slater, rather unusually, comments upon political matters, which illuminate his somewhat conservative leanings. In 1910 we learn that he intended to vote Unionist, in order to get rid of the Liberals who had been 'moved by most questionable people of socialist views' (RSd, v. 11, 20 Jan. 1910). The following year saw the coronation of George V, and Slater described himself as 'not a republican altogether'; but his judgement of the new king, from photographs, was of 'a man of small character, limited intellectual calibre [...] far from being a noble, large, impressive typical man' (RSd, v. 11, 22 June 1911). With regard to the great coal strike of 1912, he came out strongly in favour of the masters:

> I cannot but think Socialism in its greedy, merely personal aspects of trade unionism of our time is at the bottom of the unrest. I cannot think it a fact that miners are badly paid for their work [...] They have in their union funds enough to last them six months or more perhaps, and in the strikes, football fields, picture palaces, theatres and public houses etc. have been very well patronised in mining districts [...] I think it has been a very bad tendency amongst our governing classes in the House of Commons to yield again and again to persistent labour unions (RSd, v. 13, 1 Mar. 1912).

But as far as the Salvation Army was concerned, Slater's preoccupations from 1910 onwards included two contrary themes: how he might financially augment his small Army pension, and his relationship with William Booth.

With regards to his pension settlement Slater was hopeful that he might claim the copyright of the hundreds of songs and instrumental arrangements and compositions he had undertaken for the Army. Much of his diary entries from 1910 until his retirement focused upon his desire to receive what was financially due to him for the copyright of all of his music. He commented:

> I have given my best in songs and music to the Army; I have not had any allowances [...] I have a just ground for making a claim such as <u>English Law will admit and defeat</u>. (RSd, v. 11, 5 Apr. 1910)

There was a problem, however. The Salvation Army authorities apparently possessed a signed declaration from Slater renouncing all claims on copyright. But he foreswore knowledge of this, and accused the individual who gave him the form to sign of entrapment. Slater offered to appear in a Court of Inquiry over the matter (RSd, v. 12, 21 Dec. 1910). But Watson points out that 'the copyright of all written works of serving officers is vested in the Salvation Army [and] Railton helped frame the rule that stands to this day'.[107] Part of Slater's case was that Herbert Booth, William's son, had managed to secure for himself a settlement on leaving the Army in 1902: 'I know that a considerable sum was allowed to Mr H. H. Booth on account of his claims on his songs [...] The threatened legal proceedings were prevented thereby' (RSd, v. 11, 3 Apr. 1910).

Slater wrote to William Booth:

> Dear General, After the labour of many years, true, faithful, honest, in energy unstinting, and, I have every reason for thinking with a fair measure of success in the musical work of the Army, I am face to face with a very serious difficulty affecting alike the Army and myself [...] There are 2 points that have arisen, one as to the question of copyright, and another is to compensation for all my music which is in use in the Army, such as would give me in sickness and old age something definite to rely upon [...] The situation at present causes strain that threatens to come near breaking point, but I hope by your intervention in this matter, a satisfactory result may be reached. (RSd, v. 12, 21 Dec. 1910)

It might be thought in view of some of the preceding matter that William Booth and Richard Slater were hostile to each other, but on the contrary they seemed to have had a warm, if somewhat bantering, relationship during these years. At a meeting led by William Booth on 9 January 1910, Slater acted as pianist. During the prayer meeting the two men had several conversations about the pitches of choruses, and the difference between sentiment and true feeling in certain tunes. Booth expressed the wish to write a tune himself, but continued

---

[107] Watson, *Soldier Saint*, p. 247. More recently (2006) Holz has suggested a need for a contract system whereby composers would receive a standard or at least a manuscript preparation fee. See Holz, *Brass Bands of the Salvation Army*, vol. 1, p. 192.

in a bantering manner to Slater 'were I to write a tune you would spoil it by your fiddle-dee-dees' (RSd, v. 11, 9 Jan. 1910). Slater wrote in his diary entry:

> I always feel his greatness when near him, and I see how he dwarfs everyone about him by his wonderful personality. His sincerity is far above question and it was a grand sight to see him pouring out unstintingly his full energy to lead men aright on the most important of subjects. (RSd, v. 11, 9 Jan. 1910)

A few months later, Booth summed up his ambivalent feelings about Slater to his face: 'At times I feel very savage with you, but I love you all the same' (RSd, v. 11, 21 May 1910). Again while Slater was at the piano Booth came over to him and stooping down said in his ear:

> 'Do you love me?' I said 'Yes, sir!' As if not sure what I had said, he said, 'What do you say?' My response was 'I love you sincerely'. He was moved, and whispered 'And I love you! Don't put that in the papers' (the Army papers he meant) 'or else it will make some people jealous'. (RSd, v. 12, 10 Oct. 1910)

William Booth died on Tuesday 20 August 1912. Slater had the previous day with some other leading officers filed slowly by the side of the dying man's bed. Slater kissed his right temple and his left hand. In the first moment when he saw the 'tired old man', 'my emotions overcame me and I could not refrain from weeping and I could have sobbed aloud' (RSd, v. 13, 20 Aug. 1912)

On 21 July 1913 Slater wrote a letter to the new General, Bramwell Booth, requesting 'a long rest' on health grounds. He also added a reminder that 'several points regarding my own work and my future that were raised in Dec. 1910 [...] have never been brought to final decisions' (RSd, v. 13, 21 July 1913). Presumably this referred to his claim for copyright of his music. The doctor eventually diagnosed Slater as having 'a breakdown of nerves, overstrain' (RSd, v. 13, 18 Mar. 1914). Ten days later he was informed by letter from Commissioner John Carleton that his claim for compensation for copyright had been turned down by Bramwell Booth, 'the acceptance of such a principle would place the General in an absolutely impossible position, and cannot in any shape or form be entertained'. Slater confided in his diary; 'my hopes were dashed to the ground' (RSd, v. 14, 28 Mar. 1914).

It does appear that Slater wanted to claim £350 for relinquishing his claim to copyright (RSd, v. 14, 1 Dec. 1914). Instead the Salvation Army was to pay him an annual allowance in his retirement years, perhaps to provide some recompense for his compositions, short of agreeing to pay copyright. This allowance, paid over so many years, exceeded considerably the amount of £350.[108]

Slater's final days in office were spent negotiating his successor, and in the end

---

[108] Email correspondence from Doug Taylor, 24 Sept. 2008. I am indebted to Stella and Doug Taylor for this information.

it was eventually decided that both Hawkes and Goldsmith would be appointed. In spite of his setback concerning financial compensation for his published music, Richard Slater was to continue his close involvement with the Musical Department during his years of retirement as will be apparent in the succeeding chapters. I shall specifically discuss his musical legacy in the final chapter.

I now shift my attention in the next two chapters to those rank-and-file Salvationist musicians who were actively involved in the years covering Slater's working life. I shall focus on the varieties of musical participation that were available, and the development of opportunities for the teaching and learning of music within the organisation.

CHAPTER 4

Musical Participation, 1878–1913

MY purpose in this chapter is to delineate the variety of musical ensembles which generated a lively culture of musical participation in the Salvation Army. Stephanie Pitts, in her book *Valuing Musical Participation* (2005), articulates the values of musical participation in the lives of her informants drawn from a variety of musical contexts: as a potential source of confirmation and confidence; as an opportunity to demonstrate or acquire skills; as a way of promoting and preserving repertoire; as an opportunity to perform with others; as a forum for social interaction and friendships; as ways of both enhancing everyday life and escaping from it; as a source of spiritual fulfilment and pleasure. Pitts makes a particularly insightful comment about the challenge of dealing with both musical and religious experience:

> Musical involvement, like religious conviction, is difficult to put into words, and can result in an evangelical zeal that is resisted by those who lack an existing involvement or sympathy in either sphere.[1]

In my discussion of Salvationist musical participation in the years between 1878 and 1913 I shall inevitably deal with this connection between musical involvement and religious conviction. I shall consider the following questions: What opportunities were open to Salvationists for musical participation? What accounted for the eventual hegemony of brass bands within the Salvation Army? What were the social backgrounds of Salvationist band members? How considerable was the commitment expected of them? What were some of the conversion experiences of musical Salvationists? I shall conclude by considering the values of musical participation as outlined by Pitts, in the context of Salvation Army music-making during the years preceding the First World War.

✒ *Varieties of Instrumental and Vocal Participation*

It was never the intention of William Booth that brass bands should predominate in his Army. Indeed, he prefaced his first Order for Salvation Army bands with the following biblical quotations, sprinkled with numerous instrumental types:

> Psalm xcviii.6 – 'With trumpets and sound of cornet make' etc.

> Psalm cl.4 – 'Praise Him with the timbrel' etc.

---

[1] Pitts, *Valuing Musical Participation*, p. 144.

Isaiah xxxviii.20 – 'The Lord was ready to save me; therefore we will sing my songs to stringed instruments' etc.[2]

In this section I shall outline the types of instrumental ensemble other than brass bands that were in evidence during the period, together with an account of the formation of singing brigades.

'EVERY INSTRUMENT THAT WAS AVAILABLE WAS PRESSED INTO SERVICE'[3]

As we have previously noted, William Booth was keen that all who might have some ability should learn to play on a suitable instrument, and he asked that any friends who might have instruments lying idle should send them to Headquarters that they might be used by Salvationists. His list included violins, bass viols [double basses] and concertinas, as well as brass instruments and drums. There is some evidence that this musical eclecticism bore fruit, with the formation of drum and fife bands, string bands and orchestras, mandolin bands, concertina bands, mouth organ bands, and handbell ringing.

Drum and fife bands had been a formative influence on Slater's early musical development, and they were evident in such Salvation Army corps as Folkestone, Hammersmith, Tunbridge Wells, Wood Green, but there is little evidence they really flourished in later years.[4] However, Slater thought them to be suited to young people in that there was less danger of physical strain than from playing brass instruments, and they provided 'a preparatory training ground'.[5] The lack of suitable music was a problem. In July 1900 it was announced that a new tutor for drum and fife bands was to be published. The instrumentation was E♭ piccolo, B♭ flute, F flute, side drum and bass drum. Such bands had economic advantage; a brass band of 33 would cost not a penny less than £200, whilst a drum and fife band would cost a mere £16.[6]

String and orchestral bands were established in various centres, usually in combination with other instruments. Sometimes chapel musicians became Salvationists and brought their musical traditions with them, as was the case at London's Regent Hall, where string musicians from a chapel in the Holborn district transferred their allegiance and provided an orchestra for regular indoor meetings.[7] Much depended on the enthusiasm and skill of individuals. For example, Captain Lax at Leeds formed an ensemble comprising eight first violins, four second violins, a viola, two cellos, a double bass, flute and piccolo, first and

---

[2] 'Musical Instruments from The General', *War Cry*, 27 Mar. 1880.

[3] Slater, *The Salvation Army Dictionary of Music*, p. 11.

[4] Boon, *Play the Music Play!*, p. 178.

[5] *Musical Salvationist* 14 (1899–1900), p. 155.

[6] *Local Officer* 4 (1900–1), pp. 465–6.

[7] Boon, *Play the Music Play!*, p. 16.

second cornets, horn and euphonium.[8] It is no coincidence that Lax had been a professional violinist, before becoming an officer. There were other examples of such bands at Penge,[9] and at Coventry[10] where the leader of the string band, Brother Morisboys felt more was required than drum and fife bands, and so set up a violin class for young people and more specifically 'for musically inclined young women'.[11] Slater pointed out that there seemed to be no one pattern for these string groups, and the demand for special printed arrangements for string bands was too small to make such a venture financially viable. However, the pieces from the *Musical Salvationist* could easily be arranged, and a number of special arrangements had in fact appeared in the past.[12]

It is somewhat surprising that Slater did not appear to advance the cause of string playing, considering his own expertise as a violinist. Bramwell Booth appeared keen on string bands, and asked Slater if a good example of such an ensemble could be made up for the Bandmasters' Councils. Slater's reply was in the negative:

> I have been watching during the year to see what could be done [...] I do not know of one case anywhere in the country where even a simple measure of success has been reached, and as but few have made attempts, it must be because of the great difficulty of the task, and the scarcity of the right material at present in the Army, for the formation of such Bands. (RSd, v. 2, 23 Nov. 1905)

A small number of mandolin bands were established, probably the result of a general national craze for playing the mandolin in the late 19th century.[13] There were reckoned to be no more than half a dozen such bands in the Army, including one at Gloucester that in 1909 comprised 12 players.[14] The leader, Elsie Fletcher, had had a thorough musical education, and had gained four certificates including the intermediate examination of the Royal Academy of Music, and although only 17 years of age, she was already an associate of the London College of Music. It was reported that she was as at home playing Beethoven's 'Moonlight' Sonata, as she was making her own arrangements for the mandolin band from the *Musical Salvationist*.[15]

There was a considerably greater number of concertina bands. Dave Russell

[8] *Local Officer* 3 (1899–1900), pp. 461–2.

[9] Ibid., p. 464.

[10] *Bandsman and Songster*, 5 Oct. 1907, p. 5.

[11] Ibid.

[12] R. Slater, 'The Formation of String Bands', *Bandsman and Songster*, 10 July 1912, p. 6.

[13] Scholes, *The Mirror of Music*, vol. 2, p. 819.

[14] *Bandsman, Songster and Local Officer*, 18 Dec. 1909, p. 7.

[15] Ibid., 29 May 1909, p. 2.

points out that the concertina was one of the most popular instruments in the 19th century, and that from the 1880s concertina bands flourished particularly in the Yorkshire textile district.[16] An influential Salvationist advocate, Commissioner James Hay, had listened to an impressive concertina band of 26 members, largely colliers and working men playing classical music.[17] One of the attractions of the concertina for Salvationists was its portability, it was 'like an entire Brass Band in a small compass'.[18] Moreover, Hay believed that the concertina was easier to learn than brass and stringed instruments, and that women would not be debarred; in fact a women's band could be a special attraction. The cost of a small band of four trebles in C, one soprano in F, and three tenors in F, would be in the area of £30, a much smaller outlay than for an equivalent number of brass instruments. Hay advised that 16 instruments would be an ideal number for Salvationist concertina bands. He preferred the English to the Anglo-German models.[19]

A particularly notable Salvationist concertina band was found at Attercliffe, near Sheffield, with 23 male players. At Oldham a concertina band of 11 women played their instruments alternately with the band whilst on the march and in open-air meetings.[20] Sometimes concertinas comprised the larger part of orchestral bands. For example, the Norwich I Orchestral Band established in the early 1890s included 20 concertina players, alongside seven violinists, a cellist, clarinettist and drummer.[21] Occasionally the *Musical Salvationist* would publish music specifically for concertinas.

As far as young people were concerned, some of their musical needs were catered for in the Band of Love. This was a Salvationist temperance section open to children, formed on a similar pattern to the longer established Band of Hope.[22] Membership of the Band of Love was open to children who signed a pledge not to smoke, swear, steal or gamble.[23] At the Plymouth Band of Love, there were regular classes for the mouth-organ band, whilst the concertina practices helped to keep the Band of Love workers interested.[24] There were in addition regular classes for handbell playing, a well-established working-class leisure pursuit often associated with late-Victorian and Edwardian churches and chapels, with connections with brass bands in terms of repertoire and arrangements.[25]

[16] Russell, *Popular Music in England*, pp. 239–40.

[17] J. Hay, 'About Concertina Bands', *Bandsman and Songster*, 6 Apr. 1907, pp. 5, 7.

[18] Ibid., p. 7.

[19] Ibid.

[20] *Local Officer* 4 (1900–1), p. 310.

[21] *Bandsman, Songster and Local Officer*, 9 Jan. 1909, p. 5.

[22] See Harrison, *Drink and the Victorians*.

[23] See *The Young Soldier*, 10 Dec. 1892.

[24] *Local Officer* 4 (1900–1), p. 335.

[25] See Russell, *Popular Music in England*, p. 240.

Finally we should note that the use of the tambourine in the early days of the Salvation Army spread rapidly with its dual function as a musical instrument and a money-collecting tray. It was reported that by 7 October 1882, the number of tambourines sold within six weeks had reached 1,600.[26] The recommendation was that every corps should have a timbrel band; 'the value of *training* and method in beating time cannot be too strongly emphasised'.[27] William Booth was keen to have the tambourines accompanied by 'clappers, bones, fifes, banjos',[28] a combination somewhat reminiscent of blackface minstrely.

'WE DON'T WANT AT ANY PRICE TO HAVE CHOIRS'[29]

We have already encountered William Booth's antipathy to choirs, as they tended to be associated with churches, and might alienate those who were put off by formal religion. Indeed, it took until 1898 for songster (or singing) brigades to be officially recognised by the Salvation Army. William Booth gradually modified his negative opinion, so that at the 1904 International Congress in London he was reported as softening his attitude towards 'the choirs of songsters which were growing up'.[30]

By 1912, 436 singing brigades had been established, with 7,055 songsters, roughly half the numbers of bands and bandsmen.[31] A particularly thriving brigade was in evidence at the Army's premier centre in London, the Clapton Congress Hall, with 19 trebles, 12 altos, seven basses and two tenors.[32]

There is little doubt, however, that the vocal side of the Army's work played second fiddle to the instrumental side. This is evident in Richard Slater's thoughts on singing brigades recorded in his diary (RSd, v. 13, 14 June 1912). Significantly he admits his limited practical knowledge of songsters and their labours. On the positive side they had linked up many of the Army's young people; on the other hand they had checked congregational singing ('the songsters are in the habit of remaining mute during the congregational singing'), had not helped in the teaching of fresh congregational tunes, and had almost extinguished solo singing. Because their membership included a large proportion of young girls 'with as yet unformed characters' it was hardly surprising that the singing lacked depth and force. He noted a dangerous tendency for brigades to undertake long pieces that were difficult, rather than those of a simple type. In many ways this was symptomatic of a desire to entertain, rather than to aim

---

[26] Sandall, *The History of the Salvation Army*, vol. 2, p. 104.

[27] *Bandsman and Songster*, 16 Nov. 1907, p. 5.

[28] Sandall, *The History of the Salvation Army*, vol. 2, p. 104.

[29] W. Booth, 'Good Singing', p. 204.

[30] *School Music Review*, 1 Oct. 1904, p. 73.

[31] R. Slater, 'The General and Army Music', *Bandsman and Songster*, 31 Aug. 1912, p. 550.

[32] *Bandsman and Songster*, 2 Jan. 1909, p. 4.

for spiritual results. Slater bemoaned the fact that there were no criteria for the appointment of songster leaders, and they were very much left alone in their work. In the pecking order, they were subordinate to bandmasters, but this was not necessarily conducive to raising vocal efforts. What was wanted was a unified set of ideals for vocal affairs within the Army, as well as instructional material to demonstrate methods of vocal training. Although there had been a striking development in part singing, Slater discerned no conscious line of voice training or choir making. He concluded that much of the Salvation Army's vocal work was haphazard in practice.

❧ Salvation Army Brass Bands

Brass instruments were used to accompany outdoor singing in the first year of the Army's foundation, but it quickly became apparent that they could fulfil an important evangelical purpose: through their distinctive sound in open spaces they drew attention to the Christian message, and their marches and processions helped articulate the military metaphor. They soon became ubiquitous and ambitious, and have come to represent an important strand of activity in British brass playing.[33]

THE GROWTH AND DEVELOPMENT OF SALVATION ARMY BANDS

We may recollect that the first Salvation Army band consisted of four male members of the Fry family, and made its appearance in Salisbury in 1878. Its instrumentation comprised two cornets, a slide trombone and a euphonium. There was exponential growth during the years leading up to the First World War. The worldwide increase was from 18,507 band players in 1906, to 25,537 in 1913.[34]

According to Richard Slater,[35] brass instruments demonstrated their general superiority in the general musical tasks that had to be undertaken for work within the Army. He maintained that Northwich, in Cheshire, was the first corps to have a band of its own, numbering 14 instrumentalists in 1880, although Boon reports another view that this honour should be given to the band at Consett, in County Durham.[36] Another notable early Salvationist band was Carlisle, which for many years was regarded as one of the largest and best bands in the Army.

Interesting detail on the formation of an early band is supplied by Sandall.[37] At Chatham in 1881, eight brass instruments were purchased from the military,

---

[33] See T. Herbert and H. Barlow, *The Culture of Brass Project* (2008), http://www. open.ac.uk/Arts/culture-of-brass, accessed Sept. 2009.

[34] Ibid.

[35] Slater, *The Salvation Army Dictionary of Music*, p. 11.

[36] Boon, *Play the Music Play!*, pp. 12–13.

[37] Sandall, *The History of the Salvation Army*, vol. 2, p. 118.

but some were in a bad state and had to be fixed by a Salvationist soldier, who happened to be a plumber. A big drum was found in a loft, and after a month's practice on one tune, 'Who'll be the next to follow Jesus', the band 'played out' at the head of 300 soldiers.

At first there was not a standard instrumental line-up. In fact Booth was keen to expand the instrumentation available. He encouraged his bandmasters 'to add flutes and "clarionets" to the ordinary brass, and where possible he should get together a String Band'.[38] In the summary of the instrumentation of the 1895 survey of 22 Salvation Army brass bands, nine had between one and five B♭ clarinets, and six had between one and two E♭ clarinets.[39] Chalk Farm Band was apparently fairly unique in having six saxophones.[40] In a later survey in the Local Officer of 51 bands between 1901 and 1907 it was clear that greater standardisation was becoming the norm, with only four clarinets and three saxophones listed.[41] Clarinets were removed from the full scores after 1902.[42] In the 1895 survey, band membership of the 22 bands ranged from 20 to 38,[43] and by the start of the new millennium it was reckoned that the average membership of Army bands was 25.[44]

As for uniforms in the early days, bands purchased them second-hand from the military. But each set of uniforms was different: there was no overall uniformity. When Booth visited Glasgow in April 1883, six bands were present, each with its own uniform style. By 1890 a standard uniform of a blue tunic, black braid and red trimmings had been established.[45] Diane Winston makes the point that the Army's use of clothes made it possible for new members to assume new personas for the sake of duty,[46] whilst McLeod emphasises the uniform's classless nature.[47]

There is no doubt that the rise of the brass band within the Salvation Army was inexorable during these years, not only quantitatively, but also in terms of musical quality, with elite bands such as the Household Troops Band (1887–93, 1985–present) and the International Staff Band (1891–present) setting high

[38] W. Booth, 'My Model Bandmaster', Local Officer 1 (1897–8), p. 67.

[39] 'The Instrumentation of 22 Salvation Army Bands', Musical Salvationist 10 (1895–6), p. 47.

[40] Bandsman and Songster, 15 June 1907, pp. 7, 12.

[41] 'Representative Bands', Local Officer, 1901–7.

[42] See Holz, Brass Bands of the Salvation Army, vol. 2, p. 32.

[43] 'The Instrumentation of 22 Salvation Army Bands', p. 47.

[44] Local Officer 4 (1900–1), p. 60.

[45] I. Bradley, 'Blowing for the Lord', History Today 27 (1977), pp. 190–5 (p. 195).

[46] D. Winston, Red-Hot and Righteous: The Urban Religion of the Salvation Army (Cambridge, MA, 1999), p. 4.

[47] H. McLeod, Religion and Irreligion in Victorian England: How Secular was the Working Class? (Bangor, 1993), p. 22.

standards. Interestingly Booth had been keen that bands should contain both women and men, and he encouraged women musicians: 'And do not our proph-etesses lead their people with music and song under the bare heavens in proces-sions of mercy? Do they not play their music – if not their timbrels – their violins and cornets, and concertinas, and such other instruments as come to their hands?'[48] Indeed, in 1889, an attempt was made to launch a Lasses' Household Troops Band, but the response must have been disappointing as nothing came of it.[49] By the early 20th century Salvation Army bands were almost exclusively male. In the 1901–7 survey of 51 bands, out of a total number of 1,396 players, only nine were women.[50]

This male domination, however, did serve to counter the traditional imbal-ance in favour of females in the congregations of Victorian churches and chapels. Salvation Army bands, like the Boy Scouts and the Boys' Brigade of the late 19th century, refuted claims that Christianity was feminine, with their combination of religion, militarism and imperialism.[51] Callum Brown argues that much of the music of evangelical discursive culture was 'loud, powerful [and] masculine, uncompromising in its auditory symbolism of battle with evil'.[52] It created 'a characteristic male world, combining the masculinity of militaristic uniforms, the machismo of brass instruments, and the religious content of the sacred music'.[53] Pamela Walker has elaborated on this theme, arguing that 'Salvationist men embraced a new manliness'[54] enhanced by talk of knee drills, volleys and uniforms. Much of this is reminiscent of so-called muscular Christianity, which attempted 'to redefine manhood by marrying physicality to spirituality'.[55]

A nice illustration of machismo in performance was provided by a corre-spondent to the *Musical Times* in 1890 from Melbourne, where the band was getting ready for a visit by William Booth:

> With body thrown well back and the great drum supported on his swelling chest, this drummer did fearful and wonderful things with the sticks. He evolved them apparently out of the small of his back, and brought them down both together with a crash that made everyone jump; he twisted

---

[48] Sandall, *The History of the Salvation Army*, vol. 2, p. 4. The original source is William Booth's article, 'Miriam, a Forerunner of the Prophetesses of The Salva-tion Army', *War Cry*, 17 Feb. 1881.

[49] Boon, *ISB*, p. 6.

[50] 'Representative Bands', *Local Officer*, 1901–7.

[51] McLeod, *Religion and Irreligion in Victorian England*, p. 51.

[52] Brown, *The Death of Christian Britain*, p. 55.

[53] Ibid., p. 138.

[54] P. Walker, '"I live but not yet I, for Christ liveth in me": Men and Masculinity in the Salvation Army, 1865–1890', in *Manful Assertions: Masculinities in Britain since 1800*, ed. M. Roper & J. Tosh (London, 1991), pp. 92–112 (p. 92).

[55] Brown, *The Death of Christian Britain*, p. 96.

them under his shoulder-blades, and around his neck and levelled them first on one side and then on another, and then both together with dead certainty; he marked time in a bewildering series of circles and semi-circles and figures of eight until he seemed to be surrounded by a horde of flying drumsticks; finally concentrating all his energy, he turned their force in one mighty blow, and stopped, perspiring, palpitating, but triumphant.[56]

Such an emphasis on masculinity in bands appears to have run counter to the prevailing Salvationist belief in the equality of the sexes.

In summary, there were a number of reasons for the choice of brass bands by the Army: many early Salvationists had been members of brass or volunteer bands; brass bands had military connotations that were characteristic of Booth's movement; brass bands were a popular musical movement to which especially working-class people could relate;[57] bands created a preponderantly masculine culture, in which the players could embrace 'a new manliness' in connection with religion.

COMMITMENT

In order to comprehend the nature of musical participation in the Salvation Army during its early years, it is necessary to understand that it was Booth's intention to create a parallel working-class culture in which secular popular entertainment would be transformed through religion itself.[58] To do this he insisted that the Salvation Army should be musically self-sufficient and exclusive. In addition to requiring all Salvationist soldiers to abstain from intoxicating liquor and from using tobacco, there was a ban on attending or participating in cricket and football matches, or other 'wordly' activities like dancing.[59] If a bandsman was tempted to play with a band outside the ranks of the Salvation Army, woe betide him:

> Among the deserters, many have been Bandsmen in the Salvation Army [...] The poor fellow learned to play an instrument in the service of Jesus, but he turned his back on the precious Saviour, and now he plays with the local brass band. See him turning out Sundays with the ungodly herd; notice his hard work as he toils far into the night at dances [...] Will he blow his horn in hell? We think not. The unending lamentations of the lost will be the only music made by castaway souls in hell.[60]

[56] *Musical Times* 31 (1890), p. 22.

[57] D. Russell, "What is Wrong with Brass Bands? Cultural Change and the Band Movement, 1918–c. 1964', in *The British Brass Band*, ed. Herbert, pp. 68–121 (p. 77).

[58] See Rapp, 'The British Salvation Army'.

[59] *Local Officer* 4 (1900–1), p. 452.

[60] Ibid., p. 54.

The demarcation between 'inside' and 'outside' was clearly defined with respect to bands, as in this reminiscence from John Bawmber, a Lincolnsire farm labourer and keen Salvationist from the early 1900s:

> We're not too strong at Sleaford. You see we had a nice little band; the war came, the lads went to the war, they joined other bands. When they come out, 'outside' bands as pays them to play in them; our band doesn't pay, we buy our own uniforms. 'Outside' buys the uniforms for them, and pays 'em to play. We play for the love of the thing.[61]

Gaining an entrance into the everyday experience of these Salvationist musicians is difficult. There is little doubt, however, that a lot was demanded. The register of the Exeter I Band compiled between 1897 and 1906 is filled with the week-by-week attendance of the men, which included four sessions every Sunday, with open-air and indoor meetings in the morning, afternoon and evening, and four sessions in the week, including band practice and weekday open-air meetings. However, there were clearly issues about attendance. Around 1900 some loose pages were inserted into the register with a table summarising the number of practices attended in the last 12 months. Of the 23 men listed, there was a wide disparity of attendance, ranging from nine to 49 practices in the year, the average being 26. At the end of this table the Bandmaster wrote 'I trust with the coming year every Bandsman will do his best to attend each Practice held'.[62] The commitment and discipline necessary was underlined in an earlier report on the Exeter Band in the *Local Officer*:

> They contrive to make their duty a delight. Three nights a week they are at their Post, one evening is devoted to practising, and they put in full time on Sundays. Salvation Army music is strictly adhered to, and no-one out of uniform is allowed to play in the Band.[63]

To illustrate that the Exeter example is not unique I shall draw on the testimonies of seven leading bandmasters who gave evidence between 1915 and 1916 to a Commission of Enquiry about the musical life of the Salvation Army.[64] Whilst this Commission is the subject of a later chapter, I shall focus briefly now on what these Bandmasters had to say about the issue of commitment and

---

[61] Transcribed by Gordon Cox from a sound recording of an interview with Bawmber in 1951 for the Survey of English Dialects, made available by the British Library Sound Archive.

[62] 'Exeter 1 Band Register, [commenced] July 1897, S. W. Cox'. From the Cox papers, comprising a miscellany of documents relating to my grandfather, Sydney Cox, Bandmaster of the Exeter Temple Band for 54 years, from 1893 to 1947.

[63] *Local Officer* 2 (1898–9), p. 183.

[64] Commission of Enquiry into Matters Relating to Salvation Army Music, 1915–16: unpublished proceedings of the Commission, The Salvation Army International Heritage Centre, 6 vols. including Final Report.

attendance of their bandsmen, bearing in mind that they were commenting on the years immediately prior to the outbreak of war.

Three London bands were represented. Divisional Bandmaster Brand, who was also in charge of the Tottenham Band, pointed out that London bands of necessity were largely 'weekend bands', because of the distances their members had to travel. In addition to the Sunday indoor and outdoor meetings, there was usually a band of some size on Saturday nights, as well as a weekly practice.[65] A similar pattern appeared for the famed Chalk Farm Band which attended three open air and three indoor meetings every Sunday, and alternate Saturday nights. Its considerable reputation meant 'it is no unusual thing for us to be out for an engagement once a week in addition to one Band Practice per week'.[66]

The third London Band, from the Regent Hall, had its own peculiar rules, as stated by Bandmaster Twitchin, concerning those bandsmen travelling on bicycles, and general attendance:

> We have a local rule that we do not have Sunday riding; if the 'bike' breaks down they must walk, and, if it is pouring with rain they must wait until it stops; if it is raining all day, I expect there will be an evasion of this 'obligation' as we call it [...]. That kind of thing largely affects attendance. I have also got a kind of local rule that each man must attend four times out of the six required on Sunday at least [...] We have also a local rule that the band stays till ¼ to nine on Sunday night.[67]

The band held its practice on a Tuesday evening, and also was in attendance at the Saturday night open-air meeting.

Generally it appears that bandsmen in the rest of the country were required to attend for a greater amount of time in the week. At Blackpool it was the band's task to arrange the Wednesday night meeting, which was in the form of a musical variety meeting, although no further details were supplied.[68] At Warrington there was an occasional Monday night obligation.[69] The band at Portsmouth operated on Sundays with three open-air and inside meetings, and two open-air and indoor meetings on weekdays, in addition to the band practice.[70]

The only village band represented was from the South Yorkshire coal-mining community of Dinnington. The bandmaster outlined the total programme for the corps, in addition to some interesting information about the weekly practice:

[65] Ibid., 'Bandmasters' Evidence', 28 Oct. 1915, pp. 3–4.

[66] Ibid., 4 Nov. 1915, p. 37.

[67] Ibid., 18 Nov. 1915, pp. 111– 2.

[68] Ibid., 4 Nov. 1915, p. 60.

[69] Ibid., 11 Nov. 1915, p. 76.

[70] Ibid., 18 Nov. 1915, p. 133.

On Sunday, in our Corps, we do four Open-airs in the morning; sometimes five. Ours is a village Corps. In the afternoon we will have one Open-
air meeting and the inside meeting; then the Open-air and Salvation
Meeting at night. Monday Night would be taken up with a meeting, but no
Band. Tuesday night is Soldiers Meeting; Songsters' Practice on Wednes-
days, Band Practice on Thursday, and Friday is off night. Saturday night
another practice and an Open-air. I might say, we have a good arrangement at our Colliery [...] The manager tries to arrange the Men's shifts so
that we can have our practice at convenient times [...] We often have the
Band Practice on Thursday morning.[71]

THE SOCIAL BACKGROUND OF SALVATIONIST BAND MEMBERS

But who were these individuals who joined the Salvation Army and participated
in its musical life? Inglis traced a thread through the Christian evangelistic and
social reform movements of the later 19th century which were a response to a
general working-class alienation from the churches.[72] Bailey points out that the
prevalent view of historians had been to view the Army as an agency of middle-
class attitudes and interests.[73] However, increasingly work has been carried out
looking at the organisation as an expression of working-class cultural development.[74] Such research in particular focuses upon the occupational composition of Salvationists. A detailed estimate of the social background of Army
officers in 1884 discovered that a sufficient number had been colliers, navvies
and labourers to suggest there was an effective recruitment of the urban working
poor. Bramwell Booth, according to Bailey, declared in 1906 that 'It is a working
man's church, with a working man's ritual and a working-man's clergyman and
clergy woman.'[75]

This emphasis on social class also relates to the popular instrumental organisations already outlined. Pre-eminently the brass band was often referred to as
the 'working man's orchestra'.[76] Appropriately, therefore, the band anthem of
the Nottingham Salvation Army Band as sung in 1884, commenced:

> We are a band of working men
> Whom God has saved from sin and hell,
> And by His grace we mean to tell
> Of Jesus' love, of Jesus' love.

[71] Ibid., 11 Nov. 1915, p. 96.

[72] K. Inglis, *Churches and the Working Classes in Victorian England* (London, 1963).

[73] See Bailey, 'In Darkest England and the Way Out', p. 134.

[74] See Horridge, *The Salvation Army in its Early Days*.

[75] Unsourced quotation, in Bailey, 'In Darkest England and the Way Out', p. 141.

[76] Russell, *Popular Music in England*, p. 239.

> We play our instruments of brass
> For Him who saved us by His grace,
> And filled us with His love to last
> For evermore, for evermore![77]

In the 1908 issue of *Bandsman and Songster* there is an informative breakdown of the social composition of the Norland Castle Band in West London, which comprised 29 bandsmen plus ten learners. The bandmaster was asked directly, 'I should like to hear from what class of men it is your bandsmen come.' He answered

> Almost all of them are just ordinary working-men, many simply labourers [...] We have coal-heavers, painters, bricklayers' labourers, and one or two butchers; but not more than two or three are engaged in clerical work.[78]

This breakdown appears to be fairly typical. The Reading 2 band, called itself 'a working men's band', and included a plasterer, a biscuit maker, iron workers, fitters, printers, carpenters, a blacksmith, a saw sharpener, and a pianoforte tuner.[79]

From 1901 until 1907 the monthly periodical *The Local Officer* carried a regular feature entitled Representative Bands. For the historian it provides valuable data, as the 51 bands' personnel are listed, together with instruments played, and, in most cases, the occupations of the 1,396 musicians.[80] In addition, some of the listings also contain the number of years individuals had served, and sometimes the dates of their conversions. These data on occupations are particularly helpful because it should already be apparent that issues of class and status were important from the very beginning in determining the structure of the Salvation Army. The bands, as we shall see later, came from England, Scotland and Wales.

The ranking of occupations may be assigned to five social classes based upon the Registrar General's *Census 1951: Classification of Occupations* (1956).[81] Here I have followed Brown, in his *Social History of the Nonconformist Ministry* (1988), by dividing Class III into two, in order to be more precise about the distinctions between white-collar workers and shop workers, and artisans.[82]

---

[77] *Local Officer* 4 (1900–1), p. 268.

[78] *Bandsman and Songster*, 22 Feb. 1908, p. 1.79.

[79] *Local Officer* 3 (1899–1900), p. 12.

[80] 'Representative Bands', *Local Officer*, 1901–7.

[81] Registrar General, *Census 1951: Classification of Occupations* (London, 1956). Also see J. Waites, M. Drake and R. Finnegan, 'Social Mobility', in *Studying Family and Community History: 19th and 20th Centuries*, vol. 3: *Communities and Families*, ed. J. Golby (Cambridge, 1994), pp. 89–113.

[82] K. D. Brown, *A Social History of the Nonconformist Ministry in England and Wales, 1800–1930* (Oxford, 1988), p. 24.

    I Professional/Higher occupations

    II 'Intermediate' or petit bourgeois occupations

    III Skilled manual
        White-collar/shop worker
        Artisan

    IV Semi-skilled manual

    V Unskilled manual

Routh provides a helpful description of the categories.[83] Professionals include the learned professions and also the lower professions, such as artists and draughtsmen. Intermediate occupations include farmers and shopkeepers, and administrators and managers who in fact cross service and production industries. Clerical workers and white-collar workers are those engaged in paper work, and include insurance agents. Skilled manual workers are craftsmen, many of whom have served their apprenticeships. Semi-skilled workers perform tasks that can be learned in months rather than years, and include machine operators, vehicle drivers, and shop assistants. Finally, unskilled manual workers do jobs that can be learnt in hours rather than months. They include labourers who require strength and stamina rather than skill.

As Dave Russell has pointed out, all attempts at such classification contain defects.[84] For example, the frequent vagueness of occupational descriptions often makes it hard to distinguish between employer, employee and self-employed.[85] If a person is described as a 'jeweller' or a 'baker', is he or she a proprietor or an employee?[86] There is a similar vagueness about the term 'miner', which can include both skilled and semi-skilled workers, depending upon their more precise role. In this study I have followed the advice given in the 1951 census, that persons simply described as 'Coal Miner' should be allocated to the skilled category.[87]

In spite of these difficulties the data do yield valuable information about the social class and occupational composition of Salvationist bandsmen. In considering these data, I have omitted 50 individuals on the basis that no occupational details were supplied, or they were still at school. This leaves us with a total of 1346 bandsmen. The results of my analysis are shown in Table 3.

The groupings are clarified in Figure 1. These data demonstrate the over-whelming number of skilled and semi-skilled workers in the musical ranks of

[83] G. Routh, *Occupations of the People of Great Britain, 1801–1981* (Basingstoke, 1987).

[84] Russell, *Popular Music in England*, p. 251.

[85] McLeod, *Religion and Irreligion in Victorian England*, p. 30.

[86] Russell, *Popular Music in England*, p. 251.

[87] Registrar General, *Census 1951*, p. xii. For detailed discussion of the heterogeneous nature of mining work, see J. Benson, *British Coal Miners in the Nineteenth Century: A Social History* (Aldershot, 1980, r/1993).

Table 3 Occupational grouping of Salvationist band members, 1901–7

Occupational grouping	N	%
I Professional	8	0.6
II Intermediate	94	7.0
III Skilled		
White-collar/shop worker	142	10.5
Artisan	710	52.7
IV Semi-skilled	157	11.7
V Unskilled	235	17.5
	1,346	100

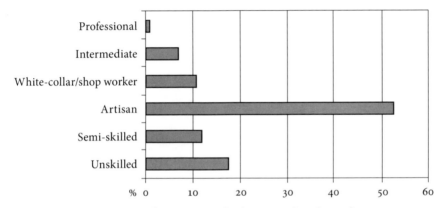

Figure 1 Occupational groupings of Salvationist band members, 1901–7

the Army, but with a significant percentage of the unskilled. By adding together categories III–V of Table 3 we are provided with a total of 92.4% of musical Salvationists who can be classified as having what can reasonably be described as working-class backgrounds. Within each grouping there were certain major occupations as in Table 4.

Some words of explanation are needed here. The relatively high number of clerks is partly due to the founding by the Salvation Army of its own Assurance Society in 1894, and its agents played an important part in the life of local corps.[88] For the skilled category, which is by far the largest, there is a wide variety of occupations, hence the difficulty of choosing just one major example.

I then looked at the occupations of 48 bandmasters (the details of three were not supplied), to see if they represented a fundamentally different balance of occupations. In Table 5 I list their occupations and the category to which I

[88] See Wiggins, *The History of the Salvation Army*, vol. 4, pp. 226–35.

Table 4 Most prevalent occupations, 1901–7 ($N = 1,346$)

Occupational grouping	Most prevalent occupation	N	%
I Professional	N/A	N/A	N/A
II Intermediate	Grocers and Greengrocers	24/94	25.5
III Skilled			
White collar/shop worker	Clerks	46/142	32.4
Artisan	Miners	95/710	13.4
IV Semi-skilled	Brickmakers	31/157	19.7
V Unskilled	Labourers	129/235	54.9

Table 5 Bandmasters' occupations by category, 1901–7 ($N = 48$)

Occupational grouping	Occupation
I Professional	Accountant
II Intermediate	Coal Merchant (2), Grocer, Merchant, Salvation Army Officer
III Skilled	
White collar/shop worker	Assurance Agent, Clerk
Artisan	Blacksmith, Blacksmith's striker, Boot maker, Boot repairer, Builder's foreman, Colourist, Contractor (2), Engine fitter, Iron moulder, Joiner, Lamp inspector, Market gardener, Miner (3), Engine tester, Fireman, Fitter, Foreman engineer, Foreman platelayer, Monumental letter cutter, Moulder, Painter (2), Photographer, Plasterer, Plumber, Rail straightener, Salvation Army Bonnet Factory, Stonemason, Turner
IV Semi-skilled	Brickmaker, Chemical worker, Gardener
V Unskilled	Coppersmith labourer, Cotton operative, Labourer (3)

have assigned them. By and large the bandmasters reflect the overall social background of Salvationist musicians, with a preponderance of skilled manual workers including a number of foremen, inspectors and contractors, with a lesser proportion of semi-skilled and unskilled workers.

Of course, it would be misleading to maintain there was a similar balance in all bands, because regional industries and crafts would make each grouping unique. For example, Salvation Army bands in mining villages would frequently be fairly homogenous. In Trealaw in the Welsh valleys the 28 members of the band included 20 miners;[89] similarly in the Tow Law band in the Durham mines there were 22 miners, although the bandmaster was a

[89] 'Representative Bands', *Local Officer*, 1901–7: Jan. 1903, p. 215.

grocer.[90] Two bands in small communities were almost exclusively composed of brick makers, with all but one of the 12 members of the Green Street Green Band in Kent in that occupation,[91] and all but three of the 16 members of the Farcet band in Cambridgeshire.[92]

The largest unit represented in the survey of Representative Bands was the Barrow-in-Furness Band with 44 members.[93] The occupations represented the heavy industry that made the town one of the country's main manufacturing centres, including engine drivers, a rail straightener, blast-furnace men, a ship-wright, a ship plater, and numerous dock labourers. There was a similar profile in the Govan Band, by the side of the Clyde.[94] And so one could go on, with the market gardeners of the Evesham Band,[95] the hatters of Luton 2,[96] the clerks of Penge,[97] the printers of St Albans[98] and the textile workers of Oldham[99] and Ashton-under-Lyne.[100]

In the 51 representative bands, there were only nine women out of a total membership of 1,396. These women came from two bands, Forest Hill in London, and Lye in Worcestershire. Whilst the two at Forest Hill were dressmakers,[101] the seven at Lye included four working at the bucket factory, one was a press worker, and two listed as 'at home'.[102]

Occupational backgrounds for the members of other musical combinations are occasionally supplied in scattered references in Salvationist periodicals. The Oldham 1 Concertina Band members were shopworkers or mill girls, rising every day at 5 a.m. to commence work at 6.[103] The 23 men of the notable Atter-cliffe Concertina Band were mostly steel workers and labourers in the mines.[104] The Bristol Divisional Singing Brigade chose to base its report of membership on a different set of criteria; some of its members previous to conversion had been gamblers, drunkards, atheists and the 'don't care' sort.[105]

[90] Ibid., Sept. 1902, p. 60.

[91] Ibid., July 1902, pp. 453–5.

[92] Ibid., Aug. 1903, p. 14.

[93] Ibid., Nov. 1902, p. 136.

[94] Ibid., Mar. 1905, p. 304.

[95] Ibid., Feb. 1902, p. 251.

[96] Ibid., May 1902, p. 377.

[97] Ibid., Dec. 1906, p. 454.

[98] Ibid., Feb. 1904, p. 256.

[99] Ibid., Mar. 1903, p. 303.

[100] Ibid., Feb. 1903, p. 254.

[101] Ibid., Jan. 1907, p. 8.

[102] Ibid., Aug. 1902, p. 15.

[103] *Local Officer* 4 (1900–1), pp. 310–11.

[104] *Bandsman, Local Officer and Songster*, 15 Aug. 1914, p. 579.

[105] *Local Officer* 3 (1899–1900), pp. 420–2.

As has been said, we learn from all these data that Salvation Army band membership at the turn of the century was predominantly male and working-class, with a preponderance of skilled and semi-skilled manual workers, but with a respectable number of the unskilled. Further research might investigate whether the overall proportion of unskilled workers during this period might be higher in the Salvation Army bands than in secular bands, and whether or not Salvation Army bands connected with higher social groups as happened with secular bands through patronage.[106]

❧ Conversion

An essential precondition of becoming a musical Salvationist (like any other kind) was to have been converted or 'saved'. The approach of the Salvation Army to conversion was among its most significant doctrinal and practical issues.[107] Salvationists believed that entire sanctification was a decisive event that could occur in a moment. There are numerous conversion stories, but here I shall focus upon four of them to illustrate the often personally profound spiritual or religious experiences that underpinned subsequent musical participation. These narratives often took the form of highly formulaic tales drawing upon a phrase or image from a scriptural passage, and in their original versions could have been oral testimonies.[108]

Charles Fry (1837–82), who I have already referred to, grew up in 'the established church', but his father, a frequenter of the tap room, had 'a growing liking for the intoxicating cup'. Fry's mother started to attend the Wesleyan chapel and prayed for the conversion of her husband and the rest of the family. Charles became passionate about music, but through ungodly connections was 'led further and further into sin', until in 1854 he was ready to leave a tea meeting in connection with the chapel where he played the cornet, when

> A dear brother, God bless him, stopped me at the door and with the utmost patience pleaded with me to stay to the prayer meeting. All the time he was removing one finger after another from my cornet until almost without knowing it, he had taken my idol from me [...] I soon fell on my knees with nine others and began crying to God for mercy [...] Just before the clock struck twelve I saw a beautiful light pathway and at the top stood my beloved Jesus, with outstretched hands and, looking smilingly at me, and above his beautiful brow was written in shining characters these words 'Come unto me all ye that labour and are heavy-laden and I will give you rest' [...] O the joy that filled my soul [...] I walked about the room and

[106] See C. Ehrlich and D. Russell, 'Victorian Music: A Perspective', *Journal of Victorian Culture* 3 (1988), pp. 111–22 (p. 114).

[107] Walker, *Pulling the Devil's Kingdom Down*, p. 65.

[108] Ibid., pp. 67–9.

sometimes fairly danced, and that's the only time in my life that I did dance.[109]

Here we note the physical separation from a musical object of idolatory, but which at the same time served as a means of evangelism. Coming to terms with this puritanical dilemma underlined the deep suspicion with which the Salvation Army hierarchy viewed the movement's growing musical life.

Not all such stories come from the context of chapel traditions. A convert to Booth's Christian Mission, 'a banjo player', provides interesting detail of the 'nigger minstrel' tradition, popular in England since 1857:[110]

> I have been one that has lived in sin and wickedness. From the age of fifteen I used to go and sit and drink in the alehouse, and have gone with a blackface and a long-tailed coat with a banjo or tambourine under my arm, from one beershop to another and sing nigger songs [...] One Sunday I heard your singing in the streets of Bradford, and I went into the theatre out of curiosity, and I liked the meetings, so I continued to go for six weeks, and then I got saved, and now I am washed in the Blood of the Lamb.[111]

But it was not only adults that could be converted. In the early days of the Salvation Army in Exeter, one of the features that would strike an outsider was the presence of two small boys, Sydney and Fred Cox, on the platform, accompanying the singing on their violins.[112] These two had been converted when they were aged 9½ and 7½ respectively. Both, according to their mother, 'were under conviction of sin' through attending the first Little Soldiers' meeting held in Exeter, 'but just not understanding what yielding up to Jesus meant, they went away unsaved'.[113] However, at the next meeting Fred 'gave his heart to the Lord'. The experience made him wary of the unsaved. A friend came to give him a music lesson, but Fred instructed his mother that he should not come again to teach him until he too had been saved. Fred was taken ill and died when he was nine. He had been saving up his money to buy a harp to play in the meetings. In his last few days he confided in his mother how glad he was that he had been saved. The headline above his mother's tribute to him, was 'Little Hallelujah Fiddler [...] who has left his violin on earth to play a harp in heaven'.

My fourth conversion story relates to the temperance issue. There are numerous accounts of Salvationist musicians overcoming the temptations of

---

[109] 'Short Sketch of the Life of Charles William Fry – By Himself', edited with additional notes by Fred. W. Fry. Unpublished MS (n.d.). Fry Family papers, The Salvation Army International Heritage Centre.

[110] See Russell, *Popular Music in England*, p. 77; Pickering, *Blackface Minstrelsy in Britain*.

[111] *Christian Mission Magazine* 9 (1877), p. 242.

[112] *The Little Soldier*, 1 Feb. 1883, p. 1.

[113] Ibid.

strong drink, nicely illustrated in the following story of Sergeant-Major Burrans of the Liverpool I Band, a B♭ bass player, and formerly a desperate drunkard and gambler:

> He remembers taking a glass of beer, holding it aloft, and exclaiming 'Talk about the Balm of Gilead! Look at that!' [...] But God used that very expression to arrest him. An address on the text 'Is there no balm in Gilead?' led him to repentance.[114]

What I have attempted to demonstrate is that the background and experiences of Salvationist musicians were many and varied, but in the main are a testimony to the roots of the Salvation Army in revivalism and Puritanism. Music was integral to the identities of these men, but within the wider perspective of personal transformation through conversion.

ໄ∾ *Conclusion*

In conclusion I shall relate the story I have told to the markers of musical participation that I outlined in the Introduction. Undoubtedly these Salvationist musicians developed considerable confidence through acquiring musical skills and demonstrating these within the regular opportunities provided for 'performance'. Particularly in the early days of the Army these opportunities embraced considerable diversity, with concertinas, drum and fife bands, handbells, mandolins, string and brass bands (including clarinets and saxophones). In this respect, and also with the often bespoke musical arrangements that were necessary at first, there appeared to be a direct connection with the old plebeian musical tradition of the church bands. There was a commitment to a specific repertoire, in this case, increasingly, to an exclusive one. Bands in particular gave male Salvationists scope for social interaction and friendships, cementing group solidarity, although, generally, musical Salvationists also shared similar backgrounds of occupations and social class. Musical participation afforded a depth of meaning and purpose to life, particularly when allied with religious devotion which as we have seen was regarded as fundamental. The rituals, the uniforms, the flags and the music potentially allowed these musicians liberation from their everyday persona, also evident in the transformative power of their conversions. Finally, musical participation as a source of spiritual fulfilment was clearly evident, although the order of priority was God, the Salvation Army, and Music.

---

[114] *Local Officer* 5 (1901–2), p. 59.

CHAPTER 5

Musical Teaching and Learning, 1878–1913

I<small>T</small> was the task of Richard Slater and his colleagues in the Musical Department to provide a system of musical instruction which would build a solid foundation for the varieties of musical participation that we have seen emerging in the pioneering days of the Salvation Army. There is no doubt that it was a mammoth educational challenge to teach thousands of children, young people and adults, most of them without formal musical training, to become proficient Salvationist musicians. This chapter is in three main parts, focusing upon pedagogical ideas, teaching and learning in practice, and the educational life stories of four Salvationist musicians. I conclude by highlighting the achievements of Slater and his colleagues in educating this musical army.

৯ *A Salvationist Musical Pedagogy*

Musical instruction was a priority in developing the potential of Salvationist vocalists and instrumentalists. To this end Richard Slater worked upon a number of educational publications, in addition to developing musical competitions and examinations to support both music practice and theory. In this section I shall investigate the development of a Salvationist pedagogy through the musical materials devised for children and young people, and the instructional publications and musical advice for adult learners.

YOUNG PEOPLE'S MUSICAL INSTRUCTION

William Booth's writing on the musical instruction of young people is illuminating. He believed that when an aptitude for music was evident in children, that capacity should be improved and practised. They should be allowed to learn such instruments as appear most likely to be useful in the public service. If children had voices for singing, they should commence by singing solos in private in order to get them ready to sing in 'the barracks' and by the bedsides of the sick and dying, or in the open-air meeting. Every musical gift should not only be used, but be improved in order to show to a dying world the love of Christ and his power to save. Simplicity was the touchstone, and every care should be taken to keep from mere performance or showing off. There was no time to waste in acquiring what were called 'accomplishments', unless they be carefully turned to account in the business of saving men.[1]

How were these ideas embodied in music instructional materials directed at

---

[1] W. Booth, 'The Education of our Children', *Local Officer* 3 (1899–1900), pp. 5–6, 46–7.

children? I shall present three examples to give a flavour of the approach taken principally by Richard Slater.

First, *The Home Pianoforte Tutor* published by the Salvation Army in 1904 was lavishly produced with gilt edging.[2] Although undoubtedly the piano did support a range of musical activities in the Salvation Army, this publication was clearly aimed at a more general market. In fact its Salvation Army provenance is not immediately apparent, as the publisher is listed simply as 'Publishing Office, 79 and 81 Fortress Road, London NW2', which was the home at that time of the Musical Department. Although its author is not mentioned, it was in fact Richard Slater, who refers to it several times in his diaries. The Tutor's subtitle was *Specially intended for use in Christian Homes [...] Including no matter of any kind which is not in keeping with the character of Christian homes.* The preface expanded on this point:

> In most other Tutors the pieces have borne such titles, and have been in such styles, as to prove objectionable to people who have been anxious that, before all else, the claims of religion should have the first place in their homes, and in all branches also of the education of their children. Such pieces as by their titles or styles are inevitably connected with the Theatre, Music Hall or Ball Room.[3]

The Tutor was organised in four parts: facts about musical notation; an introduction to the piano; matters of technic; and finally 70 sacred pieces with both tunes and verses, including such well-worn favourites as 'Nearer my God to thee', 'Saints of God', 'Stand up for Jesus', and 'When Mothers of Salem'.[4] The tunes were organised progressively in terms of difficulty, and included three duets. Slater concluded in his preface:

> Every step onward, in learning pieces under such circumstances, would thereby be an increase of the pupil's ability to minister to the religious life and exercise of the home.[5]

My second example of instructional materials for children is *The Salvation Army Band of Love International Musical Drills* (1899)[6] and its second edition, *International Musical Drills and Healthy Home Exercises* (1909).[7] Here was a direct influence from the military and from mainstream education. Many school drill texts were based upon the British Army manuals, and the teaching

---

[2] [R. Slater,] *The Home Pianoforte Tutor: Specially Intended for Use in Christian Homes* (London, [1904]).

[3] Ibid., p. 2.

[4] Many of the songs and tunes in the Pianoforte Tutor including the four cited were taken from *The Salvation Army Songs* (1899).

[5] *The Home Pianoforte Tutor*, p. 2.

[6] *The Salvation Army Band of Love International Musical Drills* (London, 1899).

[7] *International Musical Drills and Healthy Home Exercises* (London, 1909).

of drill (or callisthenics) was an accepted practice in schools in the 1870s.[8] In fact no less a person than the poet and schools inspector Matthew Arnold had pressed for the teaching of callisthenics or drill,[9] so that by 1875 schools received a special grant for the subject. Frequently school bands and drum and fife bands were encouraged to accompany the routines. In the school music catalogue of Curwen, one of the main music education publishers of the time, 13 collections of Drill Music are listed.[10]

The publication of *The Salvation Army Band of Love International Musical Drills* included an Introduction by Bramwell Booth, which is worth quoting because he emphasised the extent of the Army's ambitious educational plans:

> We provide for the *minds* of the young by teaching them under our 'Band of Love' section such useful things as Music, Shorthand, Writing, Book-keeping, Ambulance, Nursing, Cooking, Sewing, Fretwork and Drills [...] And for the *bodies* of our children experience has shown us that Drills supply a great need. Gymnasiums and playgrounds are not at the disposal of our children, who are mainly taken from the lowest classes of society; but these exercises will give them opportunity for healthy exercise and develop their muscles, while they will also teach them useful lessons in promptness, obedience and the value of united action.[11]

The book contained 212 drills with music arranged and set by Richard Slater. Those acquainted with the ordinary gymnasium were encouraged that there should be no problem in teaching the children the exercises: 'of course all the music is Salvation Army in character',[12] and was arranged for piano and any instruments pitched in B♭. A prominent part was given, unlike in other publications, to the tambourine, increasingly regarded at the time as one of the defining instruments associated with the Salvation Army. Items included 'The Lantern Drill', 'The Handkerchief Drill', and 'Living Bible Pictures'. The second edition of the book, *International Musical Drills and Healthy Home Exercises*, included instructions for standing 'at ease' and 'at attention', and for 'dismissing', 'turning by numbers' and 'marchings'. The photographs in the book illustrated the international spread of drilling through Salvation Army educational institutions in California, Holland, India and Mashonaland.[13]

My last example of instructional materials for young people is rather different. I have turned to the ninth annual number of 'Songs for Junior Anniversaries'

---

[8] See A. Penn, *Targeting Schools: Drill, Militarism and Imperialism* (London, 1999).

[9] M. Arnold, *Reports on Elementary Schools, 1852–1882* (London, 1908), pp. 152–3.

[10] *School Music in the Curwen Edition* (London, n.d.), p. 16.

[11] *The Salvation Army Band of Love International Musical Drills* (1899), p. v.

[12] *Local Officer* 2 (1898–9), p. 325.

[13] See *International Musical Drills and Healthy Home Exercises*.

contained within the *Musical Salvationist* (1910),[14] which includes four songs which have pedagogical connections or intentions. The first connects to the previous discussion about musical drills. 'Swaying and Singing' is designated 'a drill song', with words and air by a prolific Salvationist song writer, Adjutant Charles Coller. Set in a 6/4 time signature it underlines the link between music, movement and faith:

> Swaying and swinging, joyfully singing
> Songs of the Saviour strong to redeem;
> Children so zealous, will you not tell us,
> Whence comes the joy which from your faces beam?
>
> Still sweetly singing, gracefully swinging,
> To music's pulse, with faces aglow,
> Surely such training seeks but for gaining,
> Say comrades, say, what prize attracts you so?[15]

Finally the children sing 'Body and soul we give Him the whole'.

Next in this discussion of the educational implications of Salvationist song repertoire comes 'an action song', 'The Apple Pie Song', to be performed by eight to ten girls dressed in white caps and aprons and sleeves, with a table on which appropriate cooking utensils and plates of peeled apples had been placed.[16] Various actions like nodding and pointing at the various items on the table were required. Whilst the verses were secular, the chorus rammed home the message:

> The things the Army teaches are too numerous to say,
> But the dream of the General comes true ev'ry day.

Action songs as a genre were firmly established Froebel-inspired infant-school activities. They were based upon a subject chosen from daily life, and especially from the sphere in which the child lived, derived from Froebel's desire to help women educate their children more effectively as a prerequisite for a better society.[17] *School Music in the Curwen Edition* (n.d.) lists four pages of action songs.[18]

My last two examples come from the pen of Richard Slater himself. 'The Bell Song' instructs the singers in the connections between the Tonic Sol-fa method of sight singing, and the Christian faith:

---

[14] 'Songs for Junior Anniversaries' (Ninth Annual Number), *Musical Salvationist* 24 (1910), pp. 33–48.

[15] Ibid., pp. 36–7.

[16] Ibid., pp. 38–9.

[17] K. Brehony, 'F. W. A. Froebel (1782–1852)', in *Encyclopedia of Children and Childhood*, ed. P. S. Fass (New York, 2004), pp. 374–5.

[18] *School Music in the Curwen Edition*, pp. 57–60.

The *Doh* bell said 'Be strong in the faith; so conquer sin and death [...]'
The *Me* bell said 'God's above! Trust in the Father's love'.
The *Ray* bell said 'Hope on! Keep well used a cheerful song!'
The *Soh* bell, like trumpet blast, said 'Be true while life shall last'.

The song concludes with the lines 'Ding, dong, ding, dong! To the bells I listened, And they helped my soul.'[19]

This clearly relates to the growing influence of Tonic Sol-fa, and presumably might connect to the experience of school of Salvationist children. However, it was not until the 1899/1900 issue that Slater had introduced Tonic Sol-fa notation as a regular feature of the *Musical Salvationist*, with the intention of raising the profile of singing, which had been at something of a standstill compared to bands.[20]

Finally, in 'Jack', Slater portrays in a Gilbert-and-Sullivanesque type solo-and-chorus setting, the transgressions of 'the little chap' who sometimes took sugar, jam or ham 'on the sly'. He took delight in frightening his younger sister, but all this changed:

> One day when at the meeting came the light ([*repeat*] came the light),
> Jack found himself a sinner, awful sight! ([*repeat*] awful sight!)
> It made him feel afraid, To God he wept and pray'd,
> And there he gain'd the pardon of his sin.

The refrain relates that he then formed a plan to 'be a faithful Captain in The Army'.[21] Here Slater was producing a moralistic type of song popular in educational contexts, but frowned upon by reformers such as Arthur Somervell and Cecil Sharp, keen to cleanse the musical palette through national and folk songs.[22]

In these examples of a piano tutor, musical drills, and songs with educational links, we see some of the ways in which Slater attempted to marry the utilitarian musical philosophy of the Army with some of the trends evident in the wider educational arena.

INSTRUCTIONAL PUBLICATIONS

Slater and his team published their first modest educational effort in 1887, a scale sheet, and this was followed in 1890 by tutors for the cornet, the euphonium, the bombardon [Eb bass tuba], the tenor horn, the baritone horn, tenor and bass trombones. In 1891 appeared tutors for soprano cornet, clarinet and the concertina.

In addition, Slater wrote a number of textbooks in a series called *First Lessons*.

[19] *Musical Salvationist* 24 (1910), pp. 40–1.

[20] *Musical Salvationist* 14 (1899–1900), p. 153.

[21] *Musical Salvationist* 24 (1910), pp. 42–3.

[22] See Cox, *A History of Music Education in England*, chaps. 6 and 8.

His *First Lessons in Music* (*c.* 1906) was designed for class teaching or for private study. It was essentially a rudiments primer covering notes and time, staves and clefs, beating time, and musical terms. The book was often used as a preliminary to practical instruction.[23] In *First Lessons in Harmony* (1908) Slater progressed from intervals and consecutives up to chromatic chords. He advised his readers to analyse the harmonies in the Army tune book, and Bach's 371 four-part chorales. To go deeper he recommended Prout's *Harmony: Its Theory and Practice* (1889), or Riemann's *Harmony Simplified* (1895), two highly influential texts among 19th-century harmony primers.[24]

The most ambitious of this series, out of our immediate period, was *First Lessons in Harmony and Modulation*, dealing with modulation by the German sixth, the diminished seventh etc. Slater's examples were extensive and taken from the 'Great Masters', including Bach, Beethoven, Berlioz, Cherubini, Chopin, Gounod, Rossini, Schubert, Spohr. Wagner, 'the greatest of all masters of modulation', was used to illustrate the use of enharmonic modulation.[25]

Between July 1902 and September 1907 the *Musical Salvationist* regularly featured articles by Slater of general musical interest. These were then compiled by him into *The Salvation Army Dictionary of Music* (1908). This had been one of his longest and most difficult tasks.[26] In his Prefatory Note, Slater pointed out that his *Dictionary* did not aim to cover the whole field of music; it offered little on the historical and antiquarian aspects of the subject, and on matters of theory it restricted itself to meet the special needs of Army bandsmen and songsters.[27] In so doing Slater admitted it may not meet the needs of the professional musician. What is distinctive about it, is that side-by-side with entries on general musical matters (e.g. the acciaccatura, analysis, composition, false relation, the Gamut, passing discords etc.) are entries relating to the Salvation Army (history of Army bands, the Musical Board, Junior Bands, Original Army Music etc.). Occasionally Slater allows himself a touch of humour, as in the entry on 'Cacophony': 'A discordant combination of sounds applied to the efforts of learners and of incompetent Bands.'[28] Everything a Salvationist musician might need was supposed to be contained within the Dictionary's covers.

What is apparent in all this educational effort is the energy displayed by Slater and his department in publishing the numerous instrumental tutors, text books and dictionary. Through them, Army bandsmen were better able to cope with their basic instructional needs, but more than that, their musical horizons were widened and stretched to encompass more advanced work and reading.

[23] R. Slater, *First Lessons in Music* (London, [*c.* 1906]).

[24] R. Slater, *First Lessons in Harmony* (London, 1908).

[25] R. Slater, *First Lessons in Harmony and Modulation* (London, 1929), p. 49.

[26] Slater, 'My Twenty-Six Years Service', pp. 3–4.

[27] Slater, *The Salvation Army Dictionary of Music*, prefatory note, n.p.

[28] Ibid., p. 19.

1 The Fry family of Salisbury, 1878

2 The Penzance Band on the occasion of the visit of William Booth (in the top hat), n.d.

3 Salvation Songsters, 1883: Slater with violin, Hill with double-bass, and Fry with the harp. Songster No. 15 is Miss Eva Booth, later to be General of the Army.

4 The Musical Department, 1883: Richard Slater, Fred Fry and Henry Hill

5 Richard Slater and his wife, Eliza, *c.* 1883

6 Richard Slater at the harmonium, n.d.

The Bandsman and Songster of The Salvation Army

WILLIAM BOOTH Founder   SAMUEL HURREN, British Commissioner   EDWARD J. HIGGINS, General

No. 984—Vol. XXIII   Registered at the General   **LONDON, APRIL 19, 1930**   Post Office as a Newspaper   **Price One Penny**

WORKERS IN CROTCHETS AND QUAVERS

PREPARING MUSIC FOR OUR BANDS AND BRIGADES

A glimpse of the Music Editorial Staff concentrated on their task. From left to right are: Captain Eric Ball, Staff-Captain Albert Jakeway, Bandsman Phil. Catelinet, and Lieut.-Colonel F. G. Hawkes (see article on page 124)

THE CIRCULATION OF <u>OUR OWN</u> IS GOING UP—but it might go much faster if YOUR Band and Brigade would only show more personal interest.

7 The Music Editorial Board at work, 1930:
(*left to right*) Eric Ball, Albert Jakeway, Philip Catelinet, Frederick Hawkes

8 Eric Ball, 1937

SAXOPHONE SEXTETT.

TRUMPET QUINTETT.

THE CHALK FARM BAND

9 Chalk Farm Band in the 1930s led by Bandmaster Punchard

✿ Teaching and Learning in Practice

In this section I am concerned with 'what was taught and what was learned',[29] in other words moving away from pedagogical ideas to pedagogical practice. In particular, emphasis will be placed upon how Salvationist musical instructors taught their students musical skills, and upon the introduction of examinations and competitions.

STEPS IN THE MUSICAL LADDER

Through reading the columns of the Salvation Army periodicals it is possible to perceive the main trends in teaching and learning in a variety of vocal and instrumental musical ensembles.

Accounts of vocal teaching are rare, but one report focuses upon the Clapton Congress Hall Songsters. For the leader, Major Edith Rogers, 'the *Musical Salvationist* was her meat and drink'. She commenced her practices by running through the four parts of a new song, then took it apart phrase by phrase, again and again. She would rehearse four or five pieces in a single practice, and a song for Sunday. In the middle of the practice was an interval for breathing exercises, as she believed 'that it is as easy to get "winded" singing as blowing'. Her weekly practice began at 8 p.m. There was a short bible reading and prayer an hour later, and the practice concluded at 10 p.m.[30]

Descriptions of teaching and learning within instrumental groupings are more common. One individual who really seemed to make string bands flourish was, as we have seen, Captain Lax, a former professional violinist. He devised his own special system, similar to tablature, to produce violinists within six weeks:

> Instead of writing the usual five-line stave, he invents one of his own of four lines. Each of these lines represents a string on the violin [...] this stave is divided into bars [...] but instead of notes, numbers are substituted which tell which finger is to be put down. After some small amount of scale practice has been gone through, an easy tune is introduced, for instance 'Nothing but thy blood can save me' [...] In this way, Captain Lax gets one or two tunes off, so that they are performable within a few weeks; and this, naturally, gives great encouragement, and a basis for further training along more orthodox lines.[31]

Like string bands, drum and fife bands had a somewhat precarious existence in the Salvation Army. However, there is an intriguing account from 1908 of

---

[29] T. W. Laqueur, *Religion and Respectability: Sunday Schools and Working-Class Culture, 1780–1850* (New Haven, CT, 1976), p. 95.

[30] *Bandsman Songster and Local Officer*, 2 Jan. 1909, p. 4.

[31] *Local Officer* 3 (1899–1900), pp. 461–2.

teaching such a band consisting of 20 boys, with an average age of ten years.[32] First of all the band leader had to teach himself, learning all he could from the published Tutor, and seeking information from different people. When the 20 boys gathered for the first time, he impressed on them the principles of Army Bandsmanship, God first, Salvation Army second, and Music last. Each boy was then handed an instrument together with a slip on which was written a two-octave scale, with the fingering of each note written underneath. After blowing their first note, they progressed to a half scale, then a full scale, and were taught the first principles of music in order that they could then learn to play at sight:

> We had four nights practice a week, and soon formed two classes, one for 'forwards' and the other for 'backwards'. We gave two nights per week to each, and in seven weeks they were playing in the Junior Hall, leading the singing. We started with such simple tunes as 'Nearer my God to thee', 'Spanish Chant', and 'Evening Hymn' and advanced to really difficult music, but we only used two scales, D and A.[33]

When it comes to considering teaching and learning within the Army's brass bands, clearly young people's bands were a priority. In his hints on how to form and train junior brass bands, Fred Hawkes, Slater's colleague, pointed out that the Band Lads needed to be consecrated to Army warfare, something far more important than merely a musical career. Thoroughness should characterise every detail of work done. The Bandmaster should not be afraid of constant repetition either in the teaching of musical theory or the practising of tunes:

> They are accustomed to being taught and acquire habits of study at school [...] Encourage the boys to ask questions in connexion with anything they do not fully understand.[34]

Nevertheless a firm hand was needed:

> We have heard of several attempts at forming Junior Bands that have ended disastrously, largely on account of the failure to maintain discipline. A dozen boys playing about with brass instruments, before or after practice, or between meetings, can make as hideous a din as can well be imagined [...] Insist upon obedience, order and discipline at all times, even if it means that an example has to be made occasionally of one or more of the boys.[35]

At Wisbech it was decided to form the 'saved' boys into a class to teach them music. Eight lads were selected as 'pioneers'. They met twice a week for lessons

---

[32] *Bandsman and Songster*, 8 Feb. 1908, p. 11.

[33] Ibid.

[34] F. Hawkes, 'Junior Bands: More Hints on How to Form and Train Them', *Bandsman and Songster*, 7 Mar. 1908, p. 13.

[35] Ibid.

on the blackboard, but no instruments were supplied until they had learnt their scales and rudiments, and had written tunes on the board.[36]

All this is reminiscent of scenes from a once popular Salvation Army young people's book by Noel Hope, *Crotchets and Quavers or The making of the Brixwell Young People's Band* (1921). This contains an authoritative account of common routines in Salvation Army musical teaching. Although out of our immediate period, it does reflect what is found in the primary sources relating to the years up until 1913. Slater introduced the book as 'one of the most interesting and useful books bearing upon the musical life of the Salvation Army that has yet been published'.[37] Its main purpose, he continued, was to interest, instruct and guide the Band Lads, who were numbering well towards 8,000. As an aside, the book was written by Noel Hope, a nom-de-plume for Sarah L. Morewood, who worked for the Army as a journalist and wrote prolifically about its work, although not herself a Salvationist.[38] Her writing deserves further investigation.

The story concerns a number of boys persuaded to start a Salvation Army Junior Band. The main characters included Ginger, Jack, the Band-Leader and the Captain.

At the first meeting Ginger expected to see 'magnificent brass instruments of all shapes and sizes [...] what he actually saw was a row or two of chairs [...] nothing save an ordinary blackboard! A blackboard, neither better nor worse than the one he had faced in school that morning'.[39] But as Jack pointed out, 'there are the notes and that to learn first' to which Ginger replied 'Notes! [...] what do we want with notes? If I play a tin whistle by ear, can't I do the same with a brass cornet?'[40] He continued, 'Band practice? Blackboard practice [...] Learn our notes! We could all do that as we go along.'[41] In time Ginger became the blackboard orderly. The band leader promised, 'If every boy puts his best work into the next two or three lessons we ought to take up our instruments at the end of the month.' The boys thought, 'Instruments! Lost in a maze of notes, note-values, staves, rests and "time" – common and otherwise – the longed-for instruments had disappeared from view.'[42]

The Captain talked to them:

> First of all, boys, I want you to try and realize what a big thing you are taking up when you join an Army Young People's Band. Music is a wide subject [...] But you are launching out on something much wider than

[36] *Bandsman Songster and Local Officer*, 16 June 1910, p. 6.

[37] N. Hope, *Crotchets and Quavers, or The Making of the Brixwell Young People's Band* (London, 1921), p. v.

[38] C. Baird, *Noel Hope (Sarah L. Morewood)* (London, 1944).

[39] Hope, *Crotchets and Quavers*, p. 30.

[40] Ibid., pp. 30–1.

[41] Ibid., p. 37.

[42] Ibid., p. 57.

music [...] you are being trained for the biggest campaign of all – the world-wide battle between right and wrong, God and the Evil One [...] Scales and exercises are dull work, but they are all steps in the ladder, and you want to climb to the top [...] Other bands aim to make me feel jolly [...] sad [...] brave or patriotic [...] Our bands have only one object – they aim to make men better to stir them up to seek God, to encourage them to come to Him. Angels might be glad of the opportunities of an Army Band.[43]

So the boys progressed from 'open notes' to the 'use of the valves' and so to the 'full compass' of the various instruments. Exercises, intervals, scales, united scales followed each other in orderly succession: 'What a thrill went through everyone when the Band Leader announced that the Band was to make its first attempt at a tune!'[44] After the commissioning of the Band the Captain visited an old man:

Captain, I want you to thank your boys for the music they played last Sunday. I lay here a-listening and it seemed to lift me quite up, it did. I didn't feel a morsel of pain just then. I was helped nearer Heaven.[45]

As well as focusing upon young people's musical needs, there also had to be an equal emphasis upon adult learners. Some of those who became bandsmen in the Army in the early days were illiterate. Bradley cites the case of some bandsmen in South Shields whose band cards identified the names of tunes by pictures, so that 'Out on the ocean sailing' was represented by a sailing ship, and 'Oh to be over yonder' by a picture of an old man creeping towards his arm chair.[46]

The task of teaching such men could be challenging. A couple of articles were written by Arthur Goldsmith in March 1908, headed 'The Blackboard in the Classroom', which dealt with teaching adults, and with the superiority of the blackboard as a teaching aid.[47] At the head of the first page is a picture of the men gathered intently around the blackboard. There was initial resistance to the idea of the blackboard, reminiscent as it was of school. But progress is made:

We give below an illustration of a class of band recruits obtaining an introduction into the mysteries of the rudiments of music [...] Judging from the dress of the majority – we should say all the men are employed during the day in hard, laborious work [...] Look at these men. With what eagerness they are following the movements of their instructor the deputy bandmaster. They have watched him as he has drawn the lines of the stave [...]

---

[43] Ibid., pp. 69–70.

[44] Ibid., p. 120.

[45] Ibid., p. 172.

[46] Bradley, 'Blowing for the Lord', p. 195.

[47] A. Goldsmith, 'The Blackboard in the Classroom', *Bandsman and Songster*, 21 Mar. 1908, pp. 1, 4; 28 Mar. 1908, pp. 4, 7.

then that curly thing which they saw the Deputy make [...] Then the other signs, sharp, flat and natural [...] the whole thing became alive to them. Likely enough some of the more enthusiastic [...] on reaching home would get a piece of paper, and laboriously try to make some of the characters which they had seen during the evening. So they would gradually branch out.[48]

It was important in such lessons to stipulate that there must be absolute silence, and that any questions should be reserved for a certain time devoted to clearing up any difficulties that might arise. A recommended strategy was to draw the stave on the blackboard, with six different kinds of notes; then after questioning, to rub out everything and get each member to write some note or stave on the board.

It appears that some basic musical knowledge was required of those who wanted to enter a band. At Marylebone, no one was allowed into the band until they had knowledge of the seven scales, and had mastered their instruments.[49] This grounding in theory, which would include some instrumental instruction, was generally reckoned to take six months.

At Luton Temple considerable headway had been made. Bandmaster Powell, first and foremost, endeavoured to get the right priorities in place: God's honour first, music second. A special night was set apart for beginner tuition. Before the learners attended their first practice they were supplied with Slater's *First Lessons in Music*. Then certain parts were taken week by week with instructions to the learners that they had to give a satisfactory rendering on the following practice night.[50]

For our final example of preliminary musical instruction we go forward to 1915 in Hoxton, where women songsters were keen to be given a place in the band, in order to replace serving soldiers. Only one of the 17 women could read music. The corps officer promised that if they would stick to it, he would have them out playing hymn tunes in three months. The blackboard was brought into requisition with its minims and crotchets, and then came the instruments! For a period the harmony was 'distracting', but after three months and two days the women made their debut introductory festival.[51]

The experience of musical instruction coupled with an evangelical urge, was summed up well in a song sung by the bandsmen of Woolston Congress Hall, composed by their Bandmaster:[52]

[48] Ibid., p. 1.

[49] *Local Officer* 4 (1900–1), p. 308.

[50] *Bandsman Songster and Local Officer*, 11 Sept. 1909, pp. 1, 4.

[51] Ibid., 6 Nov. 1915, pp. 709–10.

[52] *Local Officer* 4 (1900–1), p. 268.

We started first with doubt and fear,
And thought we ne'er could play
Such sweet melodious harmony
As you can hear today.
But, bless the Lord! He's pulled us through,
He's led us up till now;
Down at His feet we've laid our all:
With grace He doth endow.

(Chorus) Our Bandsmen pray as well as play,
Turn out to Open-Air,
They tell the people Jesus died:
He'll save them, they declare!

Once newcomers arrived in a band, they might be fortunate to find that their band practices could, at their best, be educational encounters. At Norland Castle in West London, the band rehearsals, which lasted 8.30–10.45 p.m., followed a distinctive pattern, what the Bandmaster called the First, Second and Third Reading of the Bill.[53] The first was for mastering the notes, the second aimed to put the whole of the parts together with particular regard to expression and tempo. Another piece was then attempted, then the band went back for the third reading; 'as a rule I say there will be a penalty upon any man who causes a blur or makes a mistake. That puts the men keenly on alert [...] We finish with prayer.' The same bandmaster was keen to cultivate the imagination of his players, by drawing imaginary pictures or telling stories about the music, because ultimately the Band shall be capable of exercising 'passion' in their renderings, and need to give no thought whatever to the mechanical action by which they do it.[54]

As for the development of more advanced performance skills the *Bandsman and Songster* regularly carried detailed critiques of band festivals by Slater and Hawkes. Here is an extract from a review by Hawkes of a performance by the Chalk Farm Band of Slater's selection, *Swiss Melodies* (BJ 514, 515):

Opening correct, but not precise on *staccato* chords. All right on the A section, but a little more rhythmic spring would however have improved it. The link in the 1st time bar is taken *p* instead of *dim* [...] *Tempo* a little slow at Letter C [...] Soprano too pecking on *staccato* notes, also too loud. Tuning wavers in accompaniment here [...] Faulty again in the *tutti* close [...] Good finish, excepting final chord, which is too abrupt.[55]

The crucial figure in all of this educational endeavour was the Bandmaster. In fact William Booth had painted a picture of 'my model Bandmaster' in which he

---

53 *Bandsman and Songster*, 22 Feb. 1908, pp. 1, 5.

54 Ibid., p. 5.

55 *Bandsman and Songster*, 25 May 1907, pp. 5–6.

asked these key individuals to 'develop the gifts of his bandsmen in the way of music [...] he should develop the singing gifts of his bandsmen [...] Then there are the Juniors [...] discover their gifts and develop them, advise them.'[56] A later listing of desirable musical attributes for a bandmaster included the ability to read and play at sight, to have knowledge of the instruments, and of elementary theory. But also he had to be able to impart knowledge, to pay attention to detail, and to have the personal qualities of patience and perseverance.[57]

A notable example of the Bandmaster as Teacher was Fred Punchard of Chalk Farm, who led a band of 50 players.[58] He had a reputation for patient and persevering teaching. A solicitor's clerk by profession, Punchard's work as Bandmaster was all-consuming. Monday night was devoted to a band meeting, Tuesday evening was given over to individual instruction 6.45–7.45 p.m., followed by a general practice for 'the less efficient men' that lasted until a late hour. On Wednesday evening he instructed the Kilburn Band, and Thursday there was a united general practice. Saturday morning at 9.30 he gave a class in music to the Young People's Legion, followed by an hour's coaching 'backward men'. He put his success down to his emphasis upon 'individual instruction'.[59]

It does appear that many of the techniques used to introduce beginners to brass instruments were common across the whole banding world. Sheila and Vic Gammon quote from an account found in the *British Bandsman* of March 1888, in which the teaching method was

> To devote one night in each week for a period of two months, to exercises written upon a blackboard to be learnt and repeated by pupils, sometimes singly and sometimes together.[60]

There was little feeling of joy in this approach, but we should recollect this was symptomatic of much schooling during this period – governed by regimentation and drill and a fairly miserable experience for children.[61] There does appear to be an established pattern in the accounts of musical instruction in this chapter, of learning rudiments and musical theory from the blackboard for a considerable time, with the learners often separated into ability groups, before contact with instruments was allowed.

Once established it is probable that few of the bandsmen would practice at home very often or for long, as most technical progress would be made when playing together.

[56] W. Booth, 'My Model Bandmaster', *Local Officer* (1897–8), p. 67.

[57] *Bandsman Songster and Local Officer*, 30 Nov. 1912, p. 755.

[58] *Local Officer* 2 (1898–9), pp. 52–3.

[59] *Local Officer* 1 (1897–8), pp. 119–20.

[60] *British Bandsman*, Mar. 1888, p. 106, quoted in Gammon, 'The Musical Revolution of the Mid-Nineteenth Century', p. 145.

[61] See H. Hendrick, *Children, Childhood and English Society, 1800–1990* (Cambridge, 1997), p. 75.

Keith Swanwick, the distinguished music educator, recollected in 1988 from his own experience as a youngster in a Midlands band, that learning had been fundamentally communal in which the skills of observation, listening, trial and error, together with frequent rehearsal became the keys to success. Swanwick suspected that such learning methods persisted in the Salvation Army.[62]

EXAMINATIONS AND COMPETITIONS

As part of his educational mission Slater instituted a system of examinations and competitions principally for bandmasters and budding composers and arrangers. By November 1904 he was proposing a set of examinations for Bandmasters with three sets of certificates (RSd, v. 9, 11 Nov. 1904). A formal series of examinations in music was established in the following year in order to strengthen instruction. The candidates had to answer ten questions on Salvation Army regulations and a further ten on musical topics. Slater noted that he was kept busy marking 380 examination papers in all (RSd, v. 2, 3 Apr. 1905). The examinations took place in various centres. There was an entrance fee; the examination was observed by the Corps Officer; and a cup of tea was provided between the sittings. The different classes included Elementary and Intermediate Rudiments, and Elementary and Intermediate Harmony.[63] After the 1908 examination Slater provided a commentary:

> In harmony study [...] the nature of intervals and the matters relating to consecutives were the causes of numerous stumbles. Many seemed to be lacking the idea that each scale, both in harmony as well as melody, is a self-contained system [...] As to Italian terms in music, a good number of errors were made, for which there is no justification.[64]

These examinations in turn were supported by encouraging the development of libraries for the use of Salvation Army bandsmen.[65] The list of recommended texts is impressive in scope: Croger's *Notes on Conducting* (1903), Crowest's *The Story of Music* (1902), Lussy's *Musical Expression* (1892), Parry's *Summary of Music History* (1893), Peterson's *Catechism of Music* (1900), Prout's *Harmony* (1889), and Slater's *First Lessons* series (1906 onwards).

As we have already noted, whilst the secular banding community thrived (and still thrives) on a system of competitive performance contests and championships,[66] the Salvation Army would have none of it. However, there were a number of non-performance competitions that were allowed and

---

[62] K. Swanwick, *Music, Mind and Education* (London, 1988), p. 128.

[63] *Bandsman and Songster*, 4 May 1907, p. 8.

[64] Ibid., 27 Mar. 1909, p. 12.

[65] Ibid., 11 Aug. 1909, p. 4.

[66] See Newsome, *Brass Roots*, chap. 3; R. Newsome, *The Modern Brass Band: From the 1930s to the New Millennium* (Aldershot, 2006), chaps. 5, 10.

encouraged. Slater came to believe that a regular series of compositional competitions could encourage musical self-improvement amongst the Army's musicians.[67] They would also boost the repertoire of published material, as the prize-winners' entries were published in the *Band Journal*. An early example of such a competition was the Original Tune Competition in 1900, which attracted 32 entries, with the majority of writers being new to composition.[68] Two tunes were accepted as the winners with prizes of five shillings awarded to both composers. There was a brief critique of the overall quality in the *Local Officer* periodical:

> Several writers show independence of musical thought, while others only give reflections of memories of well-known tunes. Many fail on the ground of rhythm. They do not provide fitting accents in their music to match those of the song. Most writers, however, have put down their melodies correctly, and that is a real sign of considerable musical progress.[69]

In 1909 a competition for scoring for band attracted 74 entries, which were then placed in three classes, in addition to a disqualification for non-compliance with conditions.[70] In the same year it was reported that the winner of the March Competition was Bandsman Coles. He was congratulated for his melodious writing, but more critically there were limited harmonic resources, and the countermelody line was worked at too much.[71] As we shall see, Bramwell Coles was later to succeed Slater as head of the Army's Musical Department.[72]

But at times in his diary Slater confided his disappointment with the fruits of such competitions. In 1905 he was invited by the Bandmaster of the Staff Band to hear the marches that had been sent in:

> It was to me one of the most painful experiences in music I have ever had, and I left the room depressed in mind and exhausted in body from the effects of what I had listened to. (RSd, v. 2, 23 Aug. 1905)

By 1909 he thought the music submitted for the Musical Selection Competition was 'on the whole, a decline on former efforts, remarkably lacking in inventive power, poor in form, all being like one long medley just broken off at sections, so little distinction of arrangement or character was shown' (RSd, v. 11, 29 Dec. 1909). But the situation was that if competitions were dropped, there should be something done by the Salvation Army to train its composers and arrangers for the future. Even so, he asked rhetorically, 'is not the power to create, a very rare commodity?' (RSd, v. 11, 29 Dec. 1909)

---

[67] *Bandsman and Songster*, 13 Feb. 1909, p. 8.

[68] *Local Officer* 3 (1899–1900), p. 424.

[69] Ibid.

[70] Ibid., p. 4.

[71] *Bandsman Songster and Local Officer*, 23 Jan. 1909, p. 7.

[72] See W. Court, *'In the Firing Line': A Biography of Colonel Bramwell Coles* (Vancouver, 2006).

In relation to developing the skills of composers and arrangers, Slater conducted correspondence with several of them, providing forthright advice. For example, one novice composer expressed annoyance that his first published march had appeared in the band journal with the note 'revised by the Editor'. Slater sent a long detailed letter, pointing out in no uncertain terms that he had had to spend five whole days making corrections to the score, specifically to matters of notation and harmony:

> I think it will be wise of you to accept my word as true when I say your copies reveal such haste, carelessness and inaccuracies as to make it very necessary to revise them fit for use [...] Do not be deluded by the praise or flattery of those who cannot take what are the actual facts in your pieces [...] You have evidently over rated your music, your attainments, your degree of progress and may have been hurt by the praises of those not able to judge your work. Get more humility, love truth more, and praise less. By God's help place your claims on solid work and let His will and plan rule in all things. (RSd, v. 11, 4 Nov. 1909)

Slater concluded with some words of advice:

> You must not think you can find a short cut to a place as a good Band composer. You should master Prout's *Harmony*, and long and hard work it will be, but I can tell you of no easy way to success. (RSd, v. 11, 24 Nov. 1909)

To return to examinations and competitions; through them Slater provided a means by which Salvationist musicians, many of them unschooled in any formal sense, could improve and consolidate their musical skills. They provided, in spite of Slater's pessimism, the foundation for a thriving school of Salvationist composers and arrangers.

☙ Salvationist Musicians 'in the Making'

In this section I shall present the educational life stories of four musicians: Charles Green who became a bandmaster through the rank and file; George Marshall, a highly respected Salvationist composer and bandmaster; Oliver Cooke, a songster leader and prolific composer of Army songs; and Henry Hall who later gained a reputation as one of Great Britain's best known dance-band leaders. My intention is to demonstrate something of the variety of educational experiences that Salvationist musicians encountered.

An unusually detailed autobiographical sketch of 'a bandsman in the making' was provided by Charles Green.[73] His account is of a musical rather than a spiritual journey. Although he believed he had been born with musical gifts, he took a thorough dislike to music because of his experience in school:

---

[73] C. Green, 'A Bandsman in the Making', *Bandsman and Songster*, 4 Jan. 1908, p. 6.

I had been in the habit of singing in any key, but the school teacher insisted on our regulating our vocal organs to scientific movements, and endeavoured to make them vibrate to the equal tempered scale; but I chose the wrong method, and as a consequence I was generally, with a few others, kept back for about half an hour on music-lesson days.

Eventually the music teacher concluded it was best to abandon both teaching him music and punishing him.

Green went to work for a Scotsman, who loved piping his Scotch reels, strathspeys and jigs. After this Green was keen to learn a musical instrument, and discovered that some bands supplied instruments free. He was given a tenor horn, and taught himself. A month later the band was coming out in new uniforms, and Green was invited to make up the numbers on the march, but he was enjoined not to blow too hard, and in fact he limited himself to playing middle G.

He had to deal with discouragement:

When I was learning the slide trombone, the next door neighbours would thump the wall with all their might every time I started practising [...] By persistently practising I made such progress that instead of the old lady next door being opposed, she began quite to enjoy my practice, and would remark how heavenly it sounded to hear me playing well-known hymns whilst other boys would be roaming the streets up to all sorts of mischief.

From that date he advanced rapidly, and eventually became bandmaster of a Salvation Army band of 40 players.

My second representative Salvationist musician is Oliver Cooke, who wrote his autobiography in 15 parts, which was published weekly in the *Bandsman and Songster* under the title 'A Songster's Evolution'.[74] His story tells of the diversity of musical styles and contexts he encountered. He was born in 1873 between Oxford and Abingdon. His father was a miner and a church goer, but was also the life and soul of the village inn:

It was my father's usual practice every day to adjourn to the inn and there sang the songs, comic and sentimental, which had been in vogue in London some ten or fifteen years previously.[75]

His father, however, became a 'backslider', and started to drink. He encouraged Oliver to sing the songs he had taught him. In return the publican supplied the father with free drink. At the same time the boy was put under a music teacher to have his voice trained. He subsequently became a choir boy, but he was also a member of a minstrel troupe, with his face blackened. Poignantly Cooke remembered singing the last verse of 'The Sailor's Grave' in the pub, when his mother

[74] O. Cooke, 'A Songster's Evolution', *Bandsman and Songster*, 1913, in 15 parts.

[75] Ibid., 8 Feb. 1913, p. 95.

entered with his baby sister in her arms. She said to her husband 'You're ruining the boy – take the girl as well', and immediately left the room.[76] As a result the husband never entered a pub again. The family joined the Salvation Army. Oliver started to have some songs published in the *War Cry*. By this time he had started working in a printing office in the City. The firm printed weekly hymn-sheets and music for St Paul's Cathedral, and Cooke had to take the proofs to the house of the organist, John Stainer, every Friday. One day he accompanied Stainer to St Paul's and stood by him while Stainer played the voluntary: 'I thought I was in heaven.'[77]

But the West End lights fascinated Cooke. To earn money he started busking, singing some of the well-known ballads outside the theatres. He neglected the Army and started to drink. Later he toured some of the principal London clubs in a minstrel troupe, and thought seriously about going into the music-hall profession, and placed himself under the tuition of a well-known author and composer. However, he became convinced of the shallowness of music-hall folk. Eventually an Army officer saw that he was the worse for wear, and Cooke regarded this as a turning point. He attended a band practice and 'blotted out his sins in the prayer meeting'.[78] By the time he was writing his memoir he was playing baritone saxophone in the Nunhead Band in South London, and was becoming one of the Army's leading songster leaders and song writers.

One of the most highly regarded Army bandmasters and composers, George Marshall (1888–1956) of South Shields, entered the mines when he was 12 years of age, and is my third example of a Salvationist musician. His father, also a miner, had been the leader of the family choir and orchestra, and was the organist of the local Methodist chapel.[79] George was given an ancient violin when he was seven, being taught by his father. He would take a full score with him to a spot in a field nearby, and lying on the grass with the full score in front of him, he would imagine the seating of an imaginary symphony orchestra from which he would produce wonderful music. Encouraged by his mother to attend the Salvation Army, he was converted two years after entering the mines.

Marshall began to compose, and often when working at the coal face wrote down snatches of melody in chalk on the wall. He began to seriously study the rudiments of music, and then took up harmony. Significantly his music instructor refused to have anything more to do with him when he learnt that his first march was to be sent to the Salvation Army (the organist of Durham Cathedral, a friend of the instructor, also expressed disgust at this waste of a musical

---

[76] Ibid., 15 Feb. 1913, p. 111.

[77] *Bandsman Local Officer and Songster*, 8 Mar. 1913, p. 159.

[78] Ibid., 24 May 1913, p. 335.

[79] See A. R. Wiggins, *Triumph of Faith: George Marshall O.F.* (London, 1958). ('O.F.' stands for the Order of the Founder, the highest award the General of the Salvation Army can bestow upon Salvationists.)

talent). Tragically Marshall suffered a traumatic mining accident when he was 30 and never walked again. However, he went on to write over 100 compositions for the Army, and became a part-time member of the Army's Music Editorial Department.

My final educational life story is that of Henry Hall (1898–1989), who was to become a famous dance-band leader.[80] His father was a blacksmith, who later became a grocer, and then worked for the London Fire Brigade. A keen musician, he and his wife were Salvationists. Their ambition for their son Henry was that he would play in the local band. Attending elementary school, Henry won a scholarship to attend Trinity College of Music on Saturday mornings, where he learnt the piano and trumpet. With his natural ear he gained a first in the Student Teacher's Class before he was 13. When he was 14 he left school, and became a pageboy at the National Insurance Commission. Two men stimulated a renewed sense of musical enthusiasm in the teenager. The first of these was John Solomon, principal trumpet of the London Symphony Orchestra, who introduced Hall to the classics, to the Queen's Hall, and to miniature scores. The second influence was Arthur Goldsmith of the Salvation Army's Musical Department, where Hall's father had found him an opening and where he worked from 1914 and 1916 until war intervened and he went to serve in the Royal Field Artillery. His duties in the department were to copy music, to type from dictation and to proof read, all for 12s. 6d. per week. As a result 'I learned to read music as most people read their evening papers.'[81] One of his tasks was to copy the transcription for band that Arthur Goldsmith had made from parts of Handel's *Messiah* ('All we like sheep', BJ 888; 'And the glory of the Lord', BJ 905). What impressed Hall about Goldsmith was that 'he reminded me of a sparrow – the same alert vitality, the same quick precision of movement [...] he never forgot [...] that music was in the service of religion'.[82] Hall began to compose marches galore, songs and instrumental solos. His successor in the Musical Department was Eric Ball, to be the doyen of brass-band composers, whilst Henry Hall ironically succumbed to the pleasures of the music hall and became a central figure in the Golden Age of the Dance Band. The point is that whilst Henry Hall on his own admission did not have the religious motivation of the early Salvationists, the Army gave him a musical education and a code of 'morality' in music-making.[83]

It is difficult to acquire a full picture of the musical lives of Salvationist musicians during this period, and the way in which they were shaped by the musical education they received, and these four accounts should warn us away from simplistic attitudes.

---

[80] See Hall, *Here's to the Next Time*. Also see 'Henry Hall (1898–1989)', in *New Grove 2*, vol. 10, p. 700.

[81] Hall, *Here's to the Next Time*, p. 22.

[82] Ibid.

[83] Ibid., p. 24.

Whilst Charles Green's account may favour a stereotype of a working-class self-educated musician, it is countered by the relatively sophisticated musical backgrounds of George Marshall and Henry Hall, who received a good deal of formal tuition outside the Army. On the other hand, the story of Oliver Cooke illustrates the intersections and oppositions between the cultures of popular music, including minstrelsy and music hall, and the Salvation Army.

☙ *Conclusion*

Four points emerge from this chapter. First, the ideas held by Booth and Slater, about music in the service of religion, permeated the practice of musical instruction. There could be no doubt that 'music' was third in the list of priorities, after God and the Salvation Army. Second, there were undoubted links between general educational and musical thinking and practice, and Salvationist musical instruction. Sometimes this had something of a progressive nature, in the introduction of action songs and musical drills for children and young people. At other times it reflected the *status quo*, as in the seemingly universal practice of delaying any instrumental contact before rudiments and theory had been properly learnt. On the other hand, there was considerable encouragement for musicians to read the standard works relating to musical theory, harmony and history, which could then be turned to good account in the system of music examinations. Third, the encouragement of rank-and-file Salvationist musicians to compose their own music was a notable achievement, buttressed by the production of instructional materials, and musical competitions. It meant that the Army could become musically self-sufficient, and laid the ground for a future repertoire of considerable merit. Fourth, the lived educational experiences of Salvationist musicians 'in the making' provide evidence of a mixture of self-help, relationships between a diversity of musical styles ranging from the classics to minstrel troupes and music halls, influence of families and of 'outside' formal education structures.

Finally, the insights we gain through a concentration on what was taught and what was learned, illuminate common educational practice as it was actually carried out every week in band rooms and Salvation Army corps, and clarifies the relationships between the normative and the actual, which in this case are close, and appear to confirm Richard Slater's assertion that

> It is impossible to point to any other body of religious people that has anything similar to show as evidence of musical progress and development. A true Salvationist is sure to be musical.[84]

---

[84] *Musical Salvationist* 11 (1896–7), p. 36.

CHAPTER 6

Under the Colours, 1914–19: The War Years

So far I have focused upon the development of the musical life of the Salvation Army under the leadership of William Booth and Richard Slater. In this chapter I move forward to the war years in which Slater was succeeded by Frederick Hawkes and Arthur Goldsmith as joint Editors-in-Chief, in the Salvation Army's Musical Department. Bramwell Booth had meanwhile assumed leadership of the Army on the death of his father in 1912.

In my treatment of the years between 1914 and 1919, I shall identify three strands. First, the Salvation Army's great International Congress held in London in June 1914, an event which demonstrated something of the exponential musical growth of the organisation across much of the globe. Second, an analysis of the findings of a highly significant Commission of Enquiry into Salvation Army Music which met between 1915 and 1916. Third, the impact of the First World War on Salvationist musicians, both at home and abroad. Finally as a coda I shall refer to the immediate post-war situation in 1919.

❧ *The International Congress of 1914*

The International Congress planned for June 1914 promised to be the greatest and best. An article headed 'The Great Congress' appeared in the *Bandsman, Local Officer and Songster* on 9 May. There would be musical ensembles from Europe, the Americas and Asia, and no fewer than 200 bands would be present at the Crystal Palace, in addition to 4,000 voices. The London County Council had arranged that the Army would conduct music meetings on The Embankment on five days, featuring on its bandstands the International Head Quarters Staff Band, the New York Staff Band, the Canadian Staff Band, and the Chicago Staff Band. Over 50 bands were to march through London's West End to Hyde Park where the biggest Open-Air Meeting the Army had ever held would take place.[1]

What was distinctive about this congress was the extent of its international reach. A new band book published by the Salvation Army, had been prepared for the event, whose first six pages contained 30 National Anthems and Patriotic Airs, appearing for the first time, followed by a collection of popular national selections and marches that had been published in previous band journals, including: *English Melodies* (E. H. Hill, BJ 677), *Irish Melodies* (E. H. Hill, BJ 538), *Songs of Scotland* (Slater, BJ 428, 429), *Welsh Melodies* (E. H. Hill, BJ 586), *Songs of Germany* (Slater, BJ 694), *Songs of Sweden* (Slater, BJ 702), *Songs of Denmark* (Slater, BJ 661), *Finnish March* (Slater, BJ 624), *Songs of Holland* (Slater, BJ 497),

---

[1] 'The Great Congress', *Bandsman, Local Officer and Songster*, 9 May 1914, p. 297.

Songs of Italy (Slater, BJ 665), *Swiss Melodies* (Slater, BJ 543), *Japanese March* (Slater, BJ 479), *All Nations* (Slater, BJ 456, 457) and *Indian March* (Slater, BJ 529).[2]

But tragedy struck on 29 May, a month before the much anticipated opening when the *Empress of Ireland*, bringing the Canadian delegation to England for the Congress, collided with a Norwegian collier in the St Lawrence River, and sunk within 14 minutes. Of the 200 Salvationists on board, 167 were drowned. Among the survivors were but ten members of the Canadian Staff Band. The disaster cast a shadow over the Congress. Bandmaster Twitchin of the Regent Hall spoke of 'a great gap [...] caused by the sudden transition of the Canadian Staff Band to their Heavenly Orchestra'.[3]

The Congress went ahead, however. In the run up to the opening there was time to catch up on the progress of Salvation Army music-making within an international context. In an interview with William Gore, Leader of the Australian Staff Band in the *Bandsman, Local Officer and Songster* considerable detail was provided relating to the Australian banding scene.[4] There were 1710 Australian Salvationist bandsmen at present, and the National Staff Band in Melbourne had 30 members. The 36-strong Sydney Congress Hall Band received the ultimate accolade – 'ranks well with the best Army bands in England'.[5] The Adelaide Band had 44 members, whilst the band in Perth 'has been strengthened considerably by late arrivals from Britain'. More specifically the Hawthorn Band, 'brilliant in its interpretation [...] has been reinforced from Penge (England)'. There were scores of smaller bands, but it was pointed out that because of the size of the country, some may never get the opportunity to hear another band.

As far as American representation at the Congress was concerned, bands included: the Chicago Staff Band, founded eight years previously, and now instructed and conducted by William Broughton; the National Staff Band of New York, conducted by George Darby, who had originated from the Staffordshire town of Cannock; the Flint (Michigan) Band which had 33 players, and whose bandmaster hailed from Barrow-in-Furness, 'there is a strong English element in the band, and the remark is applicable more or less to the other bands mentioned'.[6] The American contingent also included the Coloured Songsters, 'thirteen coloured comrades [...] who will introduce to their fellow delegates and the general public some typical coon songs'. Their 'plantation songs' included: 'My didn't it rain', 'Keep a-moving', 'In my heart was a want to', 'Good-bye Pharaoh', 'The Yellow, Red and Blue', 'God's Heaven', and 'The Royal Telephone'.[7]

In Holland much of the activity had been inspired by a visit of the

---

[2] *Bandsman, Local Officer and Songster*, 6 June 1914, p. 368.

[3] Ibid., 4 July 1914, p. 418.

[4] Ibid., 13 June 1914, pp. 371, 380.

[5] Ibid., p. 371.

[6] Ibid., p. 387.

[7] Ibid., p. 373; 1 Aug. 1914, p. 491.

International Staff Band seven years previously. In addition to a National Staff Band, there were large bands in Utrecht, Amsterdam, the Hague and Rotterdam.[8]

At the opening of the Congress of the Nations at the Royal Albert Hall, it seemed that all the world was there, with over 2,000 delegates from 58 countries. Besides the Americans, Australians and the Dutch, bands came from Canada, Denmark, Germany, Sweden and Switzerland, and vocal groups from Finland, Italy, Norway and Sweden. The opening was followed on 'Salvation Saturday' with a procession to Hyde Park, including 65 bands.[9] A daily newspaper was quoted in the Salvationist press, 'London has never seen, apart from the great State spectacles, a procession more exciting and brilliant.'[10] The *Bandsman, Local Officer and Songster* reporter was overcome: 'It was the finest, biggest, completist, loudest-speaking and most dazzling thing of its kind The Army had ever attempted.'[11] It took the procession nearly an hour to pass a given point, and it provided two hours of incessant music, witnessed by one million people. A particular impression was made by the American bands: 'It is the march music perhaps, of our Yankee comrades, that peculiarly attracts the ear of the outside multitude because of the crispness of its treatment.'[12]

Immense crowds gathered at the Strand Hall to hear 'British, Continental and Overseas Music in Delightful Variety'.[13] Particular interest was evoked by the German Staff Band: 'in their dark blue tunics with gold buttons and red trimmings, these comrades looked very smart and military, and their deportment as well as their music exuded the spirit and fragrance of the one Salvation Army – plus the Fatherland'.[14] The performance of the Norwegian Male Choir comprised 'a succession of weird harmonies, intricate modulations'.[15]

Most impressive was the playing of the Swedish Band ('decidedly one of the Army's best')[16] under Klaus Østby, playing his march, *The Jolly Salvationist* (BJ 717), 'full of all sorts of surprises and thrilling effects'.[17] British bandsmen were urged to listen to this band for its 'sweet tonal effects'.[18]

Bandmaster Punchard of Chalk Farm was asked to summarise his impressions of the bands from overseas which had participated in the Congress:

[8] Ibid., 27 June 1914.

[9] Wiggins, *The History of the Salvation Army*, vol. 5, p. 204.

[10] *Bandsman, Local Officer and Songster*, 20 June 1914, p. 395.

[11] Ibid.

[12] Ibid., p. 396.

[13] Ibid., 27 June 1914, p. 409.

[14] Ibid.

[15] Ibid., p. 410.

[16] Ibid., p. 409.

[17] Ibid.

[18] Ibid., p. 411.

Most of the playing differs in general style from what we are accustomed to here. One missed that breadth of playing and depth of tone which are such features with our best bands [...] With the American bands, the instruments and distribution of parts, coupled with some Sousa-like effects [...] distinguish them from the ordinary English band [...] The delightfully crisp bright playing of the Swedish band could not fail to charm anybody who has music in him [...] The German band in their gorgeous military uniforms, and the Dutch and Swiss comrades were equally effective in their own way.[19]

Under a heading 'Congress Notelets',[20] some attention was paid to Salvationist musicians from different cultures. Signalled out for praise for their harmony singing 'in which they excel' were the Army vocalists from the island of Jamaica. Other ensembles were more problematic, seeming strange and exotic:

India, Korea, Japan and South Africa all have their 'musical' sections, but it must be confessed that the European ear does not take too kindly to much of the 'harmony' [...] The interest lies in the novelty of the thing, and the congregation is always generous in its applause, however unnerving the discord [...] Instruments of unique design and producing sounds unmusical and uncanny to the European ear, but soothing and enchanting to the Oriental were included and cleverly manipulated'.[21]

What was clear from the Congress was that there existed within the Salvation Army an increasingly lively international musical movement growing in diversity, comprising 1,674 bands, 26,000 bandsmen and 13,000 songsters.[22] For the Army's official historian, Arch. R. Wiggins, the International Congress had 'consolidated the spirit of the Army's scattered regiments'.[23] Slater, Hawkes and Goldsmith had much of which to be proud.

❧ The Commission of Enquiry

The International Congress in many ways represented the high-water mark of Salvation Army music-making. It became apparent that the Army's musical tradition had become a powerful international marker of Salvationist identity. It was in this context that Bramwell Booth set up a rather remarkable Commission

---

[19] Ibid., 4 July 1914, p. 418.

[20] Ibid., 27 June 1914, p. 412.

[21] Ibid.

[22] Wiggins, *The History of the Salvation Army*, vol. 5, p. 204.

[23] Ibid., p. 300.

of Enquiry into the music of the Salvation Army.[24] The Commission consisted of ten senior officers, and was chaired by Commissioner John Carleton. Its brief was to consider how far the development of the Army's vocal and instrumental music had been of advantage, with particular reference to the salvation of the people, and the building up of 'a simple and zealous soldiery'. More specific was the need to ascertain whether or not the typical character of Salvation Army music was being maintained, and the extent to which the vocal and instrumental music now being issued was suited to the abilities of Salvationist executants. Finally there was the matter of whether or not the regulations restricting the use of music to that published by the Army were being observed or not. Set up in 1915, the Commission was charged with reporting its findings by 31 March 1916.

The Commission interviewed five groups of individuals: Musical Experts, Bandmasters, Songster Leaders, Leading Salvation Army officers, and local Corps Officers. The interviews were transcribed verbatim, and the five typescript volumes, plus the final report, were rescued from the International Headquarters in the heart of London, after the building had been bombed in the Second World War. They still bear the marks of water damage. The transcripts enable us to eavesdrop on a fascinating record of reflections on the past and hopes for the future. Whilst not discounting the contributions of the Songster Leaders and Corps Officers, in reading the transcripts it becomes apparent that much of what they say is congruent with the views of what I regard as the major contributors for the purposes of this discussion: the Musical Experts, the Bandmasters, and the Leading Officers. I shall consider each of these groups in turn. This is, to my knowledge, the fullest account of the Commission to appear.

THE MUSICAL EXPERTS

The Musical Experts called by the Commission included the main members of the Musical Department, namely Richard Slater, Frederick Hawkes, Arthur Goldsmith, and Henry Hill, who was the Band Inspector.[25] Their responses may be grouped as follows: the merit of musical submissions to the department,

---

[24] 'Commission of Enquiry into matters relating to Salvation Army Music, 1915–16', 6 vols including the final report (typescript, The Salvation Army International Heritage Centre).

[25] The evidence for the sections on Musical Experts, Bandmasters, and Leading Salvation Army Officers comes from the interviews contained in the unpublished proceedings of the Commission. Each category of interviewees (Musical Experts etc.) and their evidence is allocated a separate volume. For ease of reference I include the interview dates of the individuals involved. The 'Musical Experts' were interviewed as follows: Brigadier Slater, Sitting No. 12, 27 Jan. 1916, pp. 2–33; Major Hawkes, Sitting No. 12, 27 Jan. 1916, pp. 34–62; Major Goldsmith, Sitting No. 12, 27 Jan. 1916, pp. 63–91; Band Inspector Hill, Sitting No. 1, 28 Oct. 1915, pp. 92–109.

whether Salvationist music should be developed or simplified, the place and standard of singing, and the use of 'outside' music, which might also include the use of music by 'the Great Masters'.

In answering the questions concerning the merit of the musical material the Musical Department received, Slater pointed out that he had wanted to 'lift' the music to a broader and higher platform, not to restrict it unduly to 'the Music Hall run'. But his department had been at the mercy of what was received. He frequently wrote down the melodies that individuals had in their heads but could not put down on paper. In this way a constituency of contributors was formed. Slater put it like this:

> It has been one of the most wonderful things of my life-time to find the vigorous capacity of Salvationists, who have had no musical training whatever; some of the very best writers, who have written the songs that have done the most good, have had no musical education. It was natural inborn talent.[26]

However, the supply had decreased in recent years because the Musical Board (Slater's *bête noir*) had insisted on too high a standard for beginner writers. But it was Slater's priority that 'we cultivate the beginner and be more interested in him than in the old-stager in the business'.[27] The other point made was that the early song-maker had been superseded by the instrumental arranger and composer who worked merely from the standpoint of bands.

Hawkes made several of the same points, but indicated that the amount of vocal compositions received far outweighed in number the supply of instrumental works. He pointed to 'the astonishing number' of Salvationist musicians making a study of harmony. Training and tuition was essential, but 'it will be a big task'.[28] It was Goldsmith's frank opinion that the musical merit of what was contributed was not great, and that the musical competitions had not really created any new writers, apart from Bramwell Coles.

It became clear in their responses that it had been they, the members of the Musical Department, who had pushed through the main musical developments of the preceding ten years. The Commission probed the Musical Experts' views on whether Salvationist music should be further developed or simplified. It was a matter of regret for Slater that in his opinion seven out of ten Salvationists would prefer a march to a selection; indeed, 'the contrasts and the higher workings of the music in the selection are beyond and above the heads of the average S.A audience'.[29] However, the present-day Salvationist was now better educated than in the past, and so required a 'higher type' of music than his forebears, but the

---

[26] Musical Experts' evidence: Slater, p. 5.

[27] Ibid., p. 6.

[28] Hawkes, p. 39.

[29] Slater, p. 7.

danger lay in losing the vigorous style of the early Army for the sake of greater sophistication. There was a need to embrace both sorts. The dilemma was that with 20,000 Salvationist bandsmen, it was necessary to keep them in a healthy progressive state. Their musical needs had to be taken into account, but to give them merely what they wanted, Slater believed, 'is bringing a very disturbing and revolutionary element into S.A. musical life'.[30]

The questioning then turned to ways in which these Musical Experts solved this dilemma in their own compositions. For example, one of the restrictions was that selections should conform to the five-minute rule. Slater was adamant this represented no difficulty whatever. He was severely practical: to expect a home-grown Salvationist musician to maintain a piece for 15 minutes with high musical interest was 'beyond the possibilities'.[31]

Hawkes was less sure, in that such a rule precluded the development of an idea. For instance there had to be an element of contrast in a piece, but often this had to be cut out in the interests of brevity. Goldsmith expressed some frustration from his own experience:

> I have just written a selection which I consider ought to take four minutes and 23 seconds. In setting out that piece of music, I have wanted to use continuity of idea, and to do that, I have wanted to put in four pieces – 'Jesus is looking for thee', 'Are you coming home tonight?', 'Art thou weary?', and 'There is life for a look'. I find, since I got on to it, that the first one was so long that I would have to cut something out, and so I have taken the one out which I thought would make the crux of the thing, to bring it within five minutes, but my musical idea has been rather flattened by it.[32]

The Commission then went on to ask about technical detail. It wondered whether or not instrumental cadenzas were really necessary, as clearly there was some concern about the opportunities available for unnecessary display connected with them. Slater's response was that almost their sole value was educational, to encourage the average bandsman to push forward his skill, but the music would not suffer if the cadenza was omitted. For Hawkes the cadenza was a compositional device for bridging over one movement to the next, often introducing a change of key, although he agreed it was not a necessity. It was Goldsmith's opinion that if used sparingly a cadenza could convey a considerable amount of sentiment and a certain amount of spiritual influence.

More fundamental was the questioning on the use of counterpoint. The following question was posed by the Commission: 'What is your judgement as to the wisdom of elaboration in part writing? Admitting this is more

---

[30] Ibid., p. 8.

[31] Ibid., p. 7.

[32] Goldsmith, p. 90.

interesting to the performer, is it helpful to the spiritual effect of the sum total in performance?'[33]

For Slater, counterpoint was life to the musician, but to the listener it could cause confusion because it obscured the melody. He was therefore against the over-elaboration of counterpoint. On the one hand counterpoint was able to intensify and enrich the emotional side of the music, but only if it was able to be kept under control by the performers: 'By giving the Bands this kind of music, you give them a razor that they can cut themselves with.'[34] Goldsmith sided with Slater. Enough progress had been made in this direction, and indeed he was endeavouring to achieve a simpler style. Like Slater he was aware that greater musical complexity could be counter-productive: 'The efforts of some poor fellows to negotiate the part writing will be anything but spiritual'.[35]

Hawkes agreed that elaboration was of little value as a thing in itself, but if it was made an integral part of a piece it had merit. Moreover, it challenged instrumentalists, particularly euphonium players, who were generally the most skilful of band musicians.

It was Goldsmith who was frank with the Commission about the ability of the Army's Musical Experts to meet increasing demands for musical complexity:

> We are not trained musicians; we are men who have absolutely trained ourselves; we have had to come up through the Army, and therefore our point of difficulty is very little in advance of the general point of difficulty of the whole Army; we are not very far in front. Perhaps Brigadier Slater, who is a trained musician [...] could easily supply the demand, but personally [...] I think we are certainly limited as to the degree of difficulty of execution that we could put up.[36]

The increasing complexity of Army music prompted the members of the Commission to ask whether or not bands should be graded as to the difficulty of music they should be allowed to play. Slater was in favour:

> The Bands that are on the top, that can play to any crowd, including the rich educated crowd, that Band should be allowed to hold its position, and gain respect for the Army, but to allow the little Band, with only half the instruments, to play the same music as the big Band, and to 'murder' it every time is ruinous to our concern [...] It is insane where any Band can play any piece without any control.[37]

---

33 Question to Musical Experts, in Slater, p. 9.

34 Musical Experts' evidence: Slater p. 9.

35 Goldsmith, p. 73.

36 Ibid., p. 67.

37 Slater, p. 14.

Goldsmith disagreed. He was in favour of simplifying the music supplied to bands, for he believed that the less able bands should be given the same opportunities as the better bands, rather than be forbidden to tackle the harder music.

When it came to the question of the place and standard of singing within the Salvation Army, there was a consensus amongst the Musical Experts that it had deteriorated. In part this was because bands played too loudly, and singers felt somewhat inferior in musicianship to the instrumentalists. Slater felt that a number of people were of the opinion that 'it is no use us singing; what is our chuckle compared with the playing of the Band?'[38] He also bemoaned the lack of vocal soloists in Army meetings. Goldsmith agreed: singing had decreased in time with the overall improvement in musical skills evident in banding. With the rise of bands, composers were particularly keen to hear their pieces in this medium.

Finally there was the perennial concern about the boundaries between 'outside' and Army music. Hawkes was in favour of incorporating into the Army repertoire such popular oratorio movements as 'The Hallelujah Chorus' from *Messiah* and 'The Heavens are Telling' from Haydn's *Creation*. Somewhat surprisingly considering his background and interests, Slater declared himself opposed to the use of classical religious items, and songs like 'The Holy City' (Stephen Adams), and 'Nazareth' (Alfred Gaul):

> I cannot understand any material religious purpose that can be served by pieces of that type, nor how the S.A. need can be met by pieces of that character; it is lovely music, but it will not minister, in my belief, to the needs of the S.A.[39]

More generally, Slater was dead set against anything that did not minister to direct religious influence, such as pianoforte, cornet or trombone solos with variations. He admitted to a conservatism in this respect, but 'the music of the Army must not be prostituted to the purposes of the concert'.[40] Hawkes was more open to cornet solos, but was against the compositional form of air and variations which encouraged the exhibiting of skill in performance.

Slater was in full agreement with the prohibition of using music from 'outside' its ranks: 'My conviction is that it is suicidal to open the door to anything that comes from outside; let the Army aim to be self-supplying and self-satisfying; let the Army believe in the capacity of its own powers to meet its own wants.'[41]

---

38 Ibid., p. 8.
39 Ibid., p. 24.
40 Ibid., p. 28.
41 Ibid., p. 26.

THE BANDMASTERS

The Commission took evidence from eight leading bandmasters.[42] Divisional Bandmaster Brand of Tottenham had led three bands since becoming a Salvationist. Bandmaster Saunders of Staines had started a band soon after his conversion; there were 22 players in his current band, but the membership was suffering from enlistments on war service. Bandmaster Punchard of Chalk Farm was in many ways a legendary figure; he had fashioned Chalk Farm into one of the premier bands of the Salvation Army. In normal times there were 50 bandsmen. Bandmaster Morris of Blackpool Citadel had, before the war, a band of 32 members. Bandmaster Tomlinson of the Yorkshire village of Dinnington represented a smaller community than the rest, and his band was usually 25 strong. Like Punchard of Chalk Farm, Bandmaster Twitchin of the Regent Hall was a household name; his band had a pre-war membership of 48 players. Finally Bandmaster Simmons of Portsmouth led a band of 42 players, a high number in war years, explained by the fact that as his men worked in the dockyards they were not allowed to enlist.

The following themes emerged from the interviews held by the Commission: the suitability or otherwise of Salvation Army music for bands; the functions of bands in their two high-profile weekly duties – playing on the march, and playing in the Sunday evening Salvation meeting; the question of whether Salvation Army music should be exclusive or not. I have previously discussed the evidence concerning the musical participation of bands and bandsmen in Chapter 4.

When asked about the suitability of Army music for their bands, there was considerable criticism. Punchard thought some of the marches were obviously the work of amateurs. He cited *The Luton March* (C. J. Greig, BJ 744):

> You will find a little bit of this and that March mixed up in it […] then we are sailing up into the sky and there is no advantage in it.[43]

As for selections, some were too long, the maximum time should be five minutes. He often chopped such selections in half for performance.

For Morris, the main contention was that the music was too difficult for the average band. What was wanted was music that was both simple and effective. Instead there were 'a lot of awkward intervals and high notes that we cannot

---

[42] Bandmasters' interviews: Divisional Bandmaster Brand, Tottenham, Sitting No. 1, 28 Oct. 1915, pp. 1–18; Bandmaster Saunders, Staines, Sitting No. 1, 28 Oct. 1915, pp. 19–34; Bandmaster Punchard, Chalk Farm, Sitting No. 2, 4 Nov. 1915, pp. 35–56; Bandmaster Morris, Blackpool, Sitting No. 2, 4 Nov. 1915, pp. 57–73; Bandmaster Lee, Warrington, Sitting No. 3, 11 Nov. 1915, pp. 74–94; Bandmaster Tomlinson, Dinnington, Sitting No. 3, 11 Nov. 1915, pp. 95–109; Bandmaster Twitchin, Regent Hall, Sitting No. 4, 18 Nov. 1915, pp. 110–31; Bandmaster Simmons, Portsmouth, Sitting No. 4, 18 Nov. 1915, pp. 132–45.

[43] Bandmaster's evidence: Punchard, p. 39.

touch'.[44] He believed that much of the music published was written for certain bands that were well equipped with able players, but the smaller combinations were overlooked.

Twitchin took a different view. At the Regent Hall he had to deal with 'the educated public'. For example, some might have attended an orchestral concert at the Queen's Hall. He rejected the idea that selections should be of a simple character, and last for only five minutes. There was scope for more elaborate treatments: 'why should not that be just as much conducive to the Salvation of the people as the brilliant flight of oratory that we always get nowadays?'[45] In his opinion, Slater's *Bible Pictures* had failed because 'how can you treat a subject like *Stilling the Storm* (BJ 601) in a selection that lasts only four or five minutes? The preacher could not treat the subject in four hours properly'.[46]

Simmons held a similar view about Slater's piece (although 'it is a very beautiful piece of music indeed'),[47] but believed that a return to simpler and plainer musical styles would cause deterioration in the bands and a lack of interest from the congregations in the music.

As far as the week-by-week work of bands was concerned, marches were obviously a popular feature. For Brand, they drew in the crowd. Many of them incorporated a hymn, and so 'must certainly awake Salvation thoughts'.[48] Simmons agreed. In Portsmouth the good lively Salvation Army march was often the only bit of religion the men got: it made them think. Twitchin felt similarly: a march could stir the emotions, and if the band was good would draw people into the hall.

Bands in the big centres often attracted 'camp followers' who attended the marches as bystanders, often in their hundreds. Twitchin supplied considerable detail in his reply to the Commission:

> I think we have got rather a large following of men at Regent Hall; they come miles to hear the Band. I can give you the distances they come; three come from Poplar every Sunday; four from Streatham; a batch of six come from round about Wandsworth and Clapham Junction way, and five come over from Wimbledon about every other Sunday. These men form themselves into a kind of body or followers of the Band, and they are, I must say, largely on my heart because they follow the Band, and there have only been one or two instances of conversion amongst them during the last two years.[49]

44 Morris, p. 63.

45 Twitchin, p. 118.

46 Ibid.

47 Simmons, p. 137.

48 Brand, p. 12.

49 Twitchin, pp. 129–30.

It was a similar story in Portsmouth, to the extent that a sergeant and five policemen were required to keep order. After the march the followers would line up both sides of the roadway outside the hall, and the band would march through them. Several of the followers would enter the hall.[50]

As for the Sunday night Salvation meeting, Brand provided a brief outline of its structure: 'Opening song; song by Songsters directly after prayers, and, generally speaking, a testimony, sometimes two speakers; the collection during which the Band plays, then the bible-reading'.[51] After the bible reading there would be the address and final song, which would then lead into the prayer meeting. Whether or not the collection was the best place for the band's solo contribution was a subject of concern amongst the bandmasters. Tomlinson maintained that playing after the collection had been taken was preferable:

> I do not think people give attention to the music while the offering is being taken up. I do not think it is fair to the men, who spend time in practising, to play when the people are not giving attention.[52]

Twitchin recounted how sometimes there was pressure from the officer in charge of a corps to make sure that the performance of the band's musical selection did not take too long a time in the Sunday evening meeting:

> About 15 months ago, I was asked by one of my Bandsmen who had just enlisted if we could play a selection called 'My Guide' [Goldsmith, BJ 676] that evening, as he wanted to take it away with him in his mind, and he wanted to feel that, if he did get into the trenches, he would have Christ as his Guide, and so on, and that the playing of the selection would help him. I said 'Yes' and we played it.[53]

It happened to last a couple of minutes longer than most selections, and this led the officer to complain, 'Fancy putting on a selection like that on a Sunday Night that takes so long.' Twitchin informed the Commission that the officer had himself preached for an hour in the same meeting. For him the band selection was entitled to the same respect as the address.

There were mixed feelings about whether Salvation Army music should be exclusive or not. Whilst Brand and Saunders were against music coming in from the 'outside', Morris, however, felt that if there was something of spiritual value in such music, it should be shared. Twitchin pointed out the dangers of keeping the door shut:

> I think we have lost many Bandsmen because we could not provide for anything in the way of advance in musical education, in the way of

[50] Simmons, p. 144.

[51] Brand, p. 9.

[52] Tomlinson, p. 100.

[53] Twitchin, p. 113.

solo-singing and playing [...] and pianoforte playing; the opportunity has not been given them; their talents have been cramped.[54]

This raised the question of whether or not music from 'The Great Masters' should be incorporated into the Salvationist repertoire. 'The Hallelujah Chorus' was provided as an example. Punchard was enthusiastic. It would appeal, and would improve the playing of bands. He felt such music could be appropriately played by two-thirds of Army bands. He listed some more possibilities: Haydn's 'When I think upon thy goodness', excerpts from Handel's *Joshua*, the euphonium solo from *Jephtha* 'Angels from the sky' ['Waft her angels through the skies'], and 'Lord incline thine ear'.[55] Morris also welcomed such a development, but there would have to be restrictions on which bands played such repertoire. It could amount to sacrilege for small bands to tackle such works.

THE CHIEF SECRETARY AND LEADING OFFICERS

A different perspective on the Army's music was provided by five leading officers called by the Commission. They all had either national or regional oversight of the evangelistic work of the Salvation Army. They were Colonel Wilson (Chief Secretary), Brigadier Rich (South London), Brigadier Langdon (Liverpool), Lt. Colonel King (Southampton), Brigadier Brown (West London).[56]

Their interviews disclose some of the tensions between Leading Officers and Salvationist musicians. Sometimes the criticism of bands and bandsmen was harsh. Wilson thought the Salvationism of bandsmen was spasmodic. The selections they played could take ten minutes, and whilst its purpose should be 'To get at the hearts of the people, instead of that it is like artillery followed by an Infantry Regiment'.[57] The people start to lose interest and 'you have to lift them up again'. He was in favour of abolishing the playing of selections in the Sunday night meetings. Brown agreed: 'these lengthy band selections I think very often cut out the good feeling of the meeting'.[58]

When asked whether or not bands increased Sunday attendance, Rich answered as follows:

54 Ibid., p. 126.

55 Punchard, p. 50.

56 Leading Officers' interviews: Colonel Wilson, Chief Secretary, 3 Feb. 1916. [No sitting specified], pp. 2–19; Brigadier Rich, Divisional Commander, South London, Sitting No. 10, 13 Jan. 1916, pp. 20–41; Brigadier Langdon, Divisional Commander, Liverpool, Sitting No. 10, 13 Jan. 1916, pp. 42–59; Lt. Colonel King, Divisional Commander, Southampton, Sitting No. 11, 20 Jan. 1916, pp. 60–84; Brigadier John Brown, Divisional Commander, West London, Sitting No. 11, 20 Jan. 1916, pp. 85–107.

57 Leading Officers' evidence: Wilson, p. 8.

58 Brown, p. 93.

I think perhaps it may be a draw to some, but, on the other hand, others are kept away by the Bands; people who are nervy and that sort of thing; it makes too much noise for them [...] some of our Bands are over-powering as you know.[59]

Whilst King admitted that much progress had been made, he thought the music could well be simplified, as at present it did not help from a Salvationist standpoint. He understood, however, that bands looked upon the Sunday night meeting as their only chance of 'performing' so it was not surprising that they should 'do a little bit of swagger'.[60] It was Rich who understood the difficulty in achieving the necessary balance that had to be struck between the spiritual and the musical:

> The tendency, you see, especially amongst the younger members of the Band, seeing the class of music they have had of recent years, is to make them musicians or professionalists [sic] [...] The difficulty is, if you get a young fellow in a Band, who is able to do the top things, and the Band does not play them, he leaves and goes to outside Bands, which is evidence he is a musician before he is a Salvationist.[61]

There were some views about using 'outside' music, and catering for different instrumental ensembles other than bands. Rich thought more could be provided for soloists, who frequently had to use 'outside' material such as variations on tunes like 'Home Sweet Home' which were sung to appropriate words in meetings. The orchestral band at Reading, according to Brown, had no choice but to use 'outside' music, as none was published by the Army. The regulation caused some difficulty for officers. For example, King had to stop one of his bands playing the Christmas classic 'Hail Smiling Morn' as 'it wasn't Army', although a couple of years later it was 'legalised'.

As for alternative instrumental groupings, King found that string bands were spasmodic, again because of lack of published material by the Army, and that concertina bands were dying out, whereas in Yorkshire and Lancashire 'years ago there used to be no Corps complete without its Concertina Band'.[62]

The testimony of Leading Officers was revealing when it touched upon 'wordly pleasures' in connection with the day-to-day lives of Salvationist musicians. Such problematic activities for the Army as going to the cinema, and smoking were touched upon. As far as sport was concerned, it appears that participation was limited to games played within and between Salvationists. Rich was asked whether he had any knowledge of Army football or cricket clubs with an exclu-

---

[59] Rich, p. 25.

[60] King, p. 70.

[61] Rich, p. 23.

[62] King, p. 84.

sive membership of bandsmen and soldiers. He admitted that one or two bands joined up for a friendly game of cricket:

> I have only known a couple or three Bands that do it, and I know that they play each other on Saturday afternoon [...] when it is arranged that one Band should go to a neighbouring place to play cricket with another, they take their instruments and help with their music at the meeting after the play is over.[63]

King shared with his questioners his own experience as a father of sons who felt somewhat aggrieved at the necessity of following such a narrow path which restricted playing sport in such a way.

RECOMMENDATIONS

It will be apparent that there was a diversity of views both within and between the three different groups of witnesses. I have isolated the following points as having particular significance:

> The dilemma between providing music that was simple, and of direct appeal to the rank-and-file soldiery, and music that had greater complexity, meeting the demands of increasingly sophisticated Salvationist musicians.

> The success of marches in attracting people to the Salvation Army's message, versus the suspicion of the band selection played in the Salvation meeting which was felt to be too long and above the heads of the congregation.

> The need to mark boundaries between 'inside' and 'outside', whether 'outside' classical music should be used, and whether 'outside' participation in sport should be permitted for bandsmen.

> A realisation that the standard of singing had deteriorated, compared with the musical advance of bands.

> A requirement to provide training and tuition for future composers.

Out of all the evidence the Commission produced both a report and a summary report.[64] In the report there was an extensive discussion of vocal and instrumental music. As far as Songster Brigades were concerned, although there was no problem in music speaking directly to the people through their singing, they could not be compared with Bands. There were a number of reasons, including a dearth of male voices, and the fact that female songsters had domestic duties to attend to. But bearing in mind that songster brigades

---

[63] Rich, p. 35.

[64] 'Report of the Commission of Enquiry into Matters Relating to Salvation Army Music, 23 March 1916', The Salvation Army International Heritage Centre; 'Summary of Report of the Musical Commission', in Holz, *Brass Bands of the Salvation Army*, vol. 1, pp. 115–17.

relatively speaking were of recent growth, the Commission felt that in future they could be of very great value.

When it came to instrumental music there was a hesitation:

> It has undoubtedly cheered and inspired our own people and has often brought hope, comfort, and encouragement to sad hearts; but, while it is indisputable, the evidence indicates that the music has not fulfilled expectations in reaching the hearts of the unsaved to the extent hoped for and earnestly desired.[65]

Two main causes were identified: an insufficient supply of suitable music, both in character and length, for Salvation services; the failure of the leaders of meetings to make any link with bandmasters or songster leaders with a view to a suitable selection of music. With regard to the first of these, it was recommended that a larger supply of Band Music was needed, which would be bright and devotional, with the introduction of a religious theme where possible, and not to exceed five minutes in length. But at the same time musical episodes should be used very sparingly, and the elaboration of parts for particular instruments 'should be eschewed'. There should be restraint from any ornateness, and 'fireworks' finales should be avoided. The second point was clearly the fault of the officers to link with their musical leaders in order to arrive at a suitable selection of music.

With regard to musical difficulty, the Commission thought some of the published scores were beyond the capacity of a number of musical groups. The Musical Department was to be instructed to provide simpler arrangements for smaller and inferior bands, as well as continuing to cater for the higher-grade bands. Moreover, present-day marches were too elaborate in arrangement, which made playing them on a march quite exhausting. There was also little or no message in them for the crowd. It was necessary to return to the older type of march, with the introduction of a well-known religious musical theme.

By and large the Orders and Regulations regarding the prohibition of unauthorised music were mostly being observed. A warning was given, however, against inviting outside choirs and musical societies into the Army hall: such a practice would be harmful to Salvationists, perhaps because there was a perceived danger that they might become infected by secular culture.

The Commission closed its report with a tribute to Salvation Army Bands. It had been impressed by the quality of bandmasters. There was acknowledgement that the social and fraternal spirit of unity existing between band members had not been fully appreciated. In many ways the spirit of the band affected the whole corps. Although music might be the common tie, the association with religious conviction could develop into a still closer unity:

---

[65] 'Report of Commission of Enquiry', p. 4.

If properly guided and controlled, this aspect of Band life is capable of producing a great spiritual influence, probably a more direct influence than that created by the music.[66]

As Holz points out, the final report is a remarkable and honest document and many of the recommendations made by the Commission did take hold, and influenced Army music right up until the 1930s.[67] But its negative conclusions about the impact of instrumental music 'on the hearts of the unsaved' must have been unsettling.

⁊ For King and Country

With the assassination of Archduke Ferdinand and the Austro-Hungarian declaration of war on Serbia on 28 July 1914, the ensuing World War was to result in a lost generation for Britain, with half a million men under the age of 30 perishing.[68] The memory of the recent International Congress must have made the implications of the conflict poignant and near to home for Salvationist musicians, as in this comment from the *Bandsman, Local Officer and Songster*:

> The majority of the members of the German Staff Band are now compulsorily serving in the Imperial Army at the Front. These comrades were great favourites at the recent International Congress.[69]

In this section I shall attempt to uncover something of the day-to-day work of Salvationist musicians both at home and overseas during the war years.

The Salvation Army was quick to react to the need for the provision of bands to accompany battalions marching to their local railway stations on their way to the battlefields. Whether supplied by the Salvation Army or not, bands were regarded by enlisting soldiers as essential on these occasions, as in this account regarding the departure of some recruits from a Scottish regiment:

> The Order came at 9.00 o'clock a.m. for them to depart at 1 o'clock, thus giving them only four hours notice [...] In view of giving his men a 'musical' send-off, the officer in charge of the detachment interviewed the S.A. officer in hopes of securing the S.A. Band. The S.A. officer consented and set out to find the men at their work with the news, he met with a ready response [...] The result was that when the soldiers paraded for departure

---

[66] Ibid., p. 17.

[67] See Holz, *Brass Bands of the Salvation Army*, vol. 1, pp. 115–17, where he provides details of the implementation of the Commission's recommendations.

[68] E. Hobsbawm, *The Age of Extremes: The Short Twentieth Century, 1914–1991* (London, 1994), pp. 22–35.

[69] *Bandsman, Local Officer and Songster*, 22 Aug. 1914, p. 531.

they were accompanied to the station by the S.A. Band in full uniform [...]
In addition to giving their services all the men lost half a day's wages in
order to give the troops a worthy send off. This is truly an example of self-
sacrifice on their part.[70]

This musical and religious send-off at railway stations became part of the
regular duties of Salvation Army bands throughout the country. They were inevitably highly charged emotional occasions, captured well in this report from the
Nunhead Band, in South London:

> Inside the station yard the band lines up, and as the dear fellows walked
> by with tears streaming down their faces as they looked back at the loved
> ones they were leaving, perhaps for ever, we played 'Auld Lang Syne' [...]
> Several, I noticed, tried to brush the tears aside and joined in singing
> [...] but it was only a broken-voiced effort [...] Scores as they passed us,
> murmured 'God bless you' [...] One dear fellow shouted 'Pray for us' [...]
> and needless to say we promised.[71]

In Exeter the band regularly turned out at 8.30 a.m. on Sunday mornings
to escort the soldiers to the cathedral for the service, a duty which entailed a
five-mile march.[72] As the war took its toll, Salvation Army bands played for
the returning wounded, including on one occasion visiting wounded Indian
soldiers to whom 'some of the band-lads sang Salvation Army choruses in
Hindustani'.[73]

Saying good bye to Salvationist comrades going to enlist on service 'for King
and Country' was painful. Brother Tasker of the Westminster Band declared in
his farewell testimony: 'That by the help of God he would do all he could in the
barrack room to show his true colours and would kneel at his bedside as at home
to pray'.[74] He was then dedicated to God under the Salvation Army flag, before
everyone sang 'God be with you till we meet again'.

In Cardiff, the Roath Band regularly marched to the military barrack square,

> Where in the darkness, but for the fitful light of a few lanterns, 150 men
> [...] were receiving final instructions before proceeding to their destina-
> tion. As the orders were 'snapped' out, one could only feel that somewhere
> in the blackness was one of 'ours', Bandsman Bramwell Bartlett [...] having
> enlisted for active service. The last order is given, we mark time, the drums
> beat, and away we go. A rush from the ranks and Bram is with us playing
> his euphonium. Our Corps Sergeant-Major carries his kit [...] The band
> is given a special stand on the platform where we play to a waiting crowd.

---

[70] *British Bandsman*, 4 Sept. 1915, p. 167.

[71] *Bandsman, Local Officer and Songster*, 12 Sept. 1914, p. 586.

[72] Ibid., 20 Feb. 1915.

[73] Ibid., 23 Oct. 1915, p. 678.

[74] Ibid., 2 Sept. 1914, pp. 585–6.

Here again Bram craves an indulgence, and is allowed to play his solo in the rendering of 'Old Times' [Slater BJ 613, 640, 671]. A cheer is raised for the Salvation Army band. We are already in single file along the platform, and as the train steams out we play 'Men of Harlech', and hearts of love pray that the God of grace might accompany these lithe smart lads of commerce.[75]

Sometimes there were reports from soldiers returning from the trenches. One of them, a bandsman from Bury, recollected that a few minutes before going into an engagement, he and 17 others, sang 'Abide with me'. A number of them fell, but he remained 'very bright in his soul'.[76] At a meeting in Gillingham a soldier who had returned from France asked permission to give one or two pieces on his concertina 'which had been his companion during the eight months he had been in the trenches'.[77] He used to play it when on the march to help the men forget their worries.

Gradually the columns of the *Bandsman, Local Officer and Songster* recorded those Salvationist musicians killed in action; on one occasion the column was entitled 'Christmas in Heaven'.[78] A correspondent from Bury, wrote to the magazine,

> I am sorry to report that Bandsman C. Boardman, one of our brightest and most willing members, has been killed in action at the Dardanelles [...] The Saturday night before he enlisted, he shook me by the hand and said he felt it was his duty to go. I replied 'Do what you think is right'.[79]

In the first three months of 1917, Hailstone has calculated that the death toll of Salvationist bandsmen stood at 256, including seven members of the Keighley Salvation Army Band on one day alone.[80]

As far as repertoire was concerned, clearly bands gave expression to patriotic and nationalist feeling, and indeed the new band book prepared for the International Congress conveniently fitted the bill. National anthems were a staple element. At Gillingham the patriotism of the 7,000 recruits was aroused as the band played the 'Marseillaise', 'Rule Britannia' and 'God Save the King'.[81] When the Barking Band visited the Purfleet Camp, the soldiers particularly appreciated the rendering of *English Melodies* as they persisted in singing the tunes to their own words. At the playing of the anthems of Russia, France, Belgium,

---

[75] Ibid., 10 Oct. 1914, p. 649.

[76] Ibid., 8 Jan. 1916, p. 25.

[77] Ibid., 8 Apr. 1916, p. 228.

[78] Ibid., 25 Dec. 1915, p. 817.

[79] Ibid., 11 Sept. 1915, p. 585.

[80] A. Hailstone, *The British Bandsman Centenary Book: A Social History of Brass Bands* (Baldcock, 1987), pp. 136–7.

[81] *Bandsman, Local Officer and Songster*, 26 Sept. 1914, p. 619.

Canada, Australia and Great Britain every soldier sprang to attention and gave cheers for each country.[82]

The repertoire at this time related patriotism to the militant Christian brand of the Salvation Army, so that at Lincoln, the band cheered the wounded soldiers with a mixture comprising *Soldiers of Christ* (Marshall, BJ 667), *English Melodies* (E. J. Hill, BJ 677), the 'Marseillaise' and 'Boston' and 'The Heart's Closed Door'.[83] There were occasionally 'patriotic festivals' in the citadels. For example, at Exeter 'the Band and Songsters united in giving a patriotic festival which included *Songs of Scotland* [Slater, BJ 428, 429], *Active Service* [Coles, BJ 659] *etc.* by the band; 'I love to sing of Jesus' and 'March to Victory' by the Brigade'.[84] Interestingly, the *Bandsman, Local Officer and Songster* reprinted without comment an article from the *Daily Chronicle* entitled, 'Plea for British Music: the obsession of foreign superiority',[85] which may have been inserted in order to provide some justification for the repertoire bands were choosing to play.

With 8,000 Salvationist bandsmen enlisting,[86] the bands at home were finding it difficult to survive. Fairly typical was Catford Band, much depleted, but 'still holding on'.[87] According to the *Musical Standard*, Salvation Army bands were badly affected, with nearly all the Manchester bands being broken up due to enlistment and munitions work, whilst practically all of the Chalk Farm bandsmen had joined up.[88] The *Bandsman, Local Officer and Songster* itemised for its readers the corps where women were coming to the rescue, including Hull,[89] Anderston, where nine women were filling the gap,[90] Penicuick's 'wartime band' with 'sisters' volunteering,[91] Lancashire's 'war-time' band at Colne, with eight women out of 20,[92] Hampstead's 'war-time band' consisting of eight 'sisters' and eight 'brothers'.[93] Headlines included 'Sisters to the rescue', referring to six women joining the band at Griffithstown in Wales;[94] 'How a Struggling Band of Three was converted into a Strong Fighting Force of Fifteen' referring to the presence of four women amongst the new recruits at Ware,[95] 'How women

---

[82] Ibid., 7 Nov. 1914, p. 714.

[83] Ibid., 3 Oct. 1914, pp. 633–4.

[84] Ibid., 24 Oct. 1914, p. 682.

[85] Ibid., 3 Oct. 1914, p. 627.

[86] Hailstone, *The British Bandsman Centenary Book*, p. 142.

[87] *Bandsman, Local Officer and Songster*, 2 Oct. 1915, p. 633.

[88] Reported in *Bandsman, Local Officer and Songster*, 28 July 1917, p. 323.

[89] Ibid., 22 Jan. 1916, p. 53.

[90] Ibid., 26 Aug. 1916, p. 545.

[91] Ibid., 23 Sept. 1916, p. 615.

[92] Ibid., 2 Dec. 1916, p. 773.

[93] Ibid., 27 Jan. 1917, p. 53.

[94] Ibid., 9 Oct. 1915, p. 645.

[95] Ibid., 26 May 1917, p. 249.

and boys are filling the gaps at Barnstaple';[96] and finally 'Six Fighting Bands-women of Chichester'.[97]

There were alternatives to bands, of course. It was suggested that orchestral bands might appeal to women,[98] while at Dumfries, as the corps comprised mostly women, the idea of a concertina band had been mooted, and it currently had 16 members.[99] At Bargoed there was a girls' concertina band that had been formed for just a year, with a membership of 14.[100] Meanwhile at Preston 2, with its 'Fighting Songster Brigade' 'the vocal element is being increasingly utilised'.[101]

There is evidence that Salvationist bandsmen who enlisted were sometimes able to pursue their musical interests, in the interstices of their active service. On one occasion it was reported that 'a battalion of Kitchener's men' was minus a band, and so the commanding officer strove hard to remedy this deficiency:

> In his despair he remembered there were Salvationists [...] belonging to his Regiment [...] no less than eighty warriors of the Blood and Fire were members of the rank and file [...] over fifty were Army Bandsmen! [...] From these men a band of thirty-four was speedily formed, with a full set of instruments, and today the battalion in question rejoices in a combi-nation of godly and capable musicians thanks wholly to The Salvation Army'.[102]

Salvation Army bandsmen in the forces sometimes formed bands at Salvation Army Huts. The Salvationist magazine for serving military personnel, *Under the Colors* (1917), offers a note of explanation under the heading 'Our Recreation Huts for You':

> The Salvation Army has erected [...] a considerable number of Hutments and recreation centres for Service-men, in many parts of the United Kingdom, France (where specially acceptable work is being done), Australia, South Africa, Canada East and Canada West [...] You are welcome any time of day or night.[103]

At one of these Huts, presumably in France – locations were always anonymised due to reporting restrictions – there was a band of 25 players. The instruments belonged to the Hut, and there was a notice inviting any Salvationists coming into the camp to report themselves. If bandsmen, they had to state what

[96] Ibid., 25 Aug. 1917, p. 352.

[97] Ibid., 13 Oct. 1917, p. 49.

[98] Ibid., 8 Apr. 1916, p. 230.

[99] Ibid., 2 June 1917, p. 257.

[100] Ibid., 1 Sept. 1917, p. 361.

[101] Ibid., 9 June 1917, p. 265.

[102] 102 Ibid., 9 Feb. 1915, p. 104.

[103] *Under the Colors: A Magazine for His Majesty's Sailors and Soldiers*, May 1917, p. 49.

instrument they played, and they were fixed up as soon as there was a vacancy. As the men were being constantly shifted along the Line, the personnel was constantly changing.[104]

A particularly well-known example of a mainly Salvationist ensemble was that of a Field Ambulance Band in France: 'when there is a slack period (it does not often come) the men can bring out their instruments and discourse music to the delight of all and sundry at the Ambulance station'.[105] It may very well have been this band ('a well-known Field Ambulance band') that gave a festival at Leeds Town Hall, where amongst the items played was *Italian Melodies* [Slater, *Songs of Italy*, BJ 665], but this brass band also doubled as a Kazoo band, 'its origin reminding them of tiring route marches on dirty roads […] when brass instruments were not permitted'.[106]

From a Salvation Hut in France there was an account of a band which held a practice twice a week, with a recent programme including *Marching On[ward]* (Goldsmith, BJ 840), *Welsh Melodies No. 1* (E. H. Hill, BJ 586), *Echoes of the Congress* (Slater, BJ 485), *Soldiers of Christ* (Marshall, BJ 667), *Flowing River* (Broughton, BJ 652), *Castle March* (H. Kirk, BJ 712), *Irish Melodies* (E. H. Hill, BJ 712). The correspondent, who had been up in the trenches for two years and four months, commented, 'Not a bad programme for eighteen of us!'[107]

Often there were more informal groupings, as detailed in the following letter:

> We have a decent little band composed of Salvationists from various units and regiments. On Sunday evenings we play a few marches and some of the boys' favourite hymns, and then assist in some fine meetings.[108]

But exclusively Salvationist bands were rare in the military context. More typically they were mixed. The band of the First Reserve Garrison Battalion of the Suffolk Regiment included 11 Salvationists, but what was distinctive about it was that it was a temperance band, 'for not one of its members drink intoxicating liquors. Those of the band who are not Salvationists are good steady fellows'.[109] What is interesting about the following report from France is the categorisation of individuals according to religious affiliation or temperance:

> We have a band in which there are about nine Godly men, including five Salvationists. Among four others, two learnt their music in the ranks of the Salvation Army. Out of the band of twenty-five there are sixteen abstainers.[110]

---

[104] *Bandsman, Local Officer and Songster*, 10 Feb. 1917, p. 85.

[105] Ibid., 13 Feb. 1917, p. 26.

[106] Ibid., 4 Nov. 1916, p. 714.

[107] Ibid., 15 Sept. 1917, p. 180.

[108] Ibid., 26 May 1917, p. 251.

[109] Ibid., 29 July 1916, p. 491.

[110] Ibid., 25 Nov. 1916, p. 761.

In this discussion of Salvation Army Banding in the war years, four themes have emerged. First, the enhanced profile that bands gave to the Army in its public work with soldiers going to war and with the wounded. Second, the constant threat of depletion of bands at home due to enlistment. Third, the contribution of women to the survival of Salvation Army bands. And fourth, the attempts to keep a banding tradition alive at the Front.

The significance of all this was summarised in an early editorial in the *Bandsman, Local Officer and Songster*:

> Public appreciation of Army music is today everywhere manifest. The old order of outward repugnance to our methods, resistance to our message, and opposition to our aggressive tactics have disappeared. The Army procession has its place, for instance, with the most conventional religious service. Our Officers are respected; our works of mercy and benevolence held up to public esteem.[111]

With the armistice terms being read to the House of Commons on 11 November 1918, the war came to an end. From the July 1919 issue of the *Bandsman, Local Officer and Songster* (in print again, although on a monthly rather than a weekly basis, after almost a year's absence due to the national paper-shortage), the recovery for bands was being celebrated:[112] 'Eastbourne Band now rejoices in being up to pre-war strength'; 'East Grinstead soon to have a good band again'; 'Hendon Band is forging ahead'; 'Haggerston Band is once again fighting true: Though the war was responsible for entirely smashing the little combination, yet it has got together again'. Of course sadness was mixed with relief. At Barking a tea and musical festival was held to welcome home those who had been on active service: 'Forty-four lads have been on service, and forty have been spared, four made the supreme sacrifice.'[113]

A rallying call was made by A. J. Gilliard, who was to become a distinguished Salvation Army officer:

> We stand on the threshold of a new era in the history of Salvation Army bands [...] During the period of the war most of our bands were compelled to call a halt, to dig themselves in, and fight hard to maintain their positions. Numbers dwindled – in some cases to the point of disappearance [...] But now the summer has come. The weary months of holding on are gone and the order is changed [...] The world for Christ – that is our goal! [...] Never in the history of the Salvation Army has it received the honour and respect it receives today [...] 'Reconstruction' is the slogan in England today. All are called upon to help build a fairer structure above the ruins of the old. Who more fitting than Salvationists.[114]

[111] Ibid., 12 Dec. 1914, p. 792.

[112] Ibid., July 1919, pp. 22–3.

[113] Ibid., pp. 26–7.

[114] Ibid., Aug. 1919, p. 36.

CHAPTER 7

Eric Ball and the Inter-War Years, 1919–39

Towards the Golden Age of Salvation Army Music

THE Salvation Army experienced a minor period of expansion after the First World War, extending through the 1920s and petering out in the early 1930s.[1] One of the contributing factors which might have deterred marginal and potential recruits, was the crisis of leadership the movement experienced between 1927–9. As John Larsson puts it, in his recent highly detailed account,

> In 1929 a constitutional storm that had long been gathering suddenly burst, sweeping from office General Bramwell Booth, the son and successor to William Booth.[2]

The crisis focused on the need for reform, which included the abandonment of autocratic rule, dynastic succession and sole trusteeship. The trigger for the crisis was the serious illness of Bramwell Booth, who as sole trustee of the Army, was deemed to be 'unfit for the discharge of the public and administrative duties of his office'. As a result, in 1929 a High Council of international leaders met in Sunbury, and ended the despotic rule of the Booth family. It was a traumatic time for all concerned. The new General elected by the High Council was Commissioner Edward Higgins, and he was succeeded in 1934 by the charismatic sister of Bramwell, Commander Evangeline Booth.

In contrast as far as Salvationist music-making was concerned, these years were ones of progress and consolidation. In particular a Bands Department was formed in 1921 under the leadership of Alfred Braine, himself a former bandmaster and a member of the International Staff Band.[3] This appointment provided for the need of a central administration to advise and guide Salvationist musicians. It was a similar appointment that Slater had declined way back in 1905. Instead of one Musical Department catering for all the Army's musical needs, there were now two; the Bands Department led by Braine, and the Music Editorial Department under the joint direction of Frederick Hawkes and Arthur Goldsmith.

By 1922 there were Salvationist bands established in four continents (see Table 6).[4]

---

[1] Robertson, 'The Salvation Army: The Persistence of Sectarianism', p. 103.

[2] Larsson, *1929*, p. vii. Also see The Salvation Army, *The Why and Wherefore of The High Council of the Salvation Army, 1928–29* (London, 1928).

[3] See Boon, *Play the Music Play!*, pp. 166–7.

[4] *Bandsman, Local Officer and Songster*, 28 Oct. 1922, p. 349.

Table 6 International distribution of Salvation Army bands, 1922

United Kingdom	
England	761
Scotland	102
Wales	70
Europe	
Denmark	32
Finland	18
Germany	25
Holland	38
Norway	42
Sweden	141
Switzerland	65
Americas	
Canada East	87
Canada West	31
United States	210
South America	3
Australasia	
Australia East	104
Australia West	100
New Zealand	54
Africa	
South Africa	31
Miscellaneous small countries	12

On 12 February 1927 it was proudly announced that 'Halesworth is the Thousandth Band' [within the British Territory], and to mark the occasion this band from a Suffolk market town was presented with a set of instruments.[5] Three years later that number was expanded to include 48 new bands. There was a great deal of confidence: '34,327 Bandsmen do Duty Every Week throughout the World, 39,658 Songsters Sing the Songs of Zion every Sunday'.[6]

Salvationist musicians received royal approval on 15 February 1928 when the Duke and Duchess of York (later King George VI and Queen Elizabeth) attended a composers' festival at Clapton Congress Hall. The Duke observed 'the music of The Salvation Army is symbolic of the spirit which

[5] Ibid., 12 Feb. 1927, p. 57.
[6] Ibid., 25 Jan. 1930, p. 27.

animates that great Organization. It is martial, it is cheery, and best of all, it is inspiring'.[7]

Bands, songsters and vocal and instrumental soloists embraced the opportunities provided by the recording industry. In 1927 Salvation Army recordings for Columbia on the 'Regal' label were released, the first of many. With the establishment of the British Broadcasting Corporation in 1927, Salvation Army bands gradually found a niche for themselves in the schedules.

But probably the most notable characteristic during these years was the increasing self-confidence, maturity and professionalism of the Army's composers, matched in equal measure by the quality of many of the musical ensembles. In particular the period witnessed the rise of Eric Ball (1903–89) as the Salvationist composer and conductor *par excellence*, undoubtedly the most accomplished musical Salvationist of the inter-war years, and, in Holz's words, 'the dean of brass band composers in the 20th century'.[8] In this chapter I shall focus upon Eric Ball's life and work as a lens through which we can view the remarkable transformation of Salvationist music-making in the inter-war years. But first I shall outline developments in the Army's Music Editorial Department to provide an overall context for our consideration of Ball's contribution.

❧ *The Music Editorial Department*

After the war Frederick Hawkes and Arthur Goldsmith remained in place as joint heads of the Musical Department until in 1921 Goldsmith moved to a financial position within the Salvation Army, leaving Hawkes in charge of the newly named Music Editorial Department until 1936. Richard Slater continued to provide assistance to the department in his retirement, and in 1923 temporarily resumed leadership in order to provide cover for Hawkes who was undergoing a bout of ill-health. One of the department's key tasks in the early years of Hawkes' leadership was to produce in 1928 a *Band Tune Book* including 542 tunes, in anticipation of a new Song Book published in 1930. A keyboard edition was published in April 1931.[9]

There were a number of significant new appointments to the department during the inter-war years: Eric Ball, Bramwell Coles, Albert Jakeway, Philip Catelinet, and on a part-time basis, George Marshall. All these men established themselves as composers and arrangers, and came to dominate the musical world of the Salvation Army in this period. In this section I shall provide pen-portraits of Coles, Jakeway, Marshall and Catelinet, before turning to Eric Ball as the main focal point of the chapter.

Bramwell Coles (1887–1960) was born into a Salvation Army family; his

---

[7] Ibid., 25 Feb. 1928, p. 61.

[8] Holz, *Brass Bands of the Salvation Army*, vol. 2, p. 117.

[9] Steadman-Allen, 'One Hundred Years of Music Publishing', p. 17.

parents were officers. Musically he was virtually self-taught: his sisters were given piano lessons, but that instrument was considered unsuitable for boys.[10] However, at school, his teacher was amazed at how quickly he responded to tonic sol-fa exercises. No matter where the modulator moved, Coles could sound out the pitches with impressive accuracy. His father and step-mother were appointed to the Chalk Farm Corps and here Coles came under the influence of Alfred W. Punchard, bandmaster of the famed band. A distinct memory from this time was going to hear with Punchard, the John Philip Sousa Band at the Queen's Hall. This was despite some Salvationist bandsmen, including George Marshall, being suspended by the Army for attending Sousa's concerts. But for Coles the experience was a revelation: 'The playing of *The Stars and Stripes Forever* stirred every pulse and fibre in my body.'[11]

On leaving school at 14, Coles took up a position as a junior clerk at the Army's International Headquarters. All his spare time was spent studying music theory and composition, and practising the saxophone. He was a member of the famous Chalk Farm Saxophone Sextet. As we have noted previously, Coles entered a number of Salvation Army Competitions for the best prize march. His first was unsuccessful, but he showed it to Frederick Hawkes:

> Who, I cannot add, went into raptures or hailed it as a world's master-piece; as a matter of fact I gathered my knowledge of harmony was not all it might be, and I promptly bade a sad farewell to my pride and joy and cast it into the wastepaper basket.[12]

Fortunately Coles became more successful in prizewinning, and established a reputation as a composer. He subsequently became a Salvation Army officer, and served in the military during the last year of the war. On 12 March 1923 he was appointed to the Music Editorial Department to work under Slater during Hawkes' illness. Two years later he went to Canada, and returned in 1936 to take over the headship of the department from Hawkes, a position he held until 1952.

Coles' musical foundations were based upon Prout's *Harmony: Its Theory and Practice* (1889). According to one of his sons, 'for years he used Prout's book on harmony and would never bend his rules even if it sounded good'.[13] As a composer, Coles established a reputation for his marches; indeed, he was known as 'The Salvation Army's March King', and 'The Salvation Army's Sousa', a designation which he did not appreciate or like. Ray Steadman-Allen points out that Coles was very different from Sousa; he was 'painfully modest, unusually reserved [...] the largeness of sound and sacrifice of finesse that marked the

---

[10] Court, *In the Firing Line*, p. 24.

[11] Ibid., p. 32. For Sousa, see T. Herbert, 'Sousa, the Band and the "American Century"', *Journal of the Royal Musical Association* 135:1 (2010), pp. 183–90.

[12] *Bandsman and Songster*, 7 June 1930, p. 179.

[13] Court, *In the Firing Line*, p. 44.

efforts of many bands often disturbed his musical sensitivities'.[14] In Steadman-Allen's opinion, Coles had a greater compositional affinity with the British military band composer F. J. Ricketts [aka Kenneth J. Alford] (1881–1941), regarded by many as the finest composer of British military marches.[15]

Characteristically, Slater was somewhat critical of Coles' compositions: 'in spite of much overwrought efforts [they] leave unsatisfactory impressions on me' (RSd, v. 19, 16 July 1927). Coles' most famous march, *Under Two Flags* (BJ 816), was published in 1919, 'dedicated to the thousands of Salvationists who had served their country', and celebrated the Army's British roots by incorporating several national melodies. Slater judged it to be 'patchwork [...] I see nothing to suggest the Salvation Army' (RSd, v. 19, 25 Feb. 1928).

Nevertheless Coles' more extended works made a considerable impact. His meditation, *Man of Sorrows* (FS 13), was sketched out originally while he was in hospital at the end of the war. The music critic of the *Toronto Telegram* was much impressed, so much so that he made some rather extravagant parallels with the work of Wagner and Arthur Sullivan.[16] The work was included as the final item at the 1928 Composers' Festival, with the musicians positioned off-stage:

> Effectively presented in a darkened hall with carefully synchronized lantern slides depicting the passion and death of our Lord.[17]

Coles' successor as Head of the Music Editorial Department in 1952 was to be Albert Jakeway, who had entered the department on 26 November 1926. Like Coles, he was self-taught musically, and his first job was in an engineering shop. After training to be a Salvation Army officer he went on war service, after which he worked for the Army in Czechoslovakia, before joining the department. His progress as a composer was the result of much trial and error:

> During this period many problems arose in my mind relative to composition, among them the question of key-relationship. In my endeavour to explore new fields I was inclined to get 'out of bounds', but upon advice from the Music Editorial Department I was saved from danger into which disassociated key-relationship would lead me.[18]

Jakeway composed numerous songs, marches, selections and meditations. From this period perhaps the most popular was the cornet duet from 1935, *Always Cheerful* (FS 104). But in Slater's judgement Jakeway's music 'seems just

---

[14] Ibid., p. 67.

[15] For more detail on Ricketts, a.k.a. Henry Alford, see J. Richards, *Imperialism and Music: Britain 1876–1953* (Manchester, 1990), pp. 428–32.

[16] Court, *In the Firing Line*, p. 125.

[17] Ibid., p. 61.

[18] [A. R. Wiggins,] 'The Music Editorial Department: Staff-Captain Jakeway; From Engineer's Bench to Composing Desk', *Bandsman and Songster*, 22 June 1930, p. 197.

a copy of outside band music, including threadbare cadenzas' (RSd, v. 24, 19 Jan. 1936).

Reference has already been made in a previous chapter to George Marshall (1888–1956), who had sustained major injuries in a mining accident in 1914.[19] He was called upon to undertake work for the Music Editorial Department in a part-time capacity. As well as writing a number of excellent marches, he proved himself to be a most innovative composer of more extended works. The first performance of his selection *Army of the Brave* (FS 6), took place in July 1923, and was given in his presence. It was his first visit to a major London event since the mining accident which had led him to be paralysed from the waist down. Needless to say it was a very emotional occasion, linked also to the fact that the piece stemmed from the death of Marshall's brother in the war. The work was dedicated to those 'who laid down the Cross for the Crown'.[20]

Much of Marshall's music is deeply felt, stemming from his own experience. For example, *Olivet and Calvary* (BJ 881), was sketched out in the trauma of his own suffering from his mining accident. Quotations from the Passion story appear in the full score of the piece. It contains numerous chromaticisms to portray 'darkness over all the earth'.[21] (See Example 4.)

In the opinion of Holz, Marshall's meditation *Horbury* (FS 62), published in 1930, was the finest and most representative meditation of the period.[22] Eric Ball summed up Marshall's achievement in this work with an insightful and credible parallel to the work of César Franck:

> In his hands the tune 'Horbury' – 'Nearer my God to Thee' – leaves its ecclesiastical surroundings, and is heard wending its way where it is needed – amongst the chromatic half-lights of unhappy human thought and despair [...] when I hear Marshall's best music, I am reminded of César Franck, who also exploited like effects, and 'redeemed' them by sheer spiritual insight and integrity'.[23]

The last member to join the department before the onset of World War II, was Philip Catelinet (1910–95), who in 1930 was working as a junior assistant.[24] He composed a considerable number of pieces for brass band, including the cornet duet *Deliverance* (BJ 1051), which also includes a brief reference to 'Little Brown Jug'!, and the air varié, *A Sunbeam* (FS 115), written in 1937 for children

---

[19] See Wiggins, *Triumph of Faith*; [A. R. Wiggins,] 'The Music Editorial Department: Divisional Bandmaster George Marshall – the Miner-Musician', *Bandsman and Songster*, 19 July 1930, p. 229.

[20] Wiggins, 'The Music Editorial Department [...] George Marshall', p. 229.

[21] Ibid.

[22] Holz, *Brass Bands of the Salvation Army*, vol. 1, p. 156.

[23] In Wiggins, *Triumph of Faith*, p. 50.

[24] [A. R. Wiggins,] 'The Music Editorial Department: Conclusion', *Bandsman and Songster*, 26 July 1930, p. 239.

Example 4 George Marshall, *Olivet and Calvary* (1922),

piano transcription by Captain Ray [Steadman] Allen (1957), bars 137–52

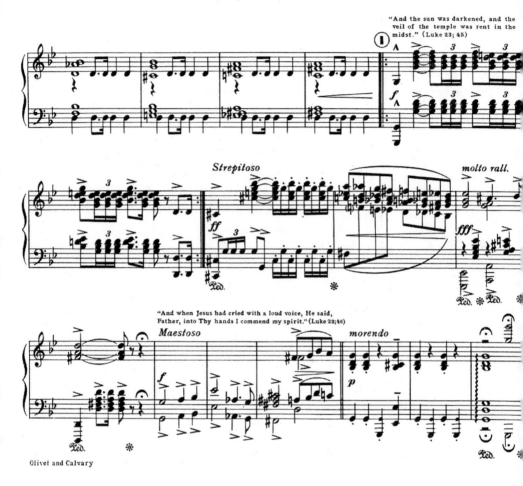

Olivet and Calvary

to enjoy, with its programmatic sequence: Dawn; The Clock Strikes 7; Playtime; School; Release (the children make their way home with shouts of merriment). For Steadman-Allen, Catelinet's music was 'beautifully constructed academically, and sometimes [in] his very tunefulness, you overlook the fact that underneath it there's a very solid structure, of knowing where he's going'.[25] Catelinet's subsequent career lay outside the Salvation Army; 'there was a sense in which he was a little overshadowed by Eric Ball'.[26] He became a professional tuba player,

[25] R. Steadman-Allen, in 'Lieut. Colonel (Dr.) Ray Steadman-Allen OF & Dr Stephen Cobb in Conversation', *The International Staff Band of the Salvation Army Heritage Series No. 1. Music from the 1930s* (London, 2009), SPS 249 CD, transcribed by Gordon Cox.

[26] Ibid.

playing the first performance of Vaughan Williams's Tuba Concerto, and later was Professor of Brass at the Carnegie-Melon University, Pittsburgh.[27]

These were the men who, together with Eric Ball, carried the responsibility for the considerable musical progress made by the Salvation Army in the years between the two world wars.

❧ Eric Ball

Eric Ball joined the Music Editorial Department in 1920. I shall outline something of his early years before examining his work within the department. Following this I shall focus on his compositions, his published letters to a musical friend, and his involvement in recording and broadcasting.

Ball's childhood was somewhat peripatetic: 'my father was a wanderer'.[28] His parents were Salvationists, although because they were always on the move Eric had experience of worship not only in the Army, but also with the Methodists and the Church of England in which he had been baptised. He recollected that even as a child he was attracted to the mystical side of religious experience. One of his vivid memories was of meeting a woman who had been 'healed by the Spirit'.[29]

At school one of his favourite lessons was

Sight singing from the Modulator – the teacher pointing out the various symbols with a baton (or more often a cane) [...] By singing the 'movable doh', modulation from one key to another quickly became a comparatively easy matter, and to this day I have always translated the symbol of staff notation into tonic sol-fa, generally sub-consciously, but more consciously if I have wanted to 'hear' a difficult modulation.[30]

In Dartford, Kent, where his family settled for a time, he studied with a local organist, and developed an interest in composing, commencing with transcribing songs from the *Musical Salvationist* for brass instruments.[31] On leaving school he became an office-boy, and during the War he met a Belgian military officer who introduced him to aspects of music of which he had little experience, and later Ball undertook a correspondence course. Eventually he became a junior assistant at the Salvation Army's Musical Instrument Department, and in 1920 was 'promoted upstairs' to the Music Editorial Department:

[27] Hindmarsh, 'Building a Repertoire', p. 262.

[28] From interviews with Eric Ball on the Australian broadcast, *Encounter with Eric Ball* (www.salvoaudio.com/bands/ericball.htm.), transcribed by Gordon Cox.

[29] Ibid.

[30] In *Eric Ball: His Words and Wisdom*, ed. P. M. Cooke (Baldock, 1992), p. 96.

[31] From the CD 'Melvyn Knott in Conversation with Eric Ball', accompanying M. Knott, *Constant Trust: The Spirituality of the Music of Eric Ball* (Llandloes, n.d.).

There is a small office, partitioned off in a back corner of the old building – packed with three desks, a piano and a harmonium – the two incumbents were Majors Arthur Goldsmith and Frederick G. Hawkes [...] Just outside was a large area where women and girls worked trimming bonnets.[32]

Among his duties, he was required to type letters which Hawkes and Goldsmith had written out in longhand, to make copies of some scores and innumerable band parts, and of songs to which had to be added tonic sol-fa notation. In addition, songs and band pieces sent in by contributors had often to be drastically edited:

Scores were often returned to their writers with corrections, and suggestions shown in red ink – it was felt the editors had a responsibility to help and encourage their musically less-equipped contributors.[33]

Ball found Arthur Goldsmith to be the more outgoing of the two editors. Hawkes was a more conservative character. There was no doubt in Ball's mind of Hawkes' achievement: 'if Richard Slater was "The Father of Salvation Army Music", then Frederick G. Hawkes [...] was its "Architect" [...] here under Hawkes' benevolent but critical eye was my university'.[34]

As has been pointed out, Richard Slater came back from retirement to head the department temporarily during Hawkes' illness. Ball was impressed by the man:

To work under the direction of the great man was a privilege. He seemed always to concentrate on what he was doing, speak few if any unnecessary words. Yet he was quite approachable. In his lunch hour he would often play the piano, using some of the classical and other music to be found in the department.

For his part, Slater was particularly concerned about the rather frequent absences of this newcomer to the department, wondering 'is he seeking another job, or is he really ill?' (RSd, v. 17, 21 Feb. 1921). Two years later he was concerned that Ball had a tendency to consumption (RSd, v. 19, 18 Jan. 1923).

There are several mentions by Slater of his informal teaching of Ball. He gave him 'two or three short lessons in harmony' (RSd, v. 17, 21 May 1921), 'had a long talk with Eric Ball on my studies of Wagner's work' (RSd, v. 19, 16 Feb. 1923), and 'showed Ball and Coles my harmonic scheme of three full chords of the 13th, with the augmented sixth supplying all the materials of key in the major and minor modes' (RSd, v. 19, 28 Mar. 1923).

In December 1924 Ball gained the Associateship Diploma of the Royal College of Music (ARCM) in the Theory of Music. The department was keen to keep him,

[32] E. Ball, 'Eric Ball Remembers', *The Musician*, 29 Oct., 1938, p. 701.

[33] Ibid.

[34] Ibid.

and offered him a weekly increase of 10/–. Slater observed, 'Ball now thinks he has a job worth keeping, as so many capable students cannot find employment' (RSd, v. 19, 10 Aug. 1925). Ball was by now seeking out first-hand knowledge of the great musical works by attending the Queen's Hall Promenade Concerts. He was acting on the advice of some influential musicians with whom he was in contact. Slater was concerned that there might be a 'danger here in being under the influence of outside ideals' (RSd, v. 19, 16 Aug. 1926).

In 1927 Eric Ball and wife, Olive, entered the Salvation Army's Training College to become Salvation Army officers.[35] By 1928 a new band was formed by the express wish of Bramwell Booth – the Salvationist Publishing and Supplies Band, commonly referred to as the SP&S Band. Originally the intention was to demonstrate the effectiveness of a small number of players and to promote the new Second Series Band Journal which was designed to meet the needs of smaller bands. Eric Ball was appointed bandmaster, and held that post until the band's dissolution with the onset of war in 1939. According to Cooke the band had its genesis as a result of an ensemble of 16 employees of the Salvationist Publishing and Supplies led by Ball, being sent, as we have seen previously, to Halesworth to celebrate the formation of the Army's 1000th band. With its permanence established, the SP&S Band gained a full complement of players and under Ball's leadership established itself as one of the premier Salvationist Bands, and indeed a rival to the International Staff Band. In particular, it established a fine reputation with its frequent radio broadcasts and gramophone recordings.[36] By 1930 Eric Ball was considered by many to be the Salvation Army's most gifted musician, both as composer and conductor. A brief description of him by Arch Wiggins, the editor of the *Bandsman and Songster*, nicely illustrates something of Ball's charisma:

> Captain Eric Ball looks the musician he is, his shock of fair hair and his deep-set blue eyes, with their far-away look (which perhaps betrays the secret of the mystical quality to be found in much of his music), accentuates the impression.[37]

Slater still kept his eye on Ball who had requested a three-month 'furlough' (break) in 1935 in order to earn some money to help his mother and sick father, something his salary did not allow him to do. He was to make some money by orchestral scoring and copying work, and involvement in recording. It was Slater's opinion that Ball had not been dealt with justly by the authorities: after all, he had worked in the department for 16 years, with no significant promotion and increase of salary. Slater viewed Ball as someone of unquestionable importance to Salvation Army music, but thought there was a danger he might be lost

---

35 P. Cooke, *Eric Ball: The Man and his Music* (Baldock, 1992), p. 53.

36 Ibid., pp. 56–60.

37 [A. R. Wiggins,] 'The Music Editorial Department: Captain Eric Ball ARCM – A Young and Enthusiastic Composer', *Bandsman and Songster*, 5 July 1930, p. 210.

to the organisation: these three months would provide him with the opportunity of 'surveying his chances outside the Army' (RSd, v. 24, 15 July 1935).

ERIC BALL, THE COMPOSER

Eric Ball had no doubt that joining the Music Editorial Department, 'centred my interests in composition and gave direction to my work'.[38] He added that for his own delectation he had written sonatas, overtures, 'and even a Symphony or two'.[39]

These early efforts are lost. By 1930 he had published 32 compositions for bands, mostly selections and meditations, and innumerable songs and vocal pieces. Hindmarsh makes the significant point that Ball's inspiration was rooted in song:

> He responded to the meaning and character of a text with a refined sensibility. And it is this, rather than any particular originality of idiom, that distinguishes him from other brass band composers of the time.[40]

His vocal works range from solos, such as 'True Life – A Reminder',[41] which in its heartfelt lyricism is somewhat reminiscent of Edwardian moralistic drawing-room ballads, to extended vocal works, most notably his nine 'sessional songs'. These were written to celebrate specific training sessions for future Army Officers. They were performed as the climax of the Commissioning service, in which the members of the session were sent out to their posting, whether within Britain or overseas. Each session had its own name, and Ball's musical settings had to set the right mood of militaristic purpose, reflection, and rousing hope for the future. The best known of these songs is 'Torchbearers!' Published in 1933, it became the basis of one of Ball's finest marches, *Torchbearers* (BJ 1069).[42] (See Example 5.)

With the election of Evangeline Booth as General in 1934, Eric Ball in some ways became her unofficial composer.[43] He worked with her on a new revised and enlarged edition of her collection of songs, entitled *Songs of the Evangel*, which had been first published by the Salvation Army in New York in 1927.[44] The association was covered in secrecy. Bramwell Coles would collect sketches of the new work from her, which were then handed to Eric Ball to work on. Ball,

---

[38] Ibid.

[39] Cooke, *Eric Ball*, p. 45.

[40] In Hindmarsh, 'Building a Repertoire', p. 260.

[41] E. Ball, 'True Life: A Reminder', *Musical Salvationist* 37 (Feb. 1923), pp. 14–16.

[42] E. Ball, 'Torchbearers! I.T.C. Cadets' Sessional Song, 1932–33', *Musical Salvationist* 47 (Jan. 1933), pp. 5–7.

[43] See E. Ball, 'Songs of the Evangel: Eric Ball Recalls some Personal Memories of Evangeline Booth', *The Musician*, 25 Dec. 1965, p. 864.

[44] E. Booth, *Songs of the Evangel*, new and enlarged edn (London, 1934).

Example 5 Eric Ball, 'Torchbearers!: I.T.C. Cadets' Sessional Song, 1932–33', bars 32–48. Eric Ball was to use this theme again in his march, *Torchbearers* (1933).

sworn to secrecy, would then visit Evangeline to discuss, criticise and amend the songs. The result was a highly distinctive collection, enhanced by photographs of the General in various poses, together with text telling of some reminiscence connected with the song. Ball clearly gained from this contact, as he was promoted by the General a couple of years before it was due.[45]

Although Richard Slater appreciated the young man's promise, nevertheless he intimated some of his musical shortcomings to his diary. Ball's early march, *The Gospel Feast* (BJ 831), Slater found ineffective, 'because of its syncopation, complicated part-writing and overwrought style' (RSd, v. 21, 16 July 1927). However, Slater thought Ball's meditation *Hanover* (FS 42) was better; 'I think he is unfinished in episodical work [...] but gets some good contrasts and colour' (RSd, v. 21, 16 July 1927). Whilst praising the instrumental scoring of Ball's selection, *Adoration* (FS 26), Slater found 'some crude episodical passages, and halts or breaks in form' (RSd, v. 22, 15 Feb. 1928). Towards the end of his life Slater praised the wider range that Ball's music contained compared to most Salvationist repertoire, although 'too much influenced by modernism' (RSd, v. 24, 19 Jan. 1936). However, both in his diary and in conversation with Brindley Boon, it was, for Slater, the Swedish-American Salvationist composer, Erik Leidzén, who took the palm:

> Leidzén had the gift [...] of knowing where he wanted to go in his music, and taking the correct route of modulation to there. 'No short cuts for him'.[46]

In considering Ball's compositional output during the inter-war years, I shall focus upon three key works for band from the 1930s: the air varié, *The Old Wells* (FS 58, 1930); the tone poems, *Exodus* (FS 117, 1937); and *The Triumph of Peace* (FS 130, 1939).

The air varié was typically a display piece for band, patterned on similar pieces released in the secular brass band press since the 1890s. In *The Old Wells*, however, Eric Ball moved away from melodic development of the theme towards thematic development; 'it approximates more nearly the form known as Symphonic Variations'.[47] The work is based on an original Salvationist song, and presents five sharply contrasting variations. It came to the notice of Edward Elgar, as Ball related to Melvyn Knott:

> We were playing it with the SP&S Band, and we went to Canterbury, and the organist of Canterbury Cathedral, a Dr Palmer, heard this. He was the

45　Ball, 'Songs of the Evangel', p. 864. Eric Ball's positive experience with Evangeline Booth, was in marked contrast with her stormy relationship with the eminent Swedish-American Salvationist composer and arranger, Erik Leidzén. See Holz, *Erik Leidzén*, pp. 28–32.

46　Brindley Boon recollection in Holz, *Erik Leidzén*, p. 254.

47　Holz, *Brass Bands of the Salvation Army*, vol. 1, p. 148.

chairman [...] And he said, 'That's very good, I'd like to send a copy to my friend Elgar' [...] I got one sent to him and he sent it to Elgar, and Elgar wrote him a postcard in which he said 'I have enjoyed reading the Salvation Army score – free, sane and open-airish'. That was his comment [...] That's typical Elgar isn't it![48]

Eric Ball recorded the piece with the SP&S Band in 1935.

The work that fully established Ball's position as the leading Salvationist composer was his Tone Poem, *Exodus*. Telling the 'story' of the biblical Exodus, its three-part structure ('Bondage', 'The Night of the Passover', 'Deliverance') was aligned with the exposition, development and recapitulation sections of sonata form. Each major section has a quasi-three-part structure.[49] Geoffrey Brand, an influential brass band conductor from a Salvationist background, expresses vividly the impact of this remarkable work:

> I've always thought that *Exodus* [...] broke new barriers. It stopped being a succession of tunes, it had development [...] Eric had started to show us that he could develop, and that music had other things to say, other than the purely melodic interest [...] The energy, the sheer sweep of the line [...] this was Eric in his early thirties [...] when the energy was strong and you feel it in his music.[50]

The Triumph of Peace was in many ways a protest against war, with its subtitle, 'They that take the sword shall perish with the sword'. Ball recollected intense discussions with colleagues at that time around the subject of war, and the role of pacifism. He uses two conflicting themes in the work: (a) the motif of Temporal Power with the changing tonality giving at times a sense of insecurity; (b) the motif of Spiritual Power, a dignified tune set by Ball to the words 'Peace in our time O Lord', heard first as a prayer and finally forming a triumphant conclusion.[51] Ball outlined the compositional process:

> In bigger pieces I'd like to have at least classical forms in mind. The sonata form I think is tremendous, and a thing like *Triumph of Peace*, once you get the idea and start it, then a lot of it is working out the sonata form, and a lot of it is experience from the sub-conscious, and you get to know what to do.[52]

[48] 'Melvyn Knott in Conversation with Eric Ball', transcribed by Gordon Cox. Also see E. Ball, 'Master of the King's Musick – A Memoir of Sir Edward Elgar', *Bandsman and Songster*, 10 Mar. 1935, p. 75.

[49] Holz, *Brass Bands of the Salvation Army*, vol. 1, p. 145.

[50] *Encounter with Eric Ball*, transcribed by Gordon Cox.

[51] D. Turton, liner notes, *In the Firing Line: Favourites from the 78 rpm Era*. SPS151CD (London, 2001).

[52] 'Melvyn Knott in Conversation with Eric Ball', transcribed by Gordon Cox.

The work was published in January 1939, and recorded by Ball and the SP&S Band in May of that year.

As a postscript to the war, and as a demonstration of the power of Ball's music on Salvationists, his selection *Constant Trust* (BJ 1179), which had been written around 1938, became a symbol of hope to many in those years.[53] Ball agreed:

> This is true, and there was a German Salvationist, I forget his name now, he was an [Salvation Army] officer, but he was taken into the ranks of the German soldiery and he went to Africa, and he took that score with him wherever he went. I met him after the war.[54]

As well as writing such serious works, Eric Ball was also adept at composing lighter pieces, including musical monologues[55] and a pianoforte solo, 'Paraphrase – Sunshine', which included a somewhat jazzy variant on a Sunday school song.[56] Such work displayed his considerable versatility as a composer.

Eric Ball was clear about the influences on his musical style:

> My music is a bit old-fashioned – back in the romantic era. Elgar, Vaughan Williams, Sibelius, that was about as advanced as I get. As a young man, I immersed myself in Mozart, Beethoven and Schubert. Elgar was probably the strongest influence, especially *The Dream of Gerontius* and the Cello Concerto.[57]

With regard to Elgar's influence, Holz points out the striking resemblance in a passage in *Constant Trust* to 'Sanctus fortis' in *Dream of Gerontius*.[58] Robert Simpson, the distinguished composer, friend of Eric Ball, and himself from a Salvationist family, commented thus on Ball's musical style:

> The very greatest composers were 'derivative' [...] The real artist uses what he finds – he doesn't try to start from nowhere. Eric's work had its own stamp, the result of his ability to make fresh use of what he knew. His originality lay in being innocently himself.[59]

As far as Ball's own philosophy of musical composition was concerned, the following is probably the best summary:

---

53 Ibid.

54 Ibid.

55 For example, 'Music Everywhere', in The Salvation Army, *Musical Monologues* (London, 1938), vol. 1, pp. 13–15.

56 'Paraphrase-Sunshine' for piano solo, in The Salvation Army, *Favourite Compositions for the Pianoforte: Instrumental Albums No. 13* (London, 1932), pp. 4–5.

57 A. M. Taylor, *Labour and Love: An Oral History of the Brass Band Movement* (London, 1983), p. 147.

58 Holz, *Brass Bands of the Salvation Army*, vol. 1, p. 168.

59 R. Simpson, Foreword, in Cooke, *Eric Ball*, p. 7.

In my own music I think I try to make it so that each section, each mood, moves into the next mood, with some sort of logic, so that in the end no-one can see where the various sections have been joined up, no one can see where it's been sewn up. What intrigues me with the Great Masters is that how so often one thing moves into another, with a kind of, I was going to say, a 'holy logic'. A kind of clarity and a logical movement that you don't find in lesser music. I like to think of music as a speech. If Beethoven wants to say something about Freedom in his great opera, or say something in one of his symphonies, he's saying something that can't be said in any other way, and it is saying something that appeals to us in the inner being.[60]

LETTERS TO A MUSICAL FRIEND

Between January and June 1934, Eric Ball wrote a weekly column for the *Bandsman and Songster* in the form of letters to a musical friend.[61] They were always addressed to 'Dear John', who was an actual friend of Eric Ball. It is necessary to bear in mind when reading these letters that 'John' plays in a Salvation Army Band, and has taken over responsibility for a songster brigade. In addition he is keen to develop compositional skills. There are 25 letters in the series, and they provide us with a clear picture of the thinking of Eric Ball about the challenges of music-making in the Salvation Army. The letters highlight both his idealism, and the day to day problems and setbacks of musical leadership within the movement.

In his very first letter, Eric Ball questioned whether or not Salvationist music may be considered as an Art.[62] The question had been raised in his mind as a result of a comment a well-known cathedral organist had made about a programme given by the Assurance Songsters which exemplified 'the artistic expression of the spirit and ideals of the Salvation Army'.[63] For Ball this phrase heightened his concept of the status of Salvation Army music, 'and consequently helped me to repel the feeling of dissatisfaction that had crept into my spirit'.[64] He thought that the greatest masterpieces were the outcome of a sincere application to a job or work, rather than an attempt to be poetic or 'highbrow'. On a later occasion he returned to the theme of keeping the individuality of Salvation Army music, and resisting the temptation for songster brigades to imitate chapel and mission choirs.[65]

[60] *Encounter with Eric Ball*, quotation transcribed by Gordon Cox from broadcast.

[61] E. Ball, 'Letters to a Musical Friend', *Bandsman and Songster*, Jan.–June 1934.

[62] Ibid., 6 Jan. 1934, p. 5.

[63] Ibid.

[64] Ibid.

[65] Ibid., 24 Feb. 1934, p. 62.

Constantly, Ball warned of the dangers of superficiality and self-satisfaction, and his letters upon this subject provide us with a picture of some of the strains that were emerging at this time, particularly between the different generations of Salvationists.

In speaking to one such 'disillusioned' young man, the expressive but bitter phrase 'the Army of the mediocre' was used.[66] For Ball this was symptomatic of the feeling amongst young musical Salvationists that there was not enough musical development amongst Salvationists at large, and consequently they came across a good deal of complacency and self-satisfaction. Ball applied this to certain unnamed composers:

> Publication of their music has so gratified them, that they make little effort to improve their style, believing themselves to have 'arrived', and their later works are only as effective as their early efforts. One sees the same harmonic effects; the same style of modulation; the same obvious weaknesses, and so on. It is very, very easy to 'Sit at ease in Zion'.[67]

The only cure for such mediocrity was to criticise oneself unmercifully.

The generational gap was mentioned by John, in dealing with the poor behaviour of some bandsmen with regard to his songster brigade. Ball replied:

> I can visualise the type of men you mention: well-groomed, spick and span, good players, and individually decent fellows; they seem to imagine it clever to pass *sotto voce* remarks about those taking part during the meeting.[68]

For Ball one of the great strengths of the Army was that it provided opportunity for public witness by all sorts of folk, often poor and illiterate. Many of the young bandsmen, however, were convinced of their own superiority:

> nothing appeals to them [...] Your job and mine is to set a stern example by our own lives, and to pray that to our musicians everywhere may come the Vision Beautiful.[69]

As for musical superficiality, Ball cited the case of one such musician who was about to transfer to John's corps. He had a light baritone voice, and played the xylophone, vibraphone, piano accordion, saxophone, violin, piano and trombone. Such men were in great demand. The problem was that they had little time for the serious side of music-making. Ball asked John to

> Try to get him interested in the more intellectual and artistic side of music, for I believe that if he would sacrifice some of his love of popularity and

---

[66] Ibid., 3 Feb. 1934, p. 34.

[67] Ibid.

[68] Ibid., 31 Mar. 1934, p. 102.

[69] Ibid.

applause, and make himself *specialize* in some particular branch, he would be capable of doing work of some real, lasting value.[70]

But the dangers of musical superficiality were not confined to the young. Ball was exasperated about the controversy about which Salvation Army band was the best:

> It is a manifestation of unmusical minds which are more concerned with a competitive instinct than with real music-making [...] In the outside world they form a proportion to whom brass banding is just another 'sport', like dog racing or football; they are the despair of idealists and real musicians of their movement. In the Salvation Army world they form the ranks of the destructive critics, who sap our spiritual strength, and whose Utopia would be entered were our bands allowed to compete![71]

It was the keeping in balance of the musical and the spiritual elements of Salvation Army life that Ball was concerned about. Too often the musical predominated. He cited reactions amongst some bandsmen to their Easter campaigns, when Easter was celebrated by visiting other corps:

> 'Fine!' 'Best weekend I have ever had'. 'Oh, everybody reckons we were the best band they've ever heard around their district' 'Great time! And the grub!'[72]

Ball concluded that 'we must set out more earnest than ever to prove that both the musical and the spiritual sides may flourish together'.[73]

In considering these reflections on the letters to a musical friend, it is appropriate to let Eric Ball encapsulate both the frustrations and the ideals of being a musical Salvationist:

> It is [...] difficult to refrain from sarcastic comments when these dear, short-visioned folk who look askance upon change, development of any kind, pass their opinion on Army music and groan: 'What are we coming to?' 'Wherever are these composers taking us?' although they have no suggestions to offer apart from the ever-popular one of coercive restraint, beloved of dictators and others who have only one point of view – their own [...] Yet a musician, composer or performer must express himself, and if he's a Salvationist, surely he is to be trusted to have at heart the demands of the Kingdom as much as anyone.[74]

In these letters we may discern both traces of an increasing musical distance between the often musically educated younger generation and the traditional

---

[70] Ibid., 7 Apr. 1934, p. 111.

[71] Ibid., 17 Feb. 1934, p. 55.

[72] Ibid., 14 Apr. 1934, p. 119.

[73] Ibid.

[74] Ibid., 16 June 1934, p. 187.

Salvationist congregation, and a growing professionalism on the part of Salvationist composers and musicians. It may be that both of these points were connected, and that this was the reason behind the fact that by the late 1920s there were a number of bands that either split from the organisation, or fractured within themselves. The best-known example was the highly respected and proficient Coventry Band, from which in April 1939, the bandmaster and 29 bandsmen all resigned, and went on to form the nucleus of the City of Coventry Band.[75]

As far as increasing musical proficiency was concerned, *The Musician* in December 1938 proudly featured the photographs of 24 'Salvationist-Musicians who have achieved success at the four great British Institutions of Music – The Royal College, the Royal Academy, Trinity College, and the Guildhall School'.[76] Among that number appeared Eric Ball ARCM (Theory of Music), William Major LRAM (Violin), the bandmaster of Coventry who a year later resigned, and William Overton ARCM (Trumpet), later to become principal trumpet of the BBC Symphony Orchestra and professor of trumpet at the Royal Academy of Music.[77]

Such achievements were a two-edged sword as later many Salvationists took their place in the ranks of the best orchestras and ensembles. As Holz has pointed out, this was to create divided loyalties that led to the loss of a significant portion of a generation of outstanding musicians.[78]

﹒ *Recording and Broadcasting*

At this point I view the wider picture of Salvation Army involvement in recording and broadcasting, in both of which Eric Ball was a key player.

One of the main developments that in many ways transformed musical life from the 1920s onwards was the recording industry. In fact the first Salvation Army recording known to have been made was in 1896 when the Trade Headquarters Band played *The Indian March* onto a wax cylinder, which no longer exists. In 1905 several 10-inch single-sided records made by the International Staff band were advertised. The Chalk Farm Band made its first records in 1912 for Pathé Frères.[79]

By 1927 Columbia had signed up many of the leading contesting bands and

75 See K. Elliott, *The Band With a Name: A History of Coventry City Salvation Army Band from 1892 to 1993* (Baldock, 1994).

76 *The Musician*, 24 Dec. 1938, p. 824; 31 Dec. 1938, p. 841.

77 William Overton was a lifelong Salvationist. He became bandmaster of the Lewisham Band, and recorded Eric Ball's 'True Life', with the composer accompanying on the piano.

78 Holz, *Brass Bands of the Salvation Army*, vol. 1, p. 160.

79 D. Turton, 'The Heritage of Salvation Army Recordings', liner notes, *The Old Wells: Favourites from the 78 rpm Era*, SPSCD 116CD (London, 1999), n.p.

military bands on their budget label 'Regal'. Signing up the International Staff Band was a natural extension of this policy. Initially the contract was for the band to make three records over a one-year period, but as sales of the first set were good, the contract was extended to include other bands and personalities. When Columbia merged with the Gramophone Company UK Ltd to form EMI, the Regal Zonophone label was established in 1932. This was a light entertainment label, and consequently it was felt that the religious nature of Salvation Army music did not fit comfortably into its list, therefore in 1935 the Regal Zonophone Salvation Army Record series was introduced with the Army's crest on its label, and this series incorporated the earlier records, as well as new recordings. By 1957 a total of 220 10-inch 78 rpm records had been issued in the series. From 1957 until 1969 the label was also used by EMI for Salvation Army 33⅓ rpm and 45 rpm discs.[80]

For our purposes we shall consider those records made between 1927 and 1939, as they will provide useful data for judging the kinds of Salvationist music that would support such a commercial venture. The recordings were made and financed by Columbia, who owned marketing rights and copyright. The Salvation Army controlled the repertoire, and had some say regarding whether records were issued in the UK, and received a royalty.[81]

But before considering these recordings, it is helpful to turn to Eric Ball for his insider's view:

> With the Band, each recording session [...] has been preceded by intensive rehearsal, in which the special demands of the microphone have been considered. At the recording studio it is not possible to place the Band in the usual festival formation. All players face the 'mike' [...] Euphoniums cause the most trouble, they being difficult to record satisfactorily. It seems that their tone does not suit the 'mike', being liable to cause 'blasting' especially on high notes; they are therefore given a back seat. Percussion instruments are not encouraged, except for special effects [...] Once the balance has been proved satisfactory, by repeated tests, a test record is made, and 'played back' to the band for criticism. Possibly another change of position will be necessary, or an unsatisfactory passage may need a little rehearsal, but at length the word is given to make a 'Master'. One hears the warning buzz for 'Get ready' and a second buzz for 'Silence'. There is a tense moment or two; one observes the glow of a red lamp, and then the Band starts.[82]

According to Turton, the recordings were made by a direct-cut system onto wax discs and no editing could be carried out. Each side of about three minutes

[80] Email correspondence with Colin Waller, SA Regal Association, 2 Apr. 2009.

[81] Ibid.

[82] 'Letters to a Musical Friend', *Bandsman and Songster*, 20 Jan. 1935, p. 18.

had to be recorded in one take, therefore it was difficult to obtain perfection: the odd split note or loss of tuning was sometimes apparent. The limitation of three minutes per side meant that some pieces had to be reduced in length, usually by cutting out repeats.[83]

Of the 86 individual records issued between 1927 and 1939, 50 were instrumental, 25 were vocal, ten were 'mixed' (one side might be instrumental, the other vocal), and there was one speech recording.[84] As far as the instrumental recordings were concerned, the breakdown of genres, counting the separate items, is shown in Table 7.

Table 7 Instrumental recordings by musical genres

Marches	42
Instrumental solos, duets, quintets	17
Selections	7
Meditations	3
Tunes	3
Airs variés	2
Transcriptions	3
Tone poem	1
Suite	1
Bible picture	1

Clearly the march fitted the requirements of a three-minute side without a problem, but like the instrumental solos, the march matched a public mood for short, generally cheerful pieces. The larger-scale works for band were more problematic as far as popular appeal was concerned.

The bulk of the recording work was undertaken by the SP&S and International Staff bands, but others included Cambridge Heath, Chalk Farm, Clapton Congress Hall, Men's Social Work Headquarters, Regent Hall, Tottenham, and Upper Norwood (Crystal Palace) bands. Eric Ball topped the list of conductors. In association with the SP&S band, he was responsible for 28 recorded items.

As might be expected, the composers with the most recordings of their compositions and arrangements included Eric Ball, George Marshall, Bramwell Coles and Arthur Goldsmith. Eric Ball's works on record up until 1939 included: the marches, *The Gospel Feast* (BJ 831), *Torchbearers* (BJ 1069), *Forward to the Fight* (BJ 929); the selection, *The Warrior's Reward* (BJ 968); the airs variés, *The Old Wells* (FS 58), *Sound out the Proclamation* (BJ 1098); the suites, *Songs of the*

---

[83] Turton, 'The Heritage of Salvation Army Recordings'.

[84] I am indebted to Ian Barton for his Regal Zonophone website, not only for the listing of recordings, but also for the chance to listen to them on line. See www.regalzonophone.com.

Morning (FS 114), *The Pilgrim Way* (BJ 1138); the tone poem, *The Triumph of Peace* (FS 130); the cornet solo, *Glory to His Name* (FS 56). Richard Slater was represented by *The Stilling of the Storm* (BJ 601).

In breaking down the details of vocal recordings Table 8 organises the items in terms of the musical forces being recorded.

Table 8 Vocal recordings and their accompaniments

Vocal solo with string accompaniment	15
Songsters with band	15
Songsters with keyboard acc.	9
Vocal solo with keyboard acc.	8
Congregational singing with bands	5
Vocal Octette	2
Vocal solo with vocal backing	2

There was a vogue for vocal solos with string accompaniment, sometimes violin and cello, at other times a string sextet. The recordings of songsters with bands were most usually Christmas carols, several of them arranged by Eric Ball.

The Songsters in these recordings represented the following London corps: Catford, Chalk Farm, Clapton Congress Hall, Harlesden, Ilford, Leyton, Penge, Southall, Wimbledon, Wood Green. Also featured were groups from various headquarters, including the Salvation Singers, the Assurance Songsters. There was a far greater spread of composers of vocal music than for brass. It was heartening to see Richard Slater represented by three of his songs.

As far as broadcasting was concerned some context is required. On 1 January 1927 the British Broadcasting Corporation took over the work of the four-year-old British Broadcasting Company, retaining in its new charter the principle of public service. The 1920s and 1930s were to be 'the golden age of wireless'.[85] It is necessary to distinguish between Regional, National and Empire programmes. Whilst a regional scheme of broadcasts had been developed since the mid-1920s, it was not until 1932 that regional policies were finally established.[86] It was envisaged that the setting up of regional stations in the British Isles would provide a greater opportunity for local talent to receive a voice. In 1930 the term 'National Programme' began to be used in relation to the BBC.[87] After 1930 there was an established pattern of both Regional and National programmes. The first big transmission of the Empire Service was sent out on 11 November 1927 to Australia. One of the main purposes of the Service was, according to C. G. Graves, who had established it, 'to keep us in touch with the isolated man in the

---

[85] A. Briggs, *The History of Broadcasting in the United Kingdom*, vol 2: *The Golden Age of Wireless* (London, 1965), p. 6.

[86] Ibid., p. 326.

[87] Ibid., p. 308.

back of beyond to whom any contact with this country would be a very good thing'.[88]

In competition with the BBC were a number of foreign commercial radio stations, including Radio Luxembourg and Radio Normandie, which concentrated upon giving what they felt the British listener really 'wanted' in the field of light entertainment.[89] A particular feature on Radio Normandie was the use of variety and dance bands on a Sunday, something not countenanced by the BBC. Radio Normandie was able to reach the whole south coast area of England, greater in size than their French audience. Its life extended from 1928 to 1939, with the last broadcast on Thursday 7 September due to the outbreak of war.

In order to demonstrate the range of Salvation Army bands which broadcast over the radio I am going to focus upon the period January–September 1939, as this probably was the peak number of broadcasts featuring these ensembles, due to Radio Normandie instituting a regular twice-weekly series of Salvation Army broadcasts in February 1939, alongside the well-established BBC transmissions. In the following discussion I shall focus on BBC and Radio Normandie programmes respectively.

There was only one National BBC broadcast during this period, and this was given by the Cambridge Heath Band on Friday 9 June.[90] In the regular column 'Bands over the Air' in *The Musician* the programme was praised as being 'typically Army', but singled out the inclusion of Bramwell Coles' devotional piece *Discipleship* (FS 18) for special mention:

> It is thought by the compilers of the programme that if radio listeners who appreciate the inclusion of such pieces [...] would go to the trouble of expressing their appreciation to the BBC officials by post card immediately after the broadcast, Army Bands would not have such difficulty in persuading the BBC that 'religious' items are really desired by the public.[91]

Here we see the tension between the programme makers, who regarded Salvation Army band programmes as entertainment, and the Salvationists, who saw them as a vehicle for evangelism. This tension was also evident in what appeared to be a cautiousness about the playing of hymn tunes on non-religious, entertainment BBC programmes:

> The rare occasions on which our bands have been permitted to feature a hymn tune on BBC broadcasts have been greatly appreciated, and by many listeners.[92]

[88] Ibid., p. 372.

[89] Ibid., pp. 352ff.

[90] *The Musician*, 3 June 1939, p. 348.

[91] Ibid.

[92] Ibid., 10 June 1938, p. 365.

Table 9 lists the bands which appeared on the BBC's regional networks from January to September 1939.

Table 9   BBC Regional broadcasts January–September 1939

London Region	International Staff Band (2 broadcasts)
	SP&S Band
	Upper Norwood (Crystal Palace) Band
	Wood Green Band (2 broadcasts)
Midland Region	Kettering Band
West of England Region	Plymouth Exeter Hall Band
Northern Region	Castleford Young People's Band (on 'Children's Hour')
Scottish Region	Springburn Band

The SP&S band conducted by Eric Ball made its one broadcast during this period on 4 February on the BBC's London Region. The 40-minute programme was fairly characteristic of such broadcasts.[93] It commenced with Coles' march, *Sons of the Army* (BJ 759), followed by a selection of national songs, in this instance *Scottish Gems* (SS 266) by Jakeway. The essential instrumental solo was Eric Ball's own cornet solo, *Glory to His Name* (FS 56), and then two classical selections, *Gems from Gounod* (Jakeway, FS 131), and Sarastro's aria, 'In diesen heil'gen Hallen' from Mozart's *Die Zauberflöte* (announced with its Army title of 'Mercy') played on the euphonium. Finally there was a performance of Ball's own recent tone poem, *The Triumph of Peace* (FS 130), which in view of the coming global conflict was a most prescient choice. This was a typically eclectic mix, balancing the popular classics and national songs with specifically Salvationist words.

A novel off-shoot of the Springburn Band's appearance, was that a musical festival was subsequently arranged in its own citadel, described as 'Our Radio Hour'.[94] The platform was draped to represent a BBC studio, whilst an adjoining room became the 'announcer's' quarters. The microphone was wired to a loud-speaker placed in front of the platform. As well as the band playing, there was an elocutionist and a piano-accordionist. Intriguingly 'an outstanding feature was a recital of Army gramophone recordings'.[95]

As far as the Empire Broadcasts were concerned, there was just one featuring a Salvation Army Band during this period, given by the Wood Green Band on Saturday 18 February at 2.30 a.m. It was beamed to Canada, and an appreciative Salvationist listener in Toronto gave his reaction:

Just a word of cheer to the Wood Green Band [...] The programme was greatly appreciated by a host of Canadian listeners. The items came

---

[93] Ibid., 7 Jan. 1939, p. 7.

[94] Ibid., 18 Mar. 1939, p. 164.

[95] Ibid.

through beautifully, as clear as a bell. One could almost imagine himself right there in the studios at Broadcasting House.[96]

Of course, all bands being featured on the BBC had to pass an audition, and 'at all the regional studios the better bands in the area were heard, and, if successful, placed on the list for future reference'.[97] It was pointed out in *The Musician* that applications for auditions had to be made through Salvation Army channels, and not directly through the BBC.[98] The Castleford Young People's Band was the first Salvationist junior section to pass the audition.[99]

Amongst Eric Ball's works included on the BBC broadcasts during this period were: cornet solo, *Glory to his Name* (FS 56), tone poem, *The Triumph of Peace* (FS 130) (played on two broadcasts by the SP&S Band, and Wood Green Band), suite, *Songs of the Morning* (FS 114) (Springburn Band), air varié, *Sound out the Proclamation* (BJ 1098) (International Staff Band), *True Life* (BJ 945) (Upper Norwood Band).

It was announced in *The Musician* on 4 February that there was to be a regular twice-weekly series of Salvation Army broadcasts on Radio Normandie on Tuesdays, 2.15 p.m. – 2.30 p.m., and Thursdays, 2.30 p.m. – 2.45 p.m. The first programme was to be given by the Tottenham Citadel Band, and the first public recording had taken place in the citadel on 2 February.[100] The signature tune was 'Lift up the Banner', and the series was to be introduced by the British Commissioner. What is noticeable in the repertoire of these broadcasts is that side by side with marches, selections and meditations, there was usually a space for a 'song tune' (i.e. a hymn). Indeed, in an early broadcast by the Plumstead Band the song tune was 'God's love is wonderful' and the band sang the chorus, something which probably would not have been encouraged by the BBC in what it regarded as an entertainment programme.[101] A listener wrote concerning a later broadcast by the Plumstead Band:

> I thank you from my heart for the beautiful hymns you broadcast [...] which will for ever bring very precious memories to me, as they were played during my husband's last hours.[102]

What was significant about the Radio Normandie programmes was that they gave a particular opportunity and some freedom to Salvation Army bands to make a greater connection between the musical and the spiritual aspects of their work than was possible on the BBC. Furthermore there was an expansion of the

---

[96] Ibid., 25 Mar. 1939, p. 182.

[97] Boon, *Play the Music Play!*, p. 221.

[98] *The Musician*, 10 June 1939, p. 365.

[99] Boon, *Play the Music Play!*, p. 221.

[100] *The Musician*, 4 Feb. 1939, p. 70.

[101] Ibid., 25 Feb. 1939, p. 120.

[102] Ibid., 6 May 1939, p. 283.

number of broadcasting bands in the south east of the country. The repertoire was generally lighter and less challenging than that broadcast on the BBC. The work of Eric Ball was largely absent. The following bands took part in the eight months of the Radio Normandie series: Catford, Chalk Farm, Clapton Congress Hall, Croydon, Harlesden, Hendon, Ilford, Men's Social Work Headquarters, Norland Castle, Plumstead, Regent Hall, Salvation Army Assurance Society, Tottenham.

On the last day of broadcasting by Radio Normandie, Thursday 7 September, there was scheduled a 'Concert by Salvation Army Orchestra'.[103] We have no more details of this, other than the bald announcement.

🕭 *Conclusion*

The 1930s are generally regarded as 'the Golden Age of Salvation Army Music'[104] and there is no doubt that the catalyst was Eric Ball. By 1942 he had been appointed Bandmaster of the International Staff Band, and it appeared that he had secured a prominent position within the Salvation Army. At the height of his influence, however, he decided to resign as a result of his growing interest in psychic matters, which he had been studying at a high level. Mention has previously been made about his predilection for the mystical and the spiritual. He sought to extend his own religious experience through spiritualism.[105] More personally he had been deeply affected by the illness and early death of his beloved sister-in-law, Elsie Dorsett, on 15 September 1942. It was around the time of her final illness that he started to attend spiritualist meetings.[106] There were also probably a number of other motives to do with what he felt were trifling regulations. For example, he had given his spiritualist friends a lecture at the Caxton Hall on the spiritual basis of music, and he had also 'strayed' outside Salvation Army convention by taking a communion service in a Congregationalist Church. The Salvationist authorities wanted him to break off his studies and give them an undertaking that he would not speak anywhere without first asking their permission. He felt unable to comply, and went to see the General:

---

[103] See www.offshoreechoes.com/radionormandie/RadioNormandy11.htm, accessed 19 Oct. 2009.

[104] Stephen Cobb, in 'Lieut. Colonel (Dr.) Ray Steadman-Allen OF & Dr Stephen Cobb in conversation', transcribed by Gordon Cox.

[105] Spiritualism was a growing interest in the inter-war years. See J. Hazelgrove, *Spiritualism and British Society between the Wars* (Manchester, 2000).

[106] Cooke, *Eric Ball*, p. 85. Significantly Eric Ball was to dedicate one of his most deeply felt compositions *Resurgam* (FS 302) to 'Elsa', his own pet name for Elsie. Written as a test piece in 1950, it was later published by the Army after Ball's reconciliation with the organisation.

The General said to me, 'now Eric, what are you going to do about it?' I said, 'You don't want to sack me', and they said 'No'. I said, 'well, I think the time has come, I'll resign' [...] They were very kind and we parted very good friends although it was suggested and somehow it turned out they didn't want me to appear on any of their platforms for some time.[107]

The effect of Ball's resignation was profound, judging by the reactions of two young composers at that time. Norman Bearcroft 'thought the end of the world had come', whilst Ray Steadman-Allen was 'shattered'. Albert Jakeway saw Eric Ball off at St Pancras Station and likened it to 'attending his funeral'.[108] Eric Ball went on to become a major figure in the national and international brass band world outside the Salvation Army. It was not until 1952 that he achieved some reconciliation with the Army.

In the aftermath of his resignation it was the job of his shaken colleagues led by Bramwell Coles to consolidate as far as was possible the musical life of the Salvation Army during the remaining years of the war, and in the ensuing years of reconstruction. But that is beyond our story.

How can we sum up the man and his influence? In listening to his recorded interviews one senses what can only be described as 'a confiding ease', laced with a keen sense of humour, which is often self-deprecating. This also comes through in his 'Letters to a Musical Friend', which are written informally, and with a sense of empathy with his correspondent. At the same time they address directly problems of leadership, and ways of dealing with people. The tone is invariably encouraging. In his numerous recordings and broadcasts we see him blossom as the all-round musician he was, as conductor, band trainer, composer and accompanist.

But unquestionably it is as a composer that we see Eric Ball's greatest contribution as a Salvationist musician. Underlying his work was an unshakeable faith:

I've never had any difficulty, or doubt about, other realms of consciousness. We'll call it that – paradise, heaven [...] never had any difficulty about that [...] No difficulty at all.[109]

The complex set of relationships regarding Eric Ball's personal character, and his musical and religious convictions requires serious biographical attention. His mystical sense found expression in the best of his musical compositions, which represented the most sophisticated works in the repertoire at the time. Trevor Herbert puts it best when he talks about Eric Ball as probably, at least up until 1939, the most talented and prolific composer of Salvation Army music:

---

[107] *Encounter with Eric Ball*, quotation transcribed by Gordon Cox from the broadcast.

[108] Cooke, *Eric Ball*, p. 95.

[109] 'Melvyn Knott in Conversation with Eric Ball', transcribed by Gordon Cox.

He possessed a distinctive musical voice, and a total mastery of the brass band idiom, and evocations of religious, spiritual and moral themes are frequently present in his works. It is difficult to identify another composer whose work juxtaposes doctrinal and aesthetic elements more successfully and consistently.[110]

It was Eric Ball's good fortune to have started his work in the Salvation Army at the right time, so that he was able to build upon the foundations that Richard Slater had laid and to inherit the musical developments that had been fought for so tenaciously.

What is intriguing in a comparison of both men, is that both explored at one time or another areas of experience and knowledge outside the conventional boundaries of the Salvation Army: phrenology for Slater, and spiritualism for Ball.[111] In so doing, both of them demonstrated in their work for the Army, a strong streak of independence and a determination to follow their own instincts, even within such an autocratic organisation. Perhaps it is these qualities as well as their undoubted musical achievements that make a study of both men's lives and their music so compelling.

---

[110] Herbert, 'God's Perfect Minstrels', p. 210.

[111] Roger Cooter intriguingly suggests that phrenology and spiritualism had much in common. See Cooter, *The Cultural Meanings of Popular Science*, pp. 265–7.

CHAPTER 8

Richard Slater and his Musical Legacy

THE figure of Richard Slater has dominated this historical account. It will have been apparent that although he had officially retired from active service at the end of 1913 this did not mark the end of his close association with the Salvation Army and its musical life. In this final chapter I shall briefly describe his years of retirement and, in Salvationist parlance, his subsequent 'promotion to Glory'. I shall then turn to a consideration of his life and work as the 'Father of Salvation Army Music'.

❧ Slater's Final Years

Slater and his wife had chosen the Kent resort of Westgate-on-Sea, near Margate, as their place of retirement. Worryingly, he appeared to suffer from exhaustion, and indeed initially he thought his inventive powers had seized up. His daughter, Brunnhilde Rolfe, recollected that the breakdown in his musical powers lasted for five years, and that it was only after 'a dark passage' in his life that healing came.[1] However, as we have seen, this did not prevent him from being called as a key figure to give evidence to the Commission of Enquiry on Salvation Army Music in 1916. He continued to carry out work in the Music Editorial Department on an occasional basis, but noted in his diary that he felt the effects of such exertion in 'nerve excitement' and 'a sort of billiousness' (RSd, v. 17, 21 May 1921). Nevertheless, in 1923 he returned briefly to head the department to cover for Frederick Hawkes during his illness. In the same year he was awarded the highest honour bestowed to Salvationists, the Order of the Founder, for invaluable service in the Army's ministry of music and song. One of his last books, *Salvation Army Song Writers* (1929), provided notes on 70 writers and over 500 of their songs.[2] Slater continued to help out the department editorially until Hawkes' retirement in 1936. Even at the age of 82 Slater felt some disappointment at coming to the end of his official connection with the department (RSd, v. 24, 31 Jan. 1936). In his final years he continued to write articles for Salvationist periodicals,[3] and six months before he died we read that he had received three manuscript books from Salvation Army Headquarters, for which he had paid 3s. (RSd, v. 24, 11 Feb. 1939). The purchase was to enable him to make good copies of

---

[1] Mrs Lieut. Commissioner Victor Rolfe [Brunnhilde Rolfe], 'My Father', *The Musician*, 5 June 1954, pp. 360, 362.

[2] Slater, *Salvation Army Song Writers*.

[3] One of his last series was 'My Memories of William Booth', published in three separate parts, *The Musician*, 9 Apr. 1938, pp. 225, 240; 16 Apr. 1938, pp. 241, 256; 23 Apr. 1938, p. 272.

the 90 or so songs that he had been composing since his 80th birthday, 'perhaps the last of my outflows of musical ideas' (RSd, v. 24, 11 Feb. 1939).

Wagner continued to be Slater's chief preoccupation in his last years. On 10 January 1937 he completed his analysis of Wagner's Ring cycle (RSd, v. 24, 10 Jan. 1937). It had been 'a long and taxing job' in which he had gathered facts that had never been assembled together before. They provided, Slater thought, a foundation for important enquiries into Wagner's art. Almost two years later he had made a final revision of his guide to *Die Meistersinger* together with a small book of analytical details (RSd, v. 24, 31 Oct. 1938).

He listened to music on the radio, and occasionally commented upon it. He found Rutland Boughton's operetta *The Queen of Cornwall* (1924) so frustrating that he could not continue to listen. In his opinion it was uninspired, continuously complicated, and barren in melody. Its chief disadvantage was that it covered much the same ground as Wagner's *Tristan*, so comparisons were inevitable (RSd, v. 24, 31 Jan. 1935). But he gave rare praise in his comment on a performance of Verdi's Requiem conducted by Beecham: 'the work gained my verdict of being in my judgement one of the greatest of modern works' (RSd, v. 24, 4 Apr. 1935).

Slater continued to read widely during his retirement. He listed the books he had borrowed from the library on 31 May 1935. They comprised seven volumes on science and mathematics, with such titles as *Introduction to Mathematics*, *Introduction to Science*, *Modern Science*, *Progress of Science*, *New Outline of Science*, *Science Today* and *Wireless*. This was in addition to Matthew Arnold's *Essays in Criticism* (1865), and Holbrooke's *Contemporary British Composers* (1925) (RSd, v. 24, 31 May 1935). A year previously he had left a looseleaf handwritten note in his diary, headed 'Notes on dusting my books'. He reflected that he had spent most of his money on the host of volumes that constituted his library. They represented, in his opinion, most of the great writers and the range was wide, encompassing Greece, Rome, Italy, Germany, America and England. Certain of these books had become his 'chief friends', particularly those by Shakespeare, Dante, Spenser, Bacon, Locke and Emerson. Nevertheless he wondered whether or not he had been somewhat superficial in his reading. But there was no doubt of his pride in saying that the chief thing in his library was his multi-volumed record of his life (RSd, v. 23, 5 Mar. 1934).

The last entry in his diaries was simply 'still feeling far from well' (RSd, v. 24, 1 Nov. 1939). He was 'promoted to Glory' on 7 December 1939.

The local newspaper headed its tribute: 'Army Composer, Distinguished Salvationist's Death'.[4] It highlighted Slater's love for nature, and his passion for walking. Up at 7 every morning he would sometimes be at Cliftonville on the way to Ramsgate before 9 o'clock. His clothes were the plainest, and when not wearing uniform he could not be distinguished from an ordinary working

---

4 *Isle of Thanet Gazette and Thanet Times*, 15 Dec. 1939.

man. Because of this, many people had been astonished when he was pointed out or introduced to them. But Colonel Slater, the piece continued, felt that this is how his Master will appear. Such humility and sincerity, the tribute concluded, meant that he was loved without exception.

The funeral at the Margate Corps was headed by the band, and the cortège, which included Salvationists from Margate and Ramsgate, proceeded to the cemetery to the strains of the Dead March from Handel's *Saul*. Slater's musical colleagues were much in evidence; Arthur Goldsmith and Bramwell Coles prayed, and Frederick Hawkes paid a tribute.

A memorial service was held in Slater's honour at the Regent Hall in Oxford Street, headlined in the *War Cry* as 'Musicians honour the memory of Lt. Colonel R. Slater'.[5] It was conducted by the Chief of the Staff, Commissioner A. G. Cunningham, who recalled Slater's fine qualities of mind, and his abilities as a theologian. The bandmaster of the Regent Hall Band, Herbert Twitchin, pointed to the spot where 'the young man in a light-grey suit, who afterwards proved to be an accomplished musician' knelt to surrender his life to God. He recollected that

> this new convert whom none us realised was a great musician, entered the band on the 2nd cornet part, but later joined an orchestra we had at the corps. It was then we discovered him to be a master of the violin.[6]

The Bandmaster of the International Staff Band, Colonel George Fuller, declared Slater to be 'the finest musician the Army has ever had, or is likely to have'.[7] A number of International Staff Bandsmen were present as a tribute to the man. Appropriately, all the songs and choruses and the band selection *City of God* (BJ 531) had been composed by Slater.[8]

Slater's two protégés and successors as head of the Musical Department provided their own insights. Colonel Frederick Hawkes had spent over 100,000 hours working with Slater, and praised his prodigious industry, whilst Colonel Arthur Goldsmith described 'his intimate knowledge and love of classical music (he had analysed and mastered [...] the whole method of construction used by Wagner) but he had the courage to set aside the things he could have done as a composer, for the things he felt he ought to do to provide the Army with the music he saw it needed'.[9] Slater's daughter, Brunnhilde Rolfe, herself an officer, added some more personal details about her father:

> His black beard, his flashing dark eyes, his quick step and happy smile [...] Our home was simple [...] He had a warm and loving heart; yet

[5] *War Cry*, 30 Dec. 1939.

[6] B. Boon, *The Best of Both Worlds: An Autobiography* (London, [2009]), p. 104.

[7] *War Cry*, 30 Dec. 1939.

[8] Boon, *The Best of Both Worlds*, p. 104.

[9] *War Cry*, 30 Dec. 1939.

very vividly do I remember his displeasure at anything resembling lazi-
ness, selfishness or self-indulgence. What an example he was of Industry
[...] On returning home from the office he would spend as little time as
possible over his meal; then getting out his books and writing material, he
worked on into the night. He begrudged time spent in sleep and wished he
could do without it![10]

What characterised him was 'his intense joy of life [...] his delight [...] in facts
of nature'. She recollected being in Japan many years after leaving home, and
hearing Slater's song 'To heal the broken heart' being sung fervently by local
missionaries. She realised then 'that God had used his offering to spread bless-
ings right around the world'.[11]

🐝 Richard Slater: the 'Father of Salvation Army Music'

What were the achievements of this 'Father of Salvation Army Music'? It is
worth reminding ourselves that Slater was a self-made man, who was intent
upon not merely advancing his own learning, but also on transforming the lives
of others. As he grew up, he became convinced that he should make his mark on
the lives of so-called ordinary people. This was his motivation in his teaching of
music, his phrenological work, and in his lecturing in working men's clubs. His
remarkable diaries testify to the passion he felt for learning and understanding
throughout his life.

But it was to be within the Salvation Army that he came to exert his greatest
influence. Joining the Army was a somewhat curious step for him to take,
considering Slater's intellectual bent, and his outright hostility at the time to
Christianity. However, he was in some ways an atypical autodidact. The sense of
purpose that was most frequently found within that tradition resulted frequently
in the pursuance of some public passion, such as Chartism, Owenism, or the
proletarian Marxists of the early 20th century, or in becoming school teachers in
the context of common elementary schooling from the 1870s and 1880s.[12] Slater,
however, was no political radical. Far from it: he was thoroughly opposed to
socialism, and possessed a deep vein of conservatism.

Perhaps this accounted for his involvement with the Salvation Army and its
autocratic structure, there was certainly a parallel between Slater's dismissal of
socialism and William Booth's refutation of the allegation that he, Booth, was a
socialist.[13] For Booth, and probably for Slater, Salvationism and its social policy
'was intended to ameliorate the worst features of the existing order rather than to

---

[10] Ibid.

[11] Ibid.

[12] Gardner, 'The Life-long Draught', pp. 468–9.

[13] Hattersley, *Blood and Fire*, p. 354.

change it'.[14] Consequently, what seems to have attracted Slater to the Salvation Army was the possibility of accomplishing moral victories over oneself, through adherence to such a faith.

In order to assess Slater's contribution to the development of Salvationist music-making, I shall identify four key elements which underpinned his work as Head of the Army's Musical Department. The first will focus upon his creation of a musical world, the second on his privileging of brass bands within the movement, the third on Slater as composer, providing an appropriate musical repertoire, and the fourth meeting the educational needs of Salvationist musicians.

It was Richard Slater's achievement, in association with William Booth, to build an exclusive and self-sufficient musical world within the Salvation Army. Underpinning this world was the desire to evangelise that section of the population alienated from the mainstream churches. In order to do this the Army appropriated the repertoire of working class entertainment – the brass band, the melodramatic narrative, the minstrel show, and music-hall songs. In this way the Army reflected authentically the background of many of its soldiers. (It must be said, however, that Slater was not overly impressed with the musical taste of his troops, and indeed he was keen to 'lift' Salvationist compositions from the arms of the music hall.) Having appropriated popular repertoire it was then felt necessary to demarcate distinctions between 'outside' and 'inside'. For whatever reason, it was decided that the Army's music was to become exclusive to itself, and that its musicians had to commit themselves one hundred per cent to the organisation, its aims, governance, and methods. In Slater's opinion it would be disastrous to allow 'outside' music to cross the border. In later life he believed that even religious music from the classical tradition could play little part in the Army context, even although he had produced numerous arrangements from the classics in the past. (It is curious that a man of his broad intellectual sensibilities, a devotee of Wagner, a connoisseur of literature, a former free thinker, should keep to this rather narrow musical exclusivity.) The primary purpose of Salvation Army music was utilitarian, to be used as a means to an end, which was to bring about the conversion of 'sinners'. Slater's aim was to reach the masses through a musical style that had to be straightforward, simple and direct.

The second key element with which Slater had to come to terms was the primacy afforded to the brass band as the defining musical marker of the Salvation Army. In many ways this highlighting of the brass band was understandable. Certainly in the years leading up to 1914 brass bands played a central role

---

[14] Ibid., p. 373. There were however many practical links between Salvationism and Socialism, with Salvationists and Socialists working for similar social aims. See Woodall, *What Price the Poor?*, p. 180; R. Samuel, '"A Spiritual Elect?": Robert Tressell and the early Socialists', in *The Robert Tressell Lectures*, ed. D. Alfred (Oxford, 1988), pp. 55–69.

in popular musical culture: in small industrial communities in particular they were central both as agents of education and of entertainment.[15] In many ways also brass bands fitted the Salvation Army's purpose, because traditionally the bands' discipline had a quasi-military tightness. Slater's advocacy of brass bands was somewhat surprising, considering his initial ignorance of the medium, but nevertheless he rose to the challenge and developed his musical and compositional skills appropriately.

Considerable progress was made during Slater's tenure as head of the Army's Musical Department in the exponential increase in the number of bands at home, and also internationally, particularly in the British Empire. Like their secular cousins these bands of Booth's imperial army were:

> able to thrive unchecked and little-changed in those small and distant communities where immigration from places other than the United Kingdom was negligible, and where cultural links with the 'Old Country' were kept strong by being continuously renewed.[16]

Australia, Canada and New Zealand met these conditions completely. Although heartened by this internationalism, Slater was keen to centralise control, so that there was but 'one band-life' in the Salvation Army throughout the world.

The more negative aspect of the rise of the Salvation Army brass band was the relative neglect of choirs (songster brigades). In many ways this was the inheritance of William Booth's suspicion of church choirs, but it was also symptomatic of Slater's admitted inexperience with choral groups, although he was an able song writer himself and wrote prolifically for voices, with a handful of his songs surviving today. But in the Army's local hierarchy, the bandmaster was to reign supreme. It meant that choral training was considered analogous to band training, with the result that the choral tradition rarely reached the same technical standards as those of bands.

With Slater's focus mainly being on bands, and to a lesser extent on songster brigades, there appears to have been little attempt to foster the considerable variety of instrumental groupings characteristic of the Army's early years. He was dismissive of of the efforts of string bands, and there was seemingly little consideration for concertina bands, orchestras, mandolin bands. He did not use his own skills as a violinist to further the cause of string bands or orchestras.

The third element of Slater's achievement as has been noted in Chapter 3, was his compositional work in which he developed specifically Salvationist versions of musical genres (song services, marches, selections, meditations, programmatic scores) under the pressure of the Army's Musical Board. It was from

---

[15] See Russell, 'What is Wrong with Brass Bands?', p. 85.

[16] D. Bythell, 'The Brass Band in the Antipodes: The Transplantation of British Popular Culture', in *The British Brass Band*, ed. Herbert, pp. 217–44 (p. 217). Also see T. Herbert and M. Sarkisson, 'Victorian Bands and their Dissemination in the Colonies', *Popular Music* 16:2 (1997), pp. 165–78.

the Board that he received his fiercest criticisms with its tendency to berate 'advanced' music and only to see dangers in venturing beyond the beaten track. Undoubtedly it was a triumph to gain William Booth's acceptance that band music might be allowed to contain original music for which no words had been composed. But there was always the suspicion that in fact Booth himself did not use such music in his meetings.

Slater understood, however, the tensions between meeting the needs of an increasing musical sophistication amongst his musicians, and those of the rank-and-file soldiers. But he favoured simplicity of construction, and was against over-elaboration. In particular, he warned of the dangers of 'performance', and of creating concerts out of Salvation Army meetings.

It was Slater's view of himself that he was a musical liberaliser, constantly battling to allow Salvationist composers some latitude for personal expression, although his own musical style was somewhat conservative. He applied this respect for composers and arrangers to his own fight to gain what he felt was rightfully owed to him in terms of the personal financial benefits accruing from the copyright to his large corpus of musical compositions written for the Army. Slater frequently had fierce dealings with the authorities when his idealism was bolstered by his combative personality. But this same personal attribute might also be said to have been possessed by William Booth and George Railton, and was perhaps a necessary trait to translate fine words into real actions, working with a social group, 'the submerged tenth', whose conditions on the face of it seemed to be intractable.

Slater's most important contribution was to meet the educational needs of the thousands of musicians who comprised his musical Army. He had to start from scratch. The energy with which he wrote, edited and published educational resources was striking. Manuals, tutor books and theory books rolled off the presses, not to mention his unique *Salvation Army Dictionary of Music*. All this was complemented by numerous competitions for composers, examinations for bandmasters and songster leaders, not to mention the encouragement of band libraries, and the publication of specialist musical periodicals including the *Musical Salvationist*. Perhaps Slater would have been proudest of this aspect of his work, stemming from his own remarkable educational voyage, and his desire early in his life to become 'a true teacher and guide of men' (RSd, v. 3, 22 Jan. 1877).

What energised Slater was a conviction that music contained within itself both a moral and a religious dimension which could act as a means of enlightenment and inspiration. On a personal level he must have found these qualities in his lifelong passion for Wagner. He developed a philosophy which came to dominate Salvation Army music-making at least during his life time. Slater believed wholeheartedly in the power of music to act as a vital force in the service of religion. To do this, it should be simple, functional, inclusive and communal, based upon familiar and popular melodies. Through this association with religion, he believed music could energise the believer to action, and hence help regenerate and revitalise individuals and communities.

Slater's conviction in the power of music in the service of religion permeates an article he wrote in 1895, shortly after taking command of the Army's Musical Department, in which he expressed vividly his sense of the vibrancy of the Salvationist musical tradition, and his confidence in the future. It also encapsulates those qualities that made him so inspirational as the 'Father of Salvation Army Music':

> Oh, what thousands have been converted by the instrumentality of Salvation Army songs! The freedom, the life, the directness, the actual living expression in the spiritual appeals which the songs have made possible [...] Are there not hundreds of saints too, who have visited Army gatherings, obtained by their participation in them new inspiration, new strength, and a new hope, through Army songs [...] Vast as are the results already achieved for the Kingdom of God on earth by the music of the Salvation Army, we are confident that they are but as a drop in the bucket compared with what all the world will see in the future history of God's people, in every land upon which the sun shines.[17]

---

[17] R. Slater, 'The Music of the Salvation Army', *The Conqueror* 4 (1895), www.theme-online.ca/2008/the-music-of-the-salvation-army, accessed 12 Sept. 2009.

Afterword

PROFOUND changes have taken place in the musical life of the Salvation Army since the outbreak of World War II in 1939. In this Afterword I shall provide a brief outline of the situation Salvationist musicians find themselves in today (2010). But I shall do this with one eye on the past. I shall relate my impressions to the four key elements of Slater's work discussed in the final chapter: the creation of a musical world, the primacy of brass bands, the development of a suitable repertoire, and educating musical Salvationists. Finally I shall connect these developments to the discussion of musical worlds by the anthropologist Ruth Finnegan in her book *The Hidden Musicians*.

It was in 1992 that the previously separate and enclosed musical world of the Salvation Army opened onto to a pathway that connected with other traditions. It was signalled by two edicts. The first was headlined on the front page of the *Salvationist* on 22 January as 'Army Music goes public: official'. The report continued: 'The Army is to make its music available to non-Army groups. The General has decided to release all SA music on the open market.' Commissioner John Larsson, the leader of the Salvation Army in the UK, commented, 'For too long the Army has had a ghetto mentality when it comes to its music.' The four-point rationale behind the decision was outlined by Robert Redhead, one of Slater's successors, as follows: through the release of the Army's music a greater number of people would come under the influence of the Holy Spirit; musical Salvationists would be enabled to make a significant contribution to the larger Christian world; many of the Army's earlier publications were already in the public domain and more were to follow; additional revenue would be generated for the Army's work.[1] The second announcement on August 17 amended the regulations, so that 'Salvationists may participate in non-Salvation Army music groups, provided that membership of such groups does not conflict with SA principles and service'.[2]

In the most recent edition of the *Regulations and Guidelines for Musicians*, issued in 2000, there are further clarifications concerning this process of *glasnost*.[3] The demarcations between what constituted 'outside' and 'inside' are gradually dissolving, so that non-Salvationist groups may be allowed to give, or take part in, special musical events organised by the Army. Furthermore, on occasion, non-Salvationists can be included in Salvationist musical groups, subject to certain conditions. From time to time musical efficiency might well be enhanced by the occasional use of a non-Salvationist guest

[1] *Salvationist*, 25 Jan. 1992, pp. 1–2.

[2] Holz, *Brass Bands of the Salvation Army*, vol. 1, p. 177.

[3] The Salvation Army, *Regulations and Guidelines for Musicians* (London, 2000).

instructor. Finally the previous ban on songsters singing anything not passed by the Music Board is rescinded. Where non-Salvation Army music is chosen, care has to taken to ensure its suitability in conjunction with the corps officer.

The effect of all this has been dramatic. It was made clear to me when I attended what was billed as an 'afternoon concert' given by the International Staff Band on Friday 16 October 2009 at the Regent Hall, which was the place that Slater became converted, and later met and married his future wife. The concert was part of the Brass Arts Festival 2009, an annual event preceding the National Brass Band Championships in the Royal Albert Hall. What made the event special was that the Championships test piece, *The Torchbearer*,[4] was to be introduced by its composer Peter Graham. He explained that the piece was composed to commemorate the 20th anniversary of the death of Eric Ball. Its title was taken from Ball's Salvation Army march, *Torchbearers* (BJ 1069), which itself was based on his sessional song of the same name. Graham's work was a set of symphonic variations upon the first phrase of the trio of Ball's march. More than that, however, the composer had also endeavoured to retain the main compositional characteristics, harmonic flavour, and scoring techniques of Eric Ball's music. Graham's talk was illustrated by the Staff Band playing excerpts from the test piece.

The historical resonances were powerful. Here was now an integrated brass band culture, in which the figure of Eric Ball was the symbol of reconciliation. Not only was the test piece derived from a Salvationist work, parts of it were actually played by a Salvation Army band. Any talk of a separate and exclusive musical world would now be inappropriate. I wondered what Slater might have thought.

The next day I travelled to the Royal Albert Hall to attend the Brass Band Championships. This all-day event featured the top 20 bands in the country competing for the First Prize of £2,000 and The Champion Band of Great Britain Challenge Trophy. Some of these bands now included Salvationist bandsmen, no longer forbidden to cross to the 'outside'. The event has its own rituals. The adjudicators were placed in an enclosed adjudication box in the front of the hall in order that the anonymity of the contestants might be preserved. Each band in turn then endeavoured to scale the considerably challenging technical heights of *The Torchbearer*. Many in the audience, with score in hand, listened with rapt attention, and the different groups of supporters cheered on their own bands. The winner on this occasion was the Black Dyke Band. In the final concert the Cory Band played Eric Ball's Salvation Army march *Torchbearers* (BJ 1069). In a sense it had been this work that had come to

---

4 P. Graham, *The Torchbearer: Symphonic Variations on a Theme by Eric Ball*, study
score (Cheadle Hulme, 2009).

symbolise, during the weekend, the further dismantling of barriers separating secular and Salvationist bands.[5]

In discussing Slater's emphasis upon the brass band as the prime musical identifier of the Salvation Army, it is still possibly true that the public perception of the Salvation Army is most closely identified with Salvation Army bands playing Christmas carols in town precincts in the weeks leading up to Christmas. But such perceptions can fade. The following international statistics have been culled from *The Salvation Army Yearbook 2010*.[6] The overall picture is that the Salvation Army operates in 118 countries, with 1,222,326 senior soldiers, and 378,009 junior soldiers. Table 10 presents the disposition of the Army's musical forces in 2009.

Table 10   International statistics 2009

Senior band members	25,377
Young people's band members	12,239
Senior songsters	94,090
Young people's singing company members	80,940
Other senior musical group members	83,498
Other young people's group members	85,000

Inescapably, there has been a serious downward turn world-wide in the number of Salvation Army band members. A comparison with the statistics of 1984, a span of 25 years, shows a decline of 42.6% percent in the number of senior band members, and 56.8% of young people's band members.[7] As far as the UK is concerned, Holz reports that in 1999 there were 510 senior bands, a figure which was holding steady in 2004. Of these bands, it was reckoned that 66% were in the 14–20 member size.[8] In contrast, we may recollect that in 1927, celebrations had been held to mark the one-thousandth Salvation Army band in Britain. Russell has pointed to similar decline in secular bands.[9]

In spite of this decline Holz argues that as far as technical and musical standards are concerned, Salvation Army bands are today the best they have ever been.

[5] There have been many other examples of this opening out process since 1992. Perhaps most significantly the joint appearances of the International Staff Band and the Black Dyke Mills Band at the Gala Concerts of the National Brass Band Championships. The two bands have also collaborated on recording CDs of the music of Wilfred Heaton and Peter Graham. As far as vocal music is concerned, the King's Singers have recorded two CDs of Salvation Army songs.

[6] *The Salvation Army Yearbook 2010* (London, 2010), p. 29.

[7] The statistics for 1984 (reported in 1985) were 44,244 Senior Band Members, 28,350 Young People's Band Members. Taken from Holz, *Brass Bands of the Salvation Army*, vol. 1, pp. 428–9.

[8] Ibid., p. 181.

[9] Russell, 'What is Wrong with Brass Bands?', pp. 69–72.

There is a strong belief that the banding tradition provides an inclusive, flexible, and versatile vehicle for spreading the Army's message.[10] Certainly as far as inclusion is concerned regarding gender, there is a considerably greater representation of female bandmembers than in the past.

There are indeed some growth areas in banding. One of these is in what are known as Fellowship Bands, whose membership consists mostly of retirees, but in which Salvationists can now play alongside non-Salvationists 'of good character'. Furthermore there has been an increase in Salvation Army brass bands in some developing countries. Among the examples Holz cites are the Congo-Brazzaville Territorial Band, the Zambian Territorial Band, The Korea Children's Home Band, and the Brass Band from Kerala.[11]

Developments in the Democratic Republic of Congo (DRC) are particularly intriguing. The Salvation Army commenced work in the then Belgian Congo in 1934, and brass bands were soon established. Today in Kinshasa alone, most of the 52 Salvation Army corps possess a band. Roy Terry has pointed out to me that the tradition of fine brass playing established by an English Salvationist, Ray Munn, in the 1960s, has been handed down to today's Congolese players who have absorbed the music of such composers as Eric Ball and Erik Leidzén. They keep up-to-date with the Salvationist repertoire largely through recordings. At the time of the civil war of 1998–2002 many Congolese Salvationists sought refuge in Europe, and many arrived in Paris.[12] Their enthusiasm for brass bands now finds expression in a number of the Paris corps of L'Armée du Salut, most notably Boulogne-Billancourt, which has a fine band of 35 players.[13] Viewing their videos on YouTube ('Hallelujah!, Haendel', 'Captain and Lieutenant, Dance like Daniel', and 'On the King's Highway') provides compelling evidence of the ways in which these Congolese Salvationists have taken the brass band tradition and made it their own.

But more generally, as Holz states, Salvation Army bands and their culture face a tough future.[14] The days of the Salvation Army revolving around its bands have gone. Whether or not this decline has been hastened by the 1992 edicts is a moot point.

We have seen that the primacy of bands within the Salvation Army meant

[10] Holz, *Brass Bands of the Salvation Army*, vol. 1, pp. 429–30.

[11] Ibid., pp. 455–6, 474.

[12] For a succinct summary of the tragic situation leading up to the conflict between 1998 and 2002 in the DRC, see A. Lebor, *'Complicity with Evil': The United Nations in the Age of Modern Genocide* (New Haven, CT, 2006), pp. 214–18.

[13] Roy Terry to Gordon Cox, email 11 Nov. 2010. I am grateful to Roy Terry for sharing with me his knowledge of the Salvationist Congo context regarding bands. For an excellent discussion regarding 'colonial bands, bandmasters and bandsmen', see Herbert and Sarkissian, 'Victorian Bands and their Dissemination in the Colonies', pp. 170–4.

[14] Holz, *Brass Bands of the Salvation Army*, vol. 1, p. 431.

that other ensembles were somewhat sidelined. But today internationally the membership of songster brigades as seen in Table 10 far outstrips that of senior bands, and this is even more so for junior choirs (or singing companies). In common with other churches, the Army has witnessed a growth in what might be called Praise and Worship bands, and in accompanying activity in drama, dance and mine. The present *Regulations and Guidelines* list under 'Other Open Groups' something of the variety of musical ensembles, beside bands and songsters, that are now available: Gospel Groups, Home League Singers, Praise Bands, Senior Citizen Choirs, String Bands, Youth Chorales, Corps Fellowship Choruses etc.[15] Such open groups encourage both Salvationists and non-Salvationists to participate side by side. The membership of such 'other musical groups' appears to be encouraging. This statistic will doubtless include such indigenous musical ensembles, that Holz illustrates in his book, such as the Indonesian Bamboo Band, the Ladies' Flute Band from Andra Pradesh, India, and a variety of instrumental groupings from Bengal.[16]

As far as the provision of a suitable repertoire of music is concerned it will be recollected that the characteristic Salvationist musical genres such as the march, the selection and the meditation were composed for the traditional contexts of open-air meetings and marches, separate Holiness, Praise and Salvation meetings, and festivals. The open-air meetings and marches have all but disappeared due to the exigencies of increased traffic, one-way roads etc. Holiness and Salvation meetings have gradually diminished, as the main focus on a Sunday has shifted as in many churches from the evening to the morning meeting. Although the march is still a popular musical form, there are fewer selections and meditations published, in favour of 'song settings', arrangements of modern gospel songs, and 'big band' style arrangements, side by side with large-scale technically demanding concert works grouped by Holz as: preludes, preludes and fugues, and related forms; symphonic variations; tone poems; suites and sinfoniettas.[17]

As we have seen, it was the job of the Musical Department and its successor, the Music Editorial Department, to oversee the regular production of repertoire. That department in turn was renamed and reorganised in 2000 as the Music Ministries Unit, in which the music editorial duties, and the management and oversight of bands and songsters are combined. The Music Board is still in existence as the Territorial Music Council, and meets regularly to review the music submitted. The International Staff Band now records the submissions for the Council, but the songs are still demonstrated live with keyboard accompaniment.

As far as the band repertoire is concerned, the works of Slater, Hawkes and Goldsmith, are largely forgotten, whilst the music of Marshall, Catelinet and

---

[15] The Salvation Army, *Regulations and Guidelines*, p. 47.

[16] Holz, *Brass Bands of the Salvation Army*, vol. 1, pp. 473–4.

[17] Ibid., vol. 2, chap. 5.

Coles is occasionally played. The work of Eric Ball still comprises the heart of the repertoire. With regard to today's leading Salvationist composers in the UK, it is Ray Steadman-Allen who has dominated the field, with such major works as *The Holy War* (FS 298), *On Ratcliff Highway* (Judd Street Collection), and *At the Edge of Time* (Judd Street Collection).[18] We might also add such other key composers as Dudley Bright, Kenneth Downie and Peter Graham in the UK, and Bruce Broughton, James Curnow and William Himes in the USA.

With regard to educational opportunities, the field has changed due to the plethora of music educational organisations and opportunities available not only in schools, but also within the wider community. However, a key part of the Salvationist educational strategy is the development of summer music schools for vocalists and instrumentalists. A measure of its success is that since the formation of the Territorial Youth Band in 1998, some of its former members have gone on to join the International Staff Band, and 'contesting' bands including Black Dyke, Buy As You View, Carlton Main Frickley Colliery, Brighouse and Rastrick, and Fairey.[19] Perhaps the educational legacy is most apparent in the way in which the Salvation Army has provided solid musical experience and education for future professional brass players in UK symphony orchestras over the years. There are too many to mention, apart from the most recent example of Philip Cobb, who in July 2009 became principal trumpet of the London Symphony Orchestra whilst still only 21 years of age.

But as far as engaging with young people outside of the ranks of the Salvation Army, there was an intriguing article published in *The Officer* in 1998, in which Phil Wall questioned how the Salvation Army might interact, if at all, with youth subcultures which were largely anti-militaristic and non-institutional. With a move away from uniformity to diversity he notes that the traditional ways of securing commitment, such as playing in the band or singing in the songsters, face major challenges. There is a dilemma in singing 'the songs of militant and radical warfare in the contradictory comfort of a middle-class religious sub-culture'.[20] Perhaps one of the encouraging signs of progress in this direction lies a report in the *Salvationist* dated 3 January 2009, on the Rock School initiative of the Salvation Army.[21] According to the report, this music-based mentoring project for young people engages some who are faced with exclusion from school. Organised in conjunction with schools and social services teams, Rock School aims to help young people 'perform higher' through engagement with their musical interests, from Rock and Pop, Indie and Punk, DJing and Rap. Perhaps we have come full circle, bearing in mind William Booth's annexation of popular culture.

[18] K. Ashman, 'Ray Steadman-Allen', *Brass Herald* 20 (Oct.–Nov. 2007), pp. 16–17.

[19] *MMU Newsletter*, 16 Mar. 2007.

[20] P. Wall, 'A New Rhythm for a New Day', *The Officer*, Aug. 1998, pp. 16–19.

[21] See 'ALOVE Update', *Salvationist*, 3 Jan. 2009.

In comparing Salvationist music-making in the present with the past I find it helpful to draw upon Ruth Finnegan's distinction between 'musical worlds' and 'musical pathways'.[22] In many ways it was the intention of William Booth and Richard Slater to construct a self-contained musical world with its own specific and separate traditions, although, of course, no musical culture can be entirely unaffected by outside influences – just think of Slater and his enthusiasm for Wagner, or the attendance of Bramwell Coles at a Sousa concert, not to mention the Army's appropriation of vernacular culture. Nevertheless, like Finnegan's brass banders, Salvationist musicians might well have said 'It's a world on its own.'[23] Today's musical Salvationists, however, belong to a musical world which is more fluid and open, with fewer overtones of boundedness: Salvationist band-members can now play in contesting bands, outsiders can play in some circumstances with insiders, outside choirs can now perform music which was formerly exclusive to the Salvation Army. Perhaps it might be more appropriate now to talk of a Salvationist 'musical pathway' than a Salvationist 'musical world'. Although musical pathways can coincide with musical worlds, the difference is that pathways overlap and intersect: none are permanent in the sense of being changeless, some fade, others extend. Finnegan points out that there is no guarantee that established cultural pathways will carry on automatically, and her words possess a particular resonance:

> These paths may be trodden deep, but they only continue because thousands of people up and down the country put thousands of hours and an unmeasurable quantity of personal commitment into keeping them open.[24]

As well as preserving such deep paths, however, Bruno Nettl points out that 'an absolutely static musical culture is actually inconceivable: [...] change is the norm, rather than continuity'.[25] The challenge for Salvationist musicians is to cultivate the deep paths of established tradition, but at the same time to explore new possibilities, so that what results is a vibrant musical tradition that revitalises the visionary work of Richard Slater, that quintessential musical Salvationist.

---

[22] Finnegan, *The Hidden Musicians*.

[23] Ibid., p. 47.

[24] Ibid., p. 325.

[25] Nettl, *The Study of Ethnomusicology*, p. 279. Of course, present-day Salvationists are also challenged by religious change. For an introduction to theories of religious change, see C. Brown, *Religion and Society in Twentieth-Century Britain* (Harlow, 2006), pp. 8–15.

Bibliography

❧ *Richard Slater's compositions and arrangements*
referred to in the text

(For page references, see Index, Slater, Richard: Works.) All Slater's music was published by the Salvation Army, in the *Band Journal* (*BJ*), or the *Musical Salvationist*.

1889 *The Life Story of a Salvationist* (Song Service), *Musical Salvationist* 3 (1888–89), Feb., pp. 65–72

1893 *The History of the Army* (Song Service), *Musical Salvationist* 8(1893–4), Nov., pp. 121–32

1894 *The History of the Army*, *Band Journal* (hereafter BJ 253–6)

1894 *The Story of a Song* (Song Service), *Musical Salvationist* 9 (1894–5), Nov., pp. 49–60

1895 *The Life of Christ in Song* (Song Service), *Musical Salvationist* 10 (1895–6), Aug., pp. 13–24

1897 *The Salvation Army's Social Scheme* (Song Service), *Musical Salvationist* 11 (1896–7), Feb., pp. 85–96

1901 Festival Selection, *Old Song Memories* (BJ Supplement)

1902 *The Morning Hymn March* (BJ 411)

1902 Selection, *Jesus Hope of Souls Repentant* (BJ 412)

1902 March, *Our Battalions* (BJ 415)

1902 *The Festival March* (BJ 422)

1902 Selection, *Songs of Scotland* (BJ 428–429)

1902 *Lead Kindly Light: A Festival Arrangement* (BJ 436)

1904 Selection, *All Nations* (BJ 456–457)

1904 Selection, *Crown Him* (BJ 462)

1905 *Japanese March* (BJ 479)

1905 Selection, *Echoes of the Congress No. 1* (BJ 485)

1905 *Italian March* (BJ 490)

1905 Selection, *Hebrew Melodies* (BJ 491)

1905 Selection, *Songs of Holland* (BJ 497)

1906 Selection, *Swiss Melodies No. 1* (BJ 514–515)

1907 *Indian March* (BJ 529)

1907 Selection, *City of God* (BJ 531)

1908 *The Drum March* (BJ 569)

1909 *The Cornet March* (BJ 577)

1910 Bible Picture, *The Stilling of the Storm* (BJ 601)

1910 Selection, *Old Time Memories* (BJ 613, 640)

1910 Bible Picture, *The Widow of Nain* (BJ 616)

1910 *The Horn March* (BJ 617)

1910 *The Finnish March* (BJ 624)

1911 *The Bass March* (BJ 650)

1912 Selection, *Songs of Denmark* (BJ 661)

1912 Selection, *Songs of Italy* (BJ 665)

1913 Selection, *Songs of Germany No. 1* (BJ 694)

1913 Bible Picture, *Abraham's Offering* (BJ 695)

1914 Selection, *Songs of Sweden* (BJ 702)

1915 Bible Picture, *The Death of Stephen* (BJ 745)

❧ Manuscripts and other Collections

MANUSCRIPTS IN PRIVATE HANDS

Cox Family Papers

Richard Slater Diaries (24 vols)

THE SALVATION ARMY INTERNATIONAL HERITAGE CENTRE

The Commission of Enquiry into Matters relating to Salvation Army Music
  (6 vols, including the Final Report)

Fry Family Papers

Slater Papers

R. Slater, 'History of Salvation Army Music: Vocal and Instrumental' (2 vols,
  unpublished)

THE NATIONAL ARCHIVES (UK)

Census Enumerators' Returns

❧ Published Primary Sources

SALVATION ARMY PERIODICALS

All the World

Bandsman and Songster

Bandsman, Local Officer and Songster

Bandsman, Songster and Local Officer

Christian Mission Magazine

The Conqueror

Field Officer
The Little Soldier
Local Officer
MMU Newsletter (Music Ministries Unit)
Musical Salvationist
The Musician
The Officer
Salvationist
Under the Colors: A Magazine for His Majesty's Sailors and Soldiers
War Cry
The Young Soldier

OTHER PERIODICALS CONSULTED

British Bandsman
Daily Express
Daily News
Isle of Thanet Gazette and Thanet Times
Musical Times
School Music Review
The Standard
Westminster Gazette

SALVATION ARMY BAND JOURNALS

Band Journal (General Series)
Band Journal (Festival Series)
Band Journal (Second Series)
Judd Street Collection

SONG COLLECTIONS, BAND SCORES AND PIANO ALBUMS

Booth, E. *Songs of the Evangel.* New York, 1927. New and enlarged edition. London, 1934.

Booth, H. *Songs of Peace and War.* London, 1890.

[Booth, W.] *Revival Music: A Complete Compendium of Revival Music for Evangelistic Services, Open-Air meetings, and the Home Circle.* London, [1876].

[——] *Salvation Army Music (formerly published as 'Revival Music') with Supplementary Tunes.* London, 1880.

[——] *Salvation Music.* Vol. 2: *Being a Collection of the Favourite Songs of the Salvation Army.* London, 1883.

—— *The Salvation Army Songs.* London, 1899.

—— *The Salvation Army Music*. London, 1900.

Chappell, W. *Old English Ditties from Popular Music of the Olden Time*. 2 vols. London, n.d.

Graham, P. *The Torchbearer: Symphonic Variations on a Theme by Eric Ball*. Study Score. Cheadle Hume, 2009.

Kidson, F., and A. Moffatt. *A Garland of English Folk-Songs*. London, 1926.

Marshall, G. *Olivet and Calvary*. Piano transcription, R. Allen. London, 1957.

The Salvation Army. *Band Music for the Salvation Army*. London, 1884.

—— *Favorite Songs from the Singing, Speaking and Praying Brigade*. London, [1886].

—— *The Musical Salvationist Vols. 1–3, with Favorite Songs Supplement*. London, 1893.

—— *Band of Love International Musical Drills*. London, 1899.

—— *Band Book No. 1*. London, 1900.

—— *International Musical Drills and Healthy Home Exercises*. London, 1909.

—— *Favourite Compositions for the Pianoforte: Instrumental Albums No. 13*. London, 1932.

—— *Musical Monologues*, vol. 1. London, 1938.

Sankey, I. D. *Sacred Songs and Solos: With Standard Hymns Combined: 750 pieces*. London, n.d.

Songs of Italy: Containing 54 canti populari of Naples, Florence, Milan and Venice, Including some Popular Modern Songs. London, [c. 1890].

AUTOBIOGRAPHIES, BIOGRAPHIES AND MEMOIRS

Ashman, K. 'Ray Steadman-Allen', *Brass Herald* 20 (Oct.–Nov. 2007), pp. 16–17.

Atkinson, J. *Always in Step: Herbert Twitchin*. London, 1956.

Baird, C. *Noel Hope (Sarah L. Morewood)*. London, 1944.

Ball, E. 'Master of the King's Musick – A Memoir of Sir Edward Elgar', *Bandsman and Songster*, 10 Mar. 1935, p. 75.

—— 'Eric Ball Remembers', *The Musician*, 29 Oct. 1938, p. 701.

—— 'Songs of the Evangel: Eric Ball Recalls some Personal Memories of Evangeline Booth', *The Musician*, 25 Dec. 1965, p. 864.

Boon, B. *The Best of Both Worlds: An Autobiography*. London, [2009].

Booth, C. B. *Bramwell Booth*. London, 1933.

[Chalk Farm Band] *A.W.P., 1894–1938*. London, [1938].

Chappelow, A. *Shaw – 'The Chucker-Out': A Biographical Exposition and Critique and a Companion to and Commentary on 'Shaw the Villager'*. London, 1969.

Cooke, O. 'A Songster's Evolution', *Bandsman and Songster*, 1913, in 15 parts.

Cooke, P. M. *Eric Ball: The Man and his Music*. Baldock, 1992.

Court, W. *'In the Firing Line': A Biography of Colonel Bramwell Coles*. Vancouver, 2006.

Cox, G. '"A Natural Pedagogue": The Life-Long Educational Quest of Richard Slater (1854–1939), "Father of Salvation Army Music", as described in his Manuscript Diaries'. Unpublished report of the Finzi Scholarship Award, 30 Apr. 2008.

Encounter: Clear Skies: The Life and Work of Eric Ball. www.salvoaudio.com/bands/ericball.htm.

Ervine, St J. *Bernard Shaw*. London, 1956.

Fry, F. W. 'Leaves from the Diary of an Early-Day Musical Composer', *Bandsman and Songster*, 13 Jan. 1934, pp. 9–10.

Green, C. 'A Bandsman in the Making', *Bandsman and Songster*, 4 Jan. 1908, p. 6.

Green, R. J. *The Life and Ministry of William Booth, Founder of the Salvation Army*. Nashville, TN, 2005.

Hall, H. *'Here's to the Next Time!': The Autobiography of Henry Hall*. London, 1955.

'Henry Hall', in *New Grove 2*, vol. 10, p. 700.

Hattersley, R. *Blood & Fire: William and Catherine Booth and their Salvation Army*. London, 1999.

Holroyd, M. *Bernard Shaw: The Pursuit of Power*. London, 1989.

Holz, R. W. *Erik Leidzén: Band Arranger and Composer*. Lewiston, NY, 1990.

Knott, M. 'M. Knott in Conversation with Eric Ball'. CD accompanying, M. Knott, *Constant Trust: The Spirituality of the Music of Eric Ball*. Llandloes, n.d.

Lamb, A. '(James) Sidney Jones', *New Grove 2*, vol. 13, p. 199.

'Old Songs and Old Tunes: Brigadier Baugh and 'Champagne Charlie', *Bandsman, Local Officer and Songster*, 8 Aug. 1914, p. 507.

Rolfe, B. 'My Father', *The Musician*, 5 June 1954, pp. 360, 362.

Severn, J. M. *The Life Story and Experiences of a Phrenologist*. Brighton, 1929.

Shaw, G. B., *Collected Letters (1856–1910)*, ed. D. Laurence. London, 1972.

Slater, R. 'Life of Staff-Captain Slater of the Training Home', *War Cry*, 7 May 1887.

—— 'My Twenty-Six Years Service', *Bandsman and Songster*, 24 Apr. 1909, pp. 3–4.

—— 'My Memories of William Booth', *The Musician*, 9 Apr. 1938, pp. 225, 240; 16 Apr. 1938, pp. 241, 256; 23 Apr. 1938, p. 272.

Temperley, N. 'Sir George (Alexander) MacFarren', *New Grove 2*, vol. 15, pp. 471–3.

Watson, B. *Soldier Saint: George Scott Railton, William Booth's First Lieutenant*. London, 1970.

[Wiggins, A. R.] 'The Music Editorial Department: A Review of its History [...] The Beginnings of Things', *Bandsman and Songster*, 16 Apr. 1930, p. 131.

[——] 'The Music Editorial Department: A Review of its History [...] Discovery of Lieut.-Col. Hawkes', *Bandsman and Songster*, 10 May 1930, p. 147.

[——] 'The Music Editorial Department: A Review of its History [...] Lieut. Colonel Goldsmith: The Poplar Boy who became a Front-Rank Army Composer', *Bandsman and Songster*, 24 May 1930, p. 165.

[——] 'The Musical Editorial Department: Staff-Captain Jakeway: From Engineer's Bench to Composing Desk', *Bandsman and Songster*, 22 June 1930, p. 197.

[——] 'The Music Editorial Department: Captain Eric Ball ARCM – A Young and Enthusiastic Composer', *Bandsman and Songster*, 5 July 1930, p. 210.

[——] 'The Music Editorial Department: Divisional Bandmaster George Marshall – the Miner-Musician', *Bandsman and Songster*, 19 July 1930, p. 229.

[——] 'The Music Editorial Department: Conclusion', *Bandsman and Songster*, 26 July 1930, p. 23.

—— *Father of Salvation Army Music: Richard Slater.* London, 1945.

—— *Triumph of Faith: George Marshall O.F.* London, 1958.

ARTICLES, BOOKS

Arnold, M. *Reports on Elementary Schools, 1852–1882.* London, 1908.

Ball, E. 'Letters to a Musical Friend', *Bandsman and Songster,* Jan.–June 1934.

Booth, C. *Life and Labour of the People in London: Religious Influences.* Vol. 2: *London: North of the Thames: The Inner Ring.* Third Series. London, 1902.

Booth, W. 'Good Singing', *Christian Mission Magazine* 9 (1877), pp. 202–9.

—— *Orders and Regulations for the Salvation Army.* London, 1880.

—— *Orders and Regulations for Field Officers of the Salvation Army.* London, 1886.

—— *Orders and Regulations for Bands. Supplement to Orders and Regulations for Field Officers of the Salvation Army.* London, 1889.

—— *In Darkest England and the Way Out.* London, 1890.

—— 'My Model Bandmaster', *Local Officer* 1 (1897–8), p. 67.

—— 'The Education of Our Children', *Local Officer* 3 (1899–1900), pp. 3, 5–6.

—— 'Singing', *Local Officer* 3 (1899–1900), pp. 281–4.

—— 'The General Thanks his Bandsmen', *Field Officer*, Dec. 1900, p. 2.

Cobb, S. 'Lieut. Colonel (Dr.) Ray Steadman-Allen OF & Dr Stephen Cobb in Conversation', *The International Staff Band of the Salvation Army Heritage Series No. 1. Music from the 1930s.* London, 2009, SPS 249 CD.

['Comments from the Editor of the *Musical Times* about data sent from 'Richard Slater' concerning his study of Wagner's works'], *Musical Times* 24 (1883), p. 601.

Cooke, P. M. *Eric Ball: His Words and Wisdom*. Baldock, 1992.

Fowler, O. S. *How to Read Character: A New Illustrated Hand-Book of Phrenology and Physiognomy for Students & Examiners: with a Descriptive Chart*. New York, 1881.

—— and L. N. Fowler. *New Illustrated Self-Instructor in Phrenology and Physiology*. London, 1860.

Goldsmith, A. 'The Blackboard in the Classroom', *Bandsman and Songster*, 21 Mar. 1908, pp. 1, 4; 28 Mar. 1908, pp. 4, 7.

Hawkes, F. G. 'Junior Bands: More Hints on How to Form and Train Them', *Bandsman and Songster*, 7 Mar. 1908, p. 13.

—— 'Fifty Years of Army Music', *The Officer* 11:1 (Jan.–Feb. 1951), pp. 15–20.

Hay, J. 'About Concertina Bands', *Bandsman and Songster*, 6 Apr. 1907, pp. 5, 7.

Hope, N. *Crotchets and Quavers, or The Making of the Brixwell Young People's Band*. London, 1921.

'The Instrumentation of 22 Salvation Army Bands', *Musical Salvationist* 10 (1895–6), p. 47.

Kendall, G. *The Salvation Army, Exeter Corps: 12th Anniversay Review*. Exeter, 1893.

Prout, E. *Harmony, its Theory and Practice*. London, 1889.

Radio Normandy. www.offshoreechoes.com/radionormandie/RadioNormandy11.htm

Railton, G. S. *Heathen England and What to do for it*. London, 1888.

'Representative Bands', *Local Officer*, 1901–7.

Salvation Army. 'Summary Report of the Commission of Enquiry into Matters Relating to Salvation Army Music' [1916], in R. Holz, *Brass Bands of the Salvation Army*, vol. 1, pp. 115–17.

—— *The Why and Wherefore of The High Council of the Salvation Army, 1928–29*. London, 1928.

—— *Regulations and Guidelines for Musicians*. London, 2000.

—— *The Salvation Army Yearbook 2010*. London, 2010.

'Salvationist-Musicians who have achieved success in the four great British Institutions of music – the Royal College, the Royal Academy, Trinity College, and the Guildhall School', *The Musician* 24 Dec. 1938, p. 824; 31 Dec. 1938, p. 841.

Shaw, G. B. *The Perfect Wagnerite: A Commentary on the Ring of the Niblungs*. London, 1898.

—— *Major Barbara*. London, 1907/2000.

[——] 'What the Critic had to Say', *The Musician*, 3 Dec. 1960, pp. 776–7.

Slater, R. 'Music in the Salvation Army', *All the World*, Apr. 1891, pp. 286–8.

—— 'The Music of the Salvation Army', *The Conqueror* 4 (1895). www. themeonline.ca/2008/the-music-of-the-salvation-army, accessed 12 Sept. 2009.

[——] *The Home Pianoforte Tutor: Specially Intended for Use in Christian Homes.* London, [1904].

—— *First Lessons in Music.* London, [1906].

—— *First Lessons in Harmony.* London, 1908.

—— *The Salvation Army Dictionary of Music: To Meet the Needs of Bandsmen and Songsters.* London, [1908].

—— 'The Formation of String Bands', *Bandsman and Songster,* 10 July 1912, p. 6.

—— 'The General and Army Music', *Bandsman and Songster,* 31 Aug. 1912, pp. 549–50.

—— 'The First Bandmasters' Council', *Bandsman and Songster,* 18 Sept. 1926, pp. 290, 304.

—— *First Lessons in Harmony and Modulation.* London, 1929.

—— *Salvation Army Song Writers: Biographical and Historical Notes of 70 Writers and on over 500 of their Songs.* London, [1929].

—— *The Life-story of a Salvationist: Words and Music with Connected Readings.* London, n.d.

Solly, H. 'On Working Men's Clubs and Institutes', *Transactions of the National Association for the Promotion of Social Service.* Edinburgh, 1881.

Steadman-Allen, R. 'Lieut. Colonel (Dr.) Ray Steadman-Allen OF & Dr Stephen Cobb in conversation', *The International Staff Band of the Salvation Army Heritage Series No. 1. Music from the 1930s.* London, 2009, SPS 249 CD.

Wall, P. 'A New Rhythm for a New Day', *The Officer,* Aug. 1998, pp. 16–19.

🔊 Secondary Sources

Avery, G. 'Companion to our Tune Book'. 2 vols. 1972. Typescript. The Salvation Army International Heritage Centre.

Bailey, P. *Popular Culture and Performance in the Victorian City.* Cambridge, 1998.

Bailey, V. '"In Darkest England and the Way Out": The Salvation Army and Social Reform and the Labour Movement', *International Review of Social History* 29:2 (1984), pp. 133–71.

Bantock, G. H. *Studies in the History of Educational Thought and Practice.* Vol. 1: *Artifice and Nature, 1350–1765.* London, 1980.

Bebbington, D. W. *Evangelicalism in Modern Britain: A History from the 1730s to the 1980s.* London, 1989.

Benson, J. *British Coal Miners in the Nineteenth Century: A Social History.* Aldershot, 1980, r/1993.

Boon, B. *Play the Music Play! The Story of Salvation Army Bands.* London, 1966.

—— *Sing the Happy Song!: A History of Salvation Army Vocal Music*. London, 1978.

—— *ISB: The Story of the International Staff Band of the Salvation Army*. Bristol, 1985.

Bradley, I. 'Blowing for the Lord', *History Today* 27 (1977), pp. 190–5.

Brehony, K. 'F. W. A. Froebel (1782–1852)', in *Encyclopedia of Children and Childhood*, ed. P. S. Fass. New York, 2004, pp. 374–5.

Briggs, A. *The History of Broadcasting in the United Kingdom*. Vol. 2: *The Golden Age of Wireless*. London, 1965.

—— 'The Salvation Army in Sussex, 1883–1892', in *Studies in Sussex Church History*, ed. M. J. Kitch. London, 1981, pp. 189–220.

Brown, C. *The Death of Christian Britain: Understanding Secularization*. London, 2001.

—— *Religion and Society in Twentieth-Century Britain*. Harlow, 2006.

Brown, K. D. *Social History of the Nonconformist Ministry in England and Wales, 1800–1930*. Oxford, 1988.

Bythell, D. 'The Brass Band in the Antipodes: The Transplantation of British Popular Culture', in *The British Brass Band*, ed. Herbert, pp. 217–44.

Cooter, R. *The Cultural Meanings of Popular Science: Phrenology and the Organisation of Consent in Nineteenth-Century Britain*. Cambridge, 1984.

Cox, G. *Folk Music in a Newfoundland Outport*. Ottawa, 1980.

—— *A History of Music Education in England, 1872–1928*. Aldershot, 1993.

—— *Living Music in Schools, 1923–1999: Studies in the History of Music Education in England*. Aldershot, 2002.

Cunningham, H. *The Volunteer Force: A Social and Political History*. London, 1975.

Davin, A. *Growing Up Poor: Home, School and Street in London*. London, 1996.

Ehrlich, C., and D. Russell. 'Victorian Music: A Perspective', *Journal of Victorian Culture* 3 (1988), pp. 111–22.

Elliott, K. *The Band With a Name: A History of Coventry City Salvation Army Band from 1892 to 1993*. Baldock, 1994.

Erdozain, D. *The Problem of Pleasure: Sport, Recreation and the Crisis of Victorian Religion*. Woodbridge, 2010.

Finnegan, R. *The Hidden Musicians: Music-Making in an English Town*. Middletown, CT, 2007.

Gammon, V. '"Babylonian Performances": The Rise and Suppression of Popular Church Music, 1660–1887', in *Popular Culture and Class Conflict 1590–1914: Exploration in the History of Labour and Leisure*, ed. E. and S. Yeo. Brighton, 1981, pp. 62–88.

—— and S. Gammon. 'The Musical Revolution of the Mid-Nineteenth Century: From "Repeat and Twiddle" to "Precision and Snap"', in *The British Brass Band*, ed. Herbert, pp. 122–54.

Gardner, P. '"The Life-long Draught"; From Learning to Teaching and Back', *History of Education* 36:4–5 (2007), pp. 465–82.

Gilbert, A. D. *Religion and Society in Industrial England.* London, 1976.

Gillett, P. 'Ambivalent Friendships: Music-Lovers, Amateurs and Professional Musicians in the Late Nineteenth Century', in *Music and British Culture 1785–1914: Essays in Honour of Cyril Ehrlich*, ed. C. Bashford and L. Langley. Oxford, 2000, pp. 321–40.

Green, L. *How Popular Musicians Learn: A Way Ahead for Music Education.* Aldershot, 2001.

Hailstone, A. *The British Bandsman Centenary Book: A Social History of Brass Bands.* Baldock, 1987.

Hanson, T. 'Sweden', in Holz, *Brass Bands of the Salvation Army*, vol. 1, pp. 255–72.

Harrison, J. F. C. *Learning and Living, 1790–1960: A Study in the History of the English Adult Education Movement.* London, 1961.

—— *Drink and the Victorians: The Temperance Question in England, 1815–1872.* London, 1971.

Hattersley, R. 'Shaw and the Salvation Army', in programme for National Theatre production of Shaw's *Major Barbara.* London, 2008, n.p.

Hazelgrove, J. *Spiritualism and British Society between the Wars.* Manchester, 2000.

Hendrick, H. *Children, Childhood and English Society, 1800–1990.* Cambridge, 1997.

Herbert, T. (ed.), *The British Brass Band: A Musical and Social History.* Oxford, 2000.

—— 'Nineteenth-Century Bands: Making a Movement', in *The British Brass Band*, ed. Herbert, pp. 10–67.

—— 'God's Perfect Minstrels: The Bands of the Salvation Army', in *The British Brass Band*, ed. Herbert, pp. 187–216.

—— 'Sousa, the Band and the "American Century"', *Journal of the Royal Musical Association* 135:1 (2010), pp. 183–90.

—— and H. Barlow. *The Culture of Brass Project* (2008). http://www.open.ac.uk/Arts/culture-of-brass, accessed 10 Sept. 2009.

—— and M. Sarkisson. 'Victorian bands and their Dissemination in the Colonies', *Popular Music* 16:2 (1997), pp. 165–78.

—— and J. Wallace. 'Aspects of Performance Practices: The Brass Band and its Influence on other Brass-Playing Styles', in *The British Brass Band*, ed. Herbert, pp. 278–305.

Hindmarsh, P. 'Building a Repertoire: Original Compositions for the British Brass Band, 1913–1998', in *The British Brass Band*, ed. Herbert, pp. 245–77.

Hobsbawm, E. *The Age of Extremes: The Short Twentieth Century, 1914–1991.* London, 1994.

Holroyd, M. (ed.), *The Genius of Shaw: A Symposium*. New York, 1979.

Holz, R. W. 'The History of the Hymn-Tune Meditation and Related Forms in Salvation Army Instrumental Music in Great Britain and North America' (Unpublished PhD dissertation, University of Connecticut, 1981).

—— *Brass Bands of the Salvation Army: Their Mission and Music*. 2 vols. Hitchin, 2006–7.

—— *The Proclaimers: A History of the New York Staff Band, 1887–2007*. New York, 2007.

Horridge, G. *The Salvation Army in its Early Days, 1865–1900*. Godalming, 1993.

Hughes, M., and R. Stradling. *The English Musical Renaissance, 1840–1940: Constructing a National Music*. 2nd edn. Manchester, 2001.

Hunter, M., and R. Thorne (eds). *King's Cross*. London, 1990.

Inglis, K. *Churches and the Working Classes in Victorian England*. London, 1963.

Jones, G. S. *Languages of Class: Studies in English Working Class History, 1832–1982*. Cambridge, 1983.

Kift, D. *The Victorian Music Hall*. Cambridge, 1996.

Kilgarriff, M. *Sing Us One of the Old Songs: A Guide to Popular Song, 1860–1920*. Oxford, 1998.

Laqueur, T. W. *Religion and Respectability: Sunday Schools and Working-Class Culture, 1780–1850*. New Haven, CT, 1976.

Larsson, J. *1929: A Crisis that Shaped the Salvation Army's Future*. London, 2009.

Lebor, A. *'Complicity with Evil': The United Nations in the Age of Modern Genocide*. New Haven, CT, 2006.

Livings, H. *That the Medals and the Baton be Put in View*. Newton Abbott, 1975.

Matthew, H. C. G. 'The Liberal Age (1851–1914)', in *The Oxford Popular History of Britain*, ed. K. O. Morgan. London, 1996, pp. 518–82

McGuire, C. E. *Music and Victorian Philanthropy: The Tonic Sol-fa Movement*. Cambridge, 2009.

McLeod, H. *Religion and Irreligion in Victorian England: How Secular was the Working Class?* Bangor, 1993.

—— *Religion and Society in England, 1850–1914*. Basingstoke, 1996.

Middleton, R. 'Popular Music of the Lower Classes', in *The Romantic Age 1800–1914*, ed. N. Temperley, The Athlone History of Music in Britain vol. 5. London, 1981, pp. 63–91.

Murdoch, N. *Origins of the Salvation Army*. Knoxville, TN, 1994.

Musgrave, M. *The Musical Life of the Crystal Palace*. Cambridge, 2005.

National Theatre. 'Salvation Army Terminology', in programme for National Theatre production of Shaw's *Major Barbara*. London, 2008, n.p.

Nettl, B. *The Study of Ethnomusicology: Thirty-one Issues and Concepts*. 2nd edn. Champaign, IL, 2005.

Newsome, R. *Brass Roots: A Hundred Years of Brass Bands and their Music, 1836–1936*. Aldershot, 1998.

—— *The Modern Brass Band: From the 1930s to the New Millennium*. Aldershot, 2006.

Obelkevich, J. 'Music and Religion in the Nineteenth Century', in *Disciplines of Faith: Studies in Religion, Politics and Patriarchy*, ed. J. O. and L. Roper, and R. Samuel. London, 1987, pp. 550–65.

Osborne, C. 'The Music Critic', in Holroyd, *The Genius of Shaw*, pp. 65–76.

Penn, A. *Targeting Schools: Drill, Militarism and Imperialism*. London, 1999.

Picard, L. *Victorian London: The Life of a City, 1840–1870*. London, 2006.

Pickering, M. *Blackface Minstrelsy in Britain*. Aldershot, 2008.

Pitts, S. E. *Valuing Musical Participation*. Aldershot, 2005.

Rainbow, B. *The Land without Music: Musical Education in England, 1800–1860 and its Continental Antecedents*. London, 1967, r/1991.

—— *The Choral Revival in the Anglican Church, 1839–1872*. London, 1970, r/2001.

—— *John Curwen: A Short Critical Biography*. Borough Green, 1980.

—— with G. Cox, *Music in Educational Thought and Practice*. 2nd edn. Woodbridge, 2007.

Rapp, D. 'The British Salvation Army, the Early Film Industry and Urban Working-Class Adolescents, *Twentieth Century British History* 7:2 (1996), pp. 157–88.

Registrar General. *Census 1951: Classification of Occupations*. London, 1956.

Richards, J. *Imperialism and Music in Britain, 1876–1953*. Manchester, 2001.

Robertson, R. 'The Salvation Army: The Persistence of Sectarianism', in *Patterns of Sectarianism: Organisation and Ideology in Social and Religious Movements*, ed. B. Wilson. London, 1967, pp. 49–105.

Rose, J. *The Intellectual Life of the British Working Classes*. New Haven, CT, 2001.

Routh, G. *Occupations of the People of Great Britain, 1801–1981*. Basingstoke, 1987.

Royle, E. *Radicals, Secularists and Republicans: Popular Freethought in Britain, 1866–1915*. Manchester, 1980.

Russell, D. *Popular Music in England, 1840–1914: A Social History*. 2nd edn. Manchester, 1997.

—— 'What is Wrong with Brass Bands?: Cultural Change and the Band Movement', in *The British Brass Band*, ed. Herbert, pp. 68–121.

Russell, J. F., and J. H. Elliot. *The Brass Band Movement*. London, 1936.

Sadie, S. (ed.), *The New Grove Dictionary of Music and Musicians*. 2nd edn. 29 vols. London, 2001. Referred to elsewhere in this bibliography as *New Grove 2*.

Samuel, R. '"A Spiritual Elect?" Robert Tressell and the Early Socialists', in *The Robert Tressell Lectures*, ed. D. Alfred. Oxford, 1988, pp. 55–69.

Sandall, R. *The History of the Salvation Army*. Vol. 1: *1865–1878*. London, 1947.

—— *The History of the Salvation Army*. Vol. 2: *1878–1886*. London, 1950.

—— *The History of the Salvation Army*. Vol. 3: *1883–1953: Social Reform and Welfare Work*. London, 1955.

Scholes, P. *The Mirror of Music, 1844–1944: A Century of Musical Life in Britain as Reflected in the Pages of the 'Musical Times'*. 2 vols. London, 1947.

School Music in the Curwen Edition. London, n.d.

Scott, D. *The Singing Bourgeois: Songs of the Victorian Drawing Room and Parlour*. 2nd edn. Milton Keynes, 2000.

—— *Sounds of the Metropolis: The 19th Century Popular Music Revolution in London, New York, Paris and Vienna*. Oxford, 2008.

Scott, H. *The Early Doors: Origins of the Music Hall*. London, 1946.

Shipley, S. *Club Life and Socialism in Mid-Victorian London*. 2nd edn. London, 1983.

Stack, D. *Queen Victoria's Skull: George Combe and the mid-Victorian Mind*. London, 2008.

Steadman-Allen, R. 'The Evolution of Salvation Army Music', *The Musician*, July 1965 – Feb. 1966.

—— 'One Hundred Years of Music Publishing', in *Salvation Army Yearbook 1976*. London, 1976.

—— 'Music of the Salvation Army', *New Grove 2*, vol. 22, pp. 183–4.

—— *Colour and Texture in the Brass Band Score*. London, 2005.

Steedman, C. *Dust*. Manchester, 2001.

—— *Master and Servant: Love and Labour in the English Industrial Age*. Cambridge, 2007.

Swanwick, K. *Music, Mind and Education*. London, 1988.

Taiz, L. *Hallelujah Lad and Lasses: Remaking the Salvation Army in America, 1880–1930*. Chapel Hill, NC, 2001.

Taylor, A. M. *Labour and Love: An Oral History of the Brass Band Movement*. London, 1983.

Taylor, J. *From Self-Help to Glamour: Working Men's Clubs 1860–1972*. Oxford, 1972.

Thompson, E. P. 'Blood, Fire and Unction', *New Society*, 13 Mar. 1965, pp. 25–6.

—— *The Making of the English Working Class*. Harmondsworth, 1968.

—— 'Patrician Society, Plebeian Culture', *Journal of Social History* 7 (1974), pp. 382–403.

'Throw out the lifeline'. See www.nethymnal.org/htmt/h/throwout.htm

Trevelyan, G. M. *Garibaldi and the Thousand*. London, 1909.

Turton, D. 'The Heritage of Salvation Army Recordings', liner notes, *The Old Wells: Favourites from the 78 rpm Era*. SPSCD 116CD. London, 1999.

Waites, J., M. Drake and R. Finnegan. 'Social Mobility', in *Studying Family and Community History: 19th and 20th Centuries*. Vol. 3: *Communities and Families*, ed. J. Golby. Cambridge, 1994, pp. 89–113.

Walker, P. J. '"I live but not yet I, for Christ liveth in me": Men and Masculinity in the Salvation Army, 1865–1890', in *Manful Assertions: Masculinities in Britain since 1800*, ed. M. Roper and J. Tosh. London, 1991, pp. 92–112.

—— *Pulling the Devil's Kingdom Down: The Salvation Army in Victorian Britain*. Berkeley, CA, 2001.

Waters, C. *British Socialists and the Politics of Popular Culture, 1884–1914*. Manchester, 1990.

Weinreb, B., and C. Hibbert (eds). *The London Encyclopaedia*. London, 1995.

Wiggins, A. R. *The History of the Salvation Army*. Vol. 4: *1886–1904*. London, 1964.

—— *The History of the Salvation Army*. Vol. 5: *1904–1914*. London, 1968.

Wilson, A. N. *The Victorians*. London, 2007.

Winston, D. *Red-Hot and Righteous: The Urban Religion of the Salvation Army*. Cambridge, MA, 1999.

Woodall, A. *What Price the Poor? William Booth, Karl Marx and the London Residuum*. Aldershot, 2005.

Wyhe, J. van. *Phrenology and the Origins of Victorian Scientific Naturalism*. Aldershot, 2004.

Yeo, S. *Religion and Voluntary Organisations in Crisis*. London, 1976.

WEBSITES

Culture of Brass. www.open.ac.uk/Arts/culture-of-brass

Encounter with Eric Ball. www.salvoaudio.com/bands/ericball.htm (Recorded Australian Radio Broadcast, n.d.)

Radio Normandie. www.offshoreechoes.com/radionormandie/RadioNormandy11.htm

Regal Zonophone recordings of Salvation Army vocal and instrumental music, compiled by Ian May. www.regalzonophone.com

Index